THE RISE OF WOMEN

THE RISE OF WOMEN

THE GROWING GENDER GAP IN EDUCATION AND WHAT IT MEANS FOR AMERICAN SCHOOLS

THOMAS A. DIPRETE AND

CLAUDIA BUCHMANN

Russell Sage Foundation • New York

The Russell Sage Foundation

Library of Congress Cataloging-in-Publication Data

DiPrete, Thomas A.
  The rise of women : the growing gender gap in education and what it means for American schools / Thomas A. DiPrete and Claudia Buchmann.
    pages cm
  Includes bibliographical references and index.
  ISBN 978-0-87154-051-5 (pbk. : alk. paper)   1. Sex role—United States.
    2. Women in education—United States.   3. Educational equalization—United States.   I. Buchmann, Claudia.   II. Title.
    HQ1075.5.U6D57 2013
    370'.82--dc23   2012032507

Text design by Suzanne Nichols.

RUSSELL SAGE FOUNDATION
112 East 64th Street, New York, New York 10065
10 9 8 7 6 5 4 3 2 1

Contents

Tables and Figures

About the Authors

Thomas A. DiPrete is professor of sociology and codirector of the Center for the Study of Wealth and Inequality at Columbia University.

Claudia Buchmann is professor of sociology at Ohio State University.

Preface

THIS BOOK is the product of more than a decade of research that began with a hallway conversation in May 2001, when we were both professors at Duke University. Tom's youngest daughter was finishing her first year of middle school. Tom had just come from an ice cream social and ceremony that the superintendent of the Durham County Schools hosted for all of the sixth-graders who had finished the academic year with perfect report cards. Tom and his wife, Katherine, and lots of other parents took off their lunch hour on a warm May day to watch their kids eat ice cream and to search the glossy program for their child's name on the list of honored students. After ice cream, the students got in line, the superintendent began calling their names, one after another they shook his hand and received a certificate, they filed back to the waiting area . . . and the gender imbalance became impossible to ignore. It seemed that two out of every three students in the line were girls. After the event ended and Tom returned to the Sociology Department, he told Claudia about the pattern of gender inequality in academic achievement that was on display at the Durham County Schools ice cream social and about how it must have broader implications that were worthy of systematic research.

Our anecdotal experiences as parents—and before that as children and adolescents ourselves—have played a role in sensitizing us to the relationship between gender and education in more ways than just those displayed at an ice cream social over ten years ago. Tom's experience growing up as a boy was followed by his experience raising only girls, all three of whom are now college graduates. Claudia's experience growing up as a girl was followed by her experience raising first a boy and then later a girl. Over the course of that spring in 2001, Claudia had been volunteering as a teacher's helper in her son's kindergarten classroom. Every week she would go in for an hour or so and work one-on-one with the children who needed a little extra help. The activities ranged from helping students learn the alphabet with flash cards (lower-case *b*'s and *d*'s are notoriously hard for kindergarteners to distinguish) to helping them practice their handwriting or review basic math facts. As the weeks went on she became aware of the fact that all but one of the children she worked with were boys.

Our own experiences certainly did not align with the scholarly literature on gender and education. At the time, most scholarly work of which we were aware focused on aspects of education in which women trailed men (Jacobs 1996), such as gender segregation in majors (Charles and Bradley 2002; Turner and Bowen 1999), women's underrepresentation at top-tier institutions (Jacobs 1999), and their underrepresentation in science and engineering (Fox and Stephan 2001; Long 2001; Xie and Shauman 2003). The few studies that did acknowledge women's higher rates of educational attainment and better academic performance treated these facts as anomalies (Mickelson 1989) or disregarded them as irrelevant because women had not yet closed the wage gap with men. In one of our first published papers on this topic (Buchmann and DiPrete 2006), we argued that failure to analyze the ways in which women are advantaged in education (as well as those in which they continue to trail men) leads to a skewed and incomplete understanding of gender stratification in education.

Our hallway conversation at Duke began many years of research on the changing relationship between gender and education. From the start, we considered the prospect of writing a book, though early on we imagined that such a book would focus on the labor market consequences as well as the causes of the educational gender gap. As we came to appreciate the complexity of the educational gender gap, we realized that the educational story on its own merited a book-length treatment. We therefore focused not only on education and the experiences of girls and boys in K-12 education and in college but also on adult experiences as important context for understanding educational outcomes. As we continued our work, many others joined our conversation and made extremely valuable contributions to our empirical knowledge as well as to our broader understanding of the role of gender in the educational process. The volume that we produced reflects these contributions as well as our own efforts.

Our greatest debt is to the students who worked with us on the gender and education project, including Jill Bowdon, Greg Eirich, Jennifer L. Jennings, Joscha Legewie, Allison Mann, Anne McDaniel, Uri Shwed, and Lisa Williams. These collaborations have led to a number of coauthored papers and published articles in addition to dissertation chapters and a great many conversations that developed our collective thinking and contributed to the making of this book. Jennifer Jennings worked with Tom on the social and behavioral side of the gender story as we were completing the analyses and writing that led to the 2006 publications in the *American Sociological Review* and *Demography*. Jennifer was also the most persistent voice urging us forward to progress from writing research articles to producing a book on a topic that was getting increasing attention from journalists and policy institutes. Jennifer's collaborative work with Tom enriched chapter 5 in particular. Anne McDaniel wrote her dissertation on comparative aspects of the gender gap, was the lead author of our collaborative study on racial differences in the gender gap in demography, and was a coauthor on our review article in the *Annual Review of Sociology*. Anne and Tom's working paper on parental effects on the gender gap enriched chapter 6. Anne also contributed ideas to chapter 2 and helped with the production of many of the figures in the book and the online supplement. Joscha Legewie was the lead contributor in our group to the theoretical and empirical study of peer effects and their relevance for the gender gap. He provided the computations for some of the tables in chapter 6 and produced figure 7.1. He also made invaluable comments on the entire manuscript that improved the quality of this book. Allison Mann has been researching gender trends in STEM majors and gender differences in self-evaluation in both the American and the international contexts, and her work enriched chapters 2 and 8 in particular. Uri Shwed did early work on gender trends, and Jill Bowdon continues to work on the development of gender differences in self-evaluation of math and science ability over the educational life course. Finally, Greg Eirich's dissertation on parental religiosity and children's educational attainment has been a valuable source of inspiration for our scholarship.

Our work received support from various agencies and scholarly institutions, including the four universities (Duke University and the Ohio State University for Claudia; Duke, Columbia, and the University of Wisconsin–Madison for Tom) that have been our academic homes during the course of this project. Tom and Jennifer received funding from the Spencer Foundation and the American Educational Research Association for studies of social and behavioral skills in early elementary grades, the influence of teachers on these skills, their differences by gender, and the causal relationship between social and behavioral skills and academic outcomes. Claudia received a seed grant from Ohio State University's Initiative for Population Research, which is funded by a center grant from the National Institute of Child Health and Human Development. Tom and Claudia worked on the aspects of this project involving women and STEM fields with support from award R01EB010584 from the National Institute of Biomedical Imaging and Bioengineering. (The content of our papers and this book is solely our responsibility and does not necessarily represent the official views of the National Institute of Biomedical Imaging and Bioengineering or the National Institutes of Health.) Tom was privileged to spend the 2008–2009 academic year as a visiting scholar at the Russell Sage Foundation. Some of the research activity involving the education panel datasets collected by the National Center for Education Statistics was facilitated by a license to analyze the restricted version of these data sets from the NCES. Work with these data also benefited from services provided by the Center for Population Research at Columbia University, the Center for Demography and Ecology at the University of Wisconsin–Madison, and the Department of Sociology at the Ohio State University. We also thank Vidya Sampath and Galo Falchettore for research services at the Russell Sage Foundation during Tom's visiting scholar year.

Tom and Claudia were invited to write a chapter on gender and education for the Russell Sage Foundation project "US2010: America After the First Decade of the New Century." Work on this project, including especially the comments of Suzanne Bianchi, contributed to the improvement of the manuscript. The project has also benefited from comments received on the many occasions when we presented either an overview of the project or various papers from the education and gender project on more specialized topics, including: a presentation at the Visiting Scholars Speaker Series of the Russell Sage Foundation in 2008; keynote addresses at the Society of Education Asilomar conferences in 2010 and 2011; a keynote address at the 2009 British Household Panel Survey Conference; presentations at the Population Research Center of the University of Texas–Austin; the Institute for Research on Women and Gender at Columbia; the Population Studies Center of the University of Pennsylvania; the Wisconsin Center for Education Research, the Sociology Colloquium, the Institute for Research on Poverty, and the Sociology of Gender "FemSem" at the University of Wisconsin–Madison; the Center for Population Dynamics at Arizona State University, the Discipline-Based Scholarship in Education Program of Indiana University; NYU Abu Dhabi; and the Steinhardt School of Education at New York University; as well as at meetings of the Population Association of America and the American Sociological Association, and at the 2012 conference in Hong Kong organized by the Research Committee on Social Stratification (RC28) of the International Sociological Association.

Paula England and an anonymous reviewer provided exceptionally thorough and thought-provoking comments that greatly improved the manuscript. Suzanne Nichols at the Russell Sage Foundation was instrumental in making this book a reality, and we appreciate her patience with us. We also appreciate a different level of patience as well as support from our spouses, Keith and Katherine. Finally, we thank our children, Julia, Bethany, Justine, Benjamin, and Michaela, for the inspiration that initiated and informed our writing of this book.

Chapter 1

Introduction

WOMEN TYPICALLY make less money than men. They seldom occupy the most powerful offices in government or corporate America. And they still do the bulk of the child care and routine housework in the home. These and other features of gender inequality have led some observers to write of the "stalled gender revolution" (England 2010; Carlson 2011). Not long ago, women also lagged considerably behind men in their educational attainment. In the United States and most industrialized societies, however, the days when gender inequality in education meant female disadvantage are now more than twenty years in the past. In fact, women have made substantial gains in all realms of education and now generally outperform men on several key educational benchmarks. In 1970, 58 percent of college students were men, but by the 1980s the gender gap in college enrollment favored women, and in 2010, 57 percent of all college students were women (Snyder and Dillow 2012). Women are also more likely than men to persist in college, obtain degrees, and enroll in graduate school. This growing female advantage in higher education has attracted the attention of college administrators, policymakers, and the media, and researchers are trying to make sense of this reversal from a male advantage to a female advantage in educational attainment as it has unfolded not only in the United States but also in most industrialized societies.[1]

The striking gains by women in the educational arena have multiple causes. Certainly, their gains in education are part of a larger story about the changing place of women in the labor market and in society more generally. But three important features of the trend favoring females in education suggest that women's educational gains do not follow solely from their changing status in society. First, women have not merely gained educational equality with men; on many fronts they have surpassed men by a large and growing margin. Second, women have overtaken men in the total number of college degrees earned even as gender segregation in fields of study has persisted. Third, trends in the size of the gender gap have differed considerably by race and ethnicity. These three features of the gender gap in education have far-reaching implications for American society and raise important policy questions. This book examines the rise of women in education with a focus on these three complex aspects of the phenomenon.

Let's dig a bit deeper into the story of the reversal of the gender gap in college completion. It is a story about females' real gains, but also about stagnation in education for males that raises daunting challenges for American society. Just fifteen years ago, the United States boasted the highest rate of tertiary education completion in the world. Today it lags behind many other industrialized countries on this front (Organization for Economic Cooperation and Development 2010a). In light of the importance of college completion rates for national wealth, quality of life, and international competitiveness, the Obama administration has expressed concern about the stagnant rates of college degree receipt in the United States and has set regaining international leadership in higher education as a national goal. It is important to understand, however, that America's stagnation in college completion is largely due to the stagnation of men's college completion rates.

Trends in bachelor's degree completion for males and females are shown in figure 1.1. This figure is based on U.S. census data from 1940 to 2000 and on American Community Survey (ACS) data from 2010. Males from the birth cohorts of 1912 through about 1950 had a lead over females. Among cohorts born after 1940, females began closing the gap with males; their gains accelerated as women born in the late 1950s and early 1960s (who were of college age during the 1980s) overtook men in their rates of completing bachelor's degrees.[2] Women continue to increase their educational attainment along roughly the same trajectory they have followed since the 1960s. On a cohort-by-cohort basis, the male college graduation rate peaked around the birth cohort of 1950 and then remained essentially flat for about fifteen birth cohorts (DiPrete and Buchmann 2006). Thereafter, male cohorts gradually increased their rate of college completion, but these gains lagged behind the contemporaneous gains for women and the gains for male cohorts born before 1950. By 2010, twenty-six- to twenty-eight-year-old females had a more than eight-percentage-point lead in college degree receipt over their male counterparts. This constitutes an enormous change in the relative position of men and women in a very short period of time.

Women's now-sizable lead in college completion has occurred despite the scientific consensus that girls and boys have similar levels of academic aptitude. It is true that girls generally outperform boys on verbal tests and lag behind boys on math tests, especially in the population at the lower end of the test score distribution. But gender differences in mental ability as measured by test scores are simply too small to account

Figure 1.1   Proportion of Twenty-Six- to Twenty-Eight-Year-Olds with a
Bachelor's Degree, Birth Cohorts 1912 to 1984, by Birth Year

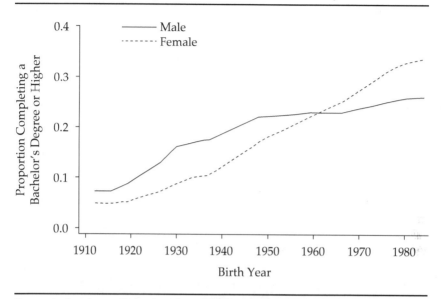

Source: Authors' compilation based on IPUMS census data, 1940 to 2000 (Ruggles et al.
2010); American Community Survey (U.S. Census Bureau 2010).

for the current gender gap in college completion. Moreover, these small
gender differences in mental ability have remained fairly stable, while
the gender gap in educational attainment has reversed from a male advantage to a female advantage that continues to grow in magnitude.

Women's rapid educational gains are certainly linked with gains in
women's real wages as well as their wages relative to men. Although a
gender gap in wages still exists—in 2010 the ratio of women's earnings
to men's earnings was 0.81 (U.S. Department of Labor 2010a)—Francine
Blau and Lawrence Kahn (2007b) show that the gender wage gap has
shrunk to roughly half the size it was in 1978, when the ratio of women's
earnings to men's earnings was only 0.61. Indeed, one important consequence of women's rising educational attainment is a reduction in their
earnings disadvantage relative to men. As Blau and Kahn (2007b) note,
women's earnings gains are particularly remarkable in light of the fact
that they have occurred during a period of rising overall wage inequality.[3] In fact, in many metropolitan labor markets today, because women's
quantitative advantage in education outweighs their disadvantage from
continuing gender segregation in the labor market, young women are
actually earning more on average than their male counterparts.[4]

This reversal of the gender wage gap in some labor market sectors
highlights men's lack of progress in increasing their "supply" of college-

educated workers in an era when economic inequality has risen to levels not seen since the 1920s and economic returns to education have risen sharply. Ironically, the stagnation in men's college completion rates occurred during a period when wages for high school–educated males declined, as a result of both technological change and the decline of the unions that had boosted the earnings of blue-collar workers. It is unclear why, in the face of these changes, more males did not complete college. Moreover, men's stagnant college completion rates exacerbated the wage decline for high school–educated workers and stimulated strong growth in the returns to a college degree (Goldin and Katz 2008). Also striking is the fact that during the period when real wages for high school–educated males were falling, the wages for high school–educated females remained stable (Appelbaum, Bernhardt, and Murnane 2003), and yet females, not males, rapidly increased their rates of college enrollment and receipt of bachelor's degrees. Men's failure to respond, as women have, to the economic incentives arising from the stagnant wages of high school–educated workers and the rising relative wages of college-educated workers is certainly puzzling and demands examination.

The Cost of the Male Shortfall in Education

As time passes, the American adult population increasingly comprises cohorts of women who lead men in educational attainment. In the 2010 American Community Survey, among fifty-five- to sixty-four-year-olds, men still lead women in bachelor's degrees (18.3 percent to 15.5 percent) and advanced degrees (13.5 percent to 11.6 percent). For forty-five- to fifty-four-year-olds, however, men trail women in bachelor's degrees by 1.4 percentage points, and they lead women in advanced degrees by less than half a percentage point. Among thirty-five- to forty-four-year-olds, the female lead in bachelor's and advanced degrees combined is over four percentage points. Among twenty-five- to thirty-four-year-olds, 11 percent of women versus 7.5 percent of men have advanced degrees; another 24.3 percent of women have bachelor's degrees compared with 20 percent of men, for a combined advantage of over ten percentage points.

Such a large gender gap in educational attainment has potentially large implications for economic outcomes as well as for other aspects of life that are enhanced by education. Here we carry out several "what if" scenarios using ACS data and simple statistical models in order to get a sense of the implications of the male shortfall in education. For example, it is well known that the likelihood of unemployment declines with level of education. Nine percent of twenty-five- to sixty-four-year-old men in the labor force were unemployed in 2010. If men had the same educational distribution as women, their unemployment rate would be half a percentage point lower. For twenty-four- to thirty-four-year-olds, among whom the male shortfall is the largest, men's unemployment rate would be one full percentage point lower if their educational attainment matched that of their female counterparts.

What about income? The median personal income for twenty-five- to sixty-four-year-old employed men in 2010 was $40,000. The gradient with education was very large: median income for men with less than a high school degree was $22,000, for men with a bachelor's degree it was $60,000, and for men with graduate degrees the median was $82,000. This steep gradient with education implies that both individual men and American society as a whole pay a heavy price for their failure to attain as much education as women. If men had women's educational distribution, their personal income would be 3.7 percent higher.[5] If the shortfall between all men and women was as large as the shortfall for the twenty-five- to thirty-four-year-old population, the missing income rises to 9.4 percent. This is a substantial sum of money to be missing from the pockets of American workers and their families.[6]

Of course, beyond economic outcomes, other aspects of life are strongly altered by education. The better-educated have better health and more stable marriages and family lives. The benefits of education can also be passed down from one generation to the next, since educated parents have more resources, financial and otherwise, to invest in their children. Failing to finish high school or obtaining only a high school diploma or GED (General Educational Development) certificate puts individuals' quality of life and that of their children at substantial risk. But some scholars maintain that the goal of "better-educated" adults should not mean "college for all." In *Beyond College for All: Career Paths for the Forgotten Half* (2001), James Rosenbaum argues that college is not an appropriate goal for all students and that there are better ways to improve the job skills of marginal students. According to the October Current Population Survey (CPS), 68 percent of high school graduates from the previous year were enrolled in college or university in 2010, and 60 percent of those were enrolled in four-year colleges (Goldin 1990). But the failure to complete college is a major problem in the United States. In earlier work (Buchmann and DiPrete 2006), we found that only 39 percent of males and 47 percent of females who attended both two-year and four-year colleges had graduated from a four-year college by the time they were about twenty-six years old (see also Bowen, Chingos, and McPherson 2009).[7]

Today about two-thirds of high school graduates pursue higher education, and about half of these students obtain a bachelor's degree by their late twenties. Thus, instead of talking about college-capable students as comprising a "top half" and a "bottom half," as Rosenbaum

(2001) has done, the data suggest that we think instead in terms of thirds. At present, nearly one-third of American cohorts (but more than one-third of American females) complete a bachelor's or advanced degree. Another third get some postsecondary education, but the great majority of this "middle" third leave the world of higher education with no degree. The bottom third of this distribution do not enroll in college and have limited prospects for doing so. In 2010, 6 percent of males age twenty-five to thirty-four received less than a year of postsecondary education, 17 percent had one year or more, and 7 percent earned an associate's degree. (The corresponding numbers for females are 6 percent, 17 percent, and 9 percent.) We do not know why so few in this middle third complete college; perhaps it has something to do with the relatively low levels of resources that typical colleges expend on their students in comparison to highly selective universities (Bowen et al. 1998; Black and Smith 2004; Hoekstra 2009; Hoxby 2009); perhaps it has to do with the skill deficits these students have as they enter college. But research suggests that at least some students with a low observed propensity to graduate from college are nonetheless better off if they do graduate (Attewell and Lavin 2007; Maurin and McNally 2008; Brand and Xie 2010). This research suggests a disconnect between the value of higher educational degrees and the failure of college-capable students to complete these degrees, even as it begs the question of why this disconnect exists—and apparently more strongly for males than for females.

Largely because of the failure of this middle third to complete college, the United States has fallen behind several other industrialized countries in the rate at which students complete tertiary education. In Japan, Australia, and Finland about 40 percent of young adults complete college.[8] The experiences of other countries and the continued strong upward trend in U.S. women's college completion rates suggest that the United States could increase its college completion rate considerably before exhausting the stock of college-capable students in each cohort. These gains could be made near the top of the middle third who have some college but do not complete college. Currently, in the United States females are achieving the most rapid increases in college completion. A deeper understanding of how they have accomplished this feat may provide insights into the causes of the current gender gap in higher education, as well as suggest strategies to increase overall rates of educational attainment in the United States.

The Goals of This Book

The rising gender gap in college completion raises some key questions. How did women manage to increase their level of educational attainment so robustly over the past twenty years? Why did the male college graduation rate stall around the 1950 birth cohort and never resume its earlier rate of increase? This slowdown in men's educational attainment is puzzling for two reasons. First, why did sons born in the last half of the twentieth century fail to benefit from their parents' human capital resources to the extent enjoyed by earlier cohorts? Across these many birth cohorts, the fraction of parents who had a college education continued to increase. The strong upward trend in parental education predicted a similarly strong upward trend in the proportion of children finishing college if the "rate of return" to parental education remained as high as it was in earlier years (Buchmann and DiPrete 2006). This predicted upward trend was realized for women but not for men. In fact, the average rate of return to parental human capital fell substantially for men born after 1950.

The second reason the slowdown in men's educational attainment is puzzling is that it occurred when the value of education for males was rising. Labor market returns to educational attainment have been rising since the mid-1970s. Returns to education in the marriage market for males also rose over this period of time, because of marital educational homogamy and because educated women earned increasing wages. Men have been less likely than women to respond to these rising incentives to get more education.

In pondering these puzzles, we must of course keep in mind the heterogeneity of both males and females. Nearly one-third of all males do graduate from a four-year college. They have taken advantage of the human capital in their home and school environments, and generally they will earn more money as a consequence of their college investment. But what about the young men in the top and middle thirds of the academic distribution who fail to graduate from college? These males share the same level of parental human and cultural capital as their sisters, and overall they have roughly the same academic ability as females (albeit with lower average grades in school). These young men generally finish high school and attain some postsecondary education, but they are less likely than females to earn a BA, despite the apparent incentives for them to do so. It is the low college completion rates of these young men that we aim to understand.

This book seeks to accomplish two goals. First, we describe the changes in the relative educational attainment of females and males in the United States over the twentieth and early twenty-first centuries and consider explanations for the reversal of the gender gap during these years. Changing college completion rates can be accounted for in terms of changes in high school completion rates, rates of transition between high school and college, and rates of college completion for students who enroll in college. As we describe these changes, we attend to the experiences of different racial and ethnic groups, especially the notably different trends in the educational gender gap for whites and blacks. These trends occurred within the context of massive expansion of the U.S. higher education system and other important societal changes, and we place the gender trends within this broader context. Part I focuses on several macro social changes during the years when the gender gap declined and then reversed. The most obvious change concerns the place of women in American society. At the beginning of the twentieth century, patriarchal culture ensured an incompatibility between higher education, marriage, and fertility for American women (Goldin 1990), who were forced to choose between having a career and having a family (Epstein 1970; Walby 1986). This patriarchal system kept the perception that women's place was in the home firmly entrenched for several decades of the twentieth century. Patriarchal culture also shaped the socialization and investment practices of families. When faced with labor markets and family systems that privilege males, a "rational" family prioritizes the education of sons (Becker 1981; Papanek 1985; Rosenzweig and Schultz 1982).[9] Over the course of the twentieth century, this patriarchal system eroded and was gradually replaced with more gender-egalitarian norms and social institutions.[10] While by no means do we maintain that women have attained equality in most realms of society, we do believe that the reduction in gender inequality in the American labor market and the shift toward greater gender-egalitarian attitudes among Americans (Brewster and Padavic 2000) have reduced parents' incentives to favor sons with educational investments.

Other important macro social changes were the growth in labor market opportunities for college-educated workers and the growing accessibility of college education for America's middle class. In the late nineteenth and early twentieth centuries, when the proportion of Americans who went to college was very small, women's rates of college completion actually slightly surpassed those of men (Goldin 1992), owing to patterns of gender segregation in the workforce. Women went to college for essentially only two careers—teaching and nursing—and these two occupations were much larger than the male-dominated careers that required a college degree, such as medicine, law, engineering, and management. The subsequent acceleration in the demand for college-educated workers was directed largely at men. The costs of higher education dropped across much of the twentieth century, especially in the twenty-five years after World War II (Goldin and Katz 2008).

Children of middle- and upper-class parents have always had an advantage in completing college, stemming partly from their higher academic performance and partly from their financial advantages. By raising the number of available places and reducing costs, educational expansion can reduce these socioeconomic advantages, but it is unlikely to eliminate them until the point at which educational attainment becomes nearly universal, which is not foreseeable for the case of college completion (Raftery and Hout 1993). At any rate, class advantages do not directly affect gender differences, because sons and daughters are equally distributed across the socioeconomic status distribution. Families' socioeconomic resources do, however, play a role in the size of the contemporary gender gap, as we discuss later.

Finally, changes in American families—specifically, changes in marriage patterns, the rise in family instability, and the changing educational incentives for both women and men that emerged as a consequence of these changes in family structure—are all related to contemporary educational gender gaps. In the first half of the twentieth century, marriage markets were defined more by class than by education. When more men than women completed college, women "married up" in educational terms. In fact, higher education was an impediment to marriage for women, because it was associated with a career orientation seen as incompatible with the roles of middle-class wife and mother (Goldin 1992). But in the second half of the twentieth century, education gradually became an important asset in the marriage market for both women and men. A college education increased the chances that a woman would ever marry and that she would have children within marriage (Qian and Preston 1993; Ellwood and Jencks 2004). Educational homogamy also increased in recent decades, as highly educated women were more likely to marry highly educated men (Schwartz and Mare 2005). College-educated women also have lower divorce rates and have experienced a stronger downward trend in divorce rates than women without a college education (Isen and Stevenson 2010).

The second goal of this book is to examine gender differences in educational performance and attainment over the life course. Parts II and III focus on families, peers, and schools as they relate to gender differences in educational attainment and performance in the contemporary era. We are especially interested in the contemporary period because the shortfall in male educational attainment is a major component of the slowdown in American educational progress, and we seek to provide insights into how the United States could raise its educational attainment rates in the future. In response to the gender revolution that occurred in American society, the educational life course of girls and boys has changed in some important respects but has remained relatively stable in others. Although managing to complete high school and then enroll in and complete college depends partly on students' plans for the future, it depends even more on their academic performance. The relative educational and occupational aspirations of boys and girls have changed over time, but as we document, there has been a high degree of stability in the gender gap in academic performance over many decades, with girls outperforming boys in one central measure: course grades.

High school course-taking patterns, however, have changed considerably over time. Early in the twentieth century, girls and boys tended to take different high school courses as soon as they reached the level where choices were possible. Girls took courses oriented toward their future status as homemakers, while boys took courses that would prepare them for the labor market. Boys also generally took more college preparatory courses than did girls, especially more math and science courses. These gender differences in course-taking exacerbated gender differences in math and science scores on standardized college entrance examinations. With the expansion of college enrollment after World War II, the fraction of students taking college preparatory courses rose, and by the 1970s the gender gap in college preparatory courses began to close. By the late 1980s girls and boys took similar courses, and girls had largely closed the performance gap in math and science courses while maintaining their performance advantage in the rest of the curriculum (Hyde et al. 2008).[11] Through the 1980s and 1990s, high schools continued to elaborate the menu of college preparatory courses and students in the top decile of the academic distribution were going noticeably further in math and science than college preparatory students had done in the 1960s and 1970s (Dalton et al. 2007).

Why do girls perform better in the classroom? We document a performance gap that begins at the start of elementary school. Girls begin school with a clear advantage in reading and rough parity with boys in math performance. Over time, boys catch up somewhat in reading and gain an advantage in mathematics, at least as measured by standardized test scores. However, teachers consistently rate girls as having stronger academic performance than predicted from their test scores alone. Early in elementary school, girls also demonstrate better social and behavioral skills than do boys, and this advantage grows over the first few years of elementary school. Moreover, higher social and behavioral skills are correlated with higher rates of cognitive learning (as documented by standardized test scores) and higher levels of academic investment (as measured by homework). Girls' greater attention to homework and stronger academic orientation translate into their higher grades in middle school. Girls predominate among students getting mostly A's in middle school, while boys predominate among students getting C's or lower. Girls' higher grades in middle school lead to their higher grades in high school and college.

As noted earlier, college completion requires a series of successful educational transitions. A college graduate must first graduate from high school, then make the transition either directly into a four-year college or indirectly through enrollment in a two-year college. The final step is the achievement of a bachelor's degree. Throughout the 1950s, 1960s, and 1970s, white males and females transitioned into college at roughly equal rates, even though males had poorer average high school grades than did females. Males were more likely to graduate from college than females, essentially because women were less likely to pursue four-year college degrees. In the 1980s, female college enrollment surpassed male enrollment, and their increasing enrollment proved to be a decisive advantage. Because there is a strong relationship between academic performance and the likelihood of graduation, and because females earn higher grades in college than males, as they increased their enrollment advantage over males, women also graduated from college in higher numbers. Understanding the female advantage in college completion, therefore, is largely a matter of understanding the female advantage in academic performance at all stages of education.

The female advantage in academic achievement may account, in part, for the irony of stagnating male rates of college completion at a time when education's value on the labor market is historically high. Boys and girls both act as though they understand the value of higher education; three-quarters of middle school boys and 80 percent of middle school girls say that they intend to get a college degree. Seventy percent of students who graduate from high school make the transition to college, but many drop out of college before they complete a degree. This pattern suggests that the problem is not due to young Americans' failure to recognize the value of college, but their failure to adequately prepare for college during the elementary and secondary school years.[12]

Alternative Perspectives

Scholars have long been interested in how and why males and females differ in their educational achievement and attainment, though perspectives and theories have changed sharply as awareness of the female advantage in education has become more widespread. Some scholars focus on sex-based biological differences, maintaining either that female brains are better suited to academic work or that males and females have different biologically based incentives that lead to educational performance and attainment differences. For example, Susan Pinker (2008) argues that females are biologically superior to males. The irony of the female biological superiority argument is that it follows a larger literature that viewed females as biologically inferior to males in cognitive ability. Research continues to search for biological explanations for the persisting gender gap in favor of boys in performance on mathematics tests (for a review, see Ceci et al. 2009). But in light of the recent gender reversal in many educational outcomes, more recent research has focused on gender identity and the ways in which environments link gender to educational outcomes.

For several decades, psychologists debated the relative importance of internal "cognitive" mechanisms and the external environment in shaping gendered development. Early on, Walter Mischel (1966) promoted a social-learning view of gender differences in which behaviors precede cognitions, such that if one is rewarded for doing boy things, one must be a boy. In contrast, Lawrence Kohlberg (1966) proposed a cognitive model organized around the ideas of gender constancy and gender identity. In his view, young children gain an understanding of gender categories through cognitive processes and their permanent placement within these categories, such that one learns that one is a boy and therefore likes to do boy things. Kohlberg's approach was advanced by Carol Lynn Martin and Charles Halverson (1981) and Sandra Bem (1981) through the development of gender-schema theory, which maintains that children form "organized networks of mental associations representing information about themselves and the sexes" (Martin, Ruble, and Szkrybalo 2002, 911). Children are motivated to behave in accordance with gender norms "as a means of defining themselves and attaining cognitive consistency" (911). All of these cognitive views embody the principle that "basic gender identity guides behavior" (913). At the same time, relative to cognitive development theory, gender schema pays more attention to the role of the environment, such that children develop schema about how to reinforce their gender identity via interaction with the environment. Some of this knowledge takes the form of gender stereotypes—learned behaviors that are "boy-like" or "girl-like" even if they do not characterize the actual behavior of most boys or most girls—that are used to evaluate behaviors positively or negatively according to one's own gender. Gender-schema theory raises two questions regarding current gendered educational outcomes. First, how do gender differences in educational outcomes derive from the gendered behavior of children or society's response to such gendered behavior? Second, how do families, peers, and schools shape gendered educational outcomes?

Sociologists have long favored the socialization model for explaining educational attainment. The Wisconsin model of status attainment argues that adolescents form their educational and occupational aspirations through socialization, with the major influence coming from parents, peers, and teachers (Hauser, Tsai, and Sewell 1983; Sewell and Hauser 1975; Sewell, Haller, and Portes 1969). Teachers influence educational ambitions and expectations, while parents influence both educational and occupational aspirations and function as role models with respect to both domains. Although this literature was not developed to explain gender differences in educational outcomes, it implies that these differences are a consequence of gender socialization. Likewise, in the

1960s and 1970s the field of psychology was dominated by a socialization perspective that saw gender as constructed by parents (Maccoby 1998). This "traditional" view was replaced with a recognition that children shape the environment within which they live and play and are thus key actors in constructing their own gender identities. In this respect, the modern psychological view of gender identity follows the recent literature that sees intelligence as produced by a mixture of biological tendencies reinforced through environmental selection. This view places less weight on parents as actors and more weight on children's hormonal drives reinforced by dyadic and group play. But it cannot account for the striking change in the gender gap in educational outcomes.

When girls had lower educational attainment than boys, the liberal sociocultural view was that the environment was to blame; girls faced discrimination in the labor market and also within their families and schools (see, for example, Bailey et al. 1992). In contrast, the conservative view was rooted in the idea that women's and men's lives constituted separate spheres, each having its own values, life goals, and dominant personality characteristics. The conservative perspective was based on a biologically driven gender essentialism. As women have attained parity and surpassed men in educational attainment, the question has become "what is wrong with boys?" and conservative commentators have shifted from biological explanations to sociocultural ones. For example, some maintain that feminists are waging a "war against boys" in schools (Sommers 2001). In this view, schools have become dominated by a feminine culture that is not supportive of the way boys behave and learn. Even some mainstream scholars allege that schools use conduct-based grading that evaluates typically feminine behavior more favorably than typically masculine behavior (Entwisle, Alexander, and Olson 2007).

With the growing realization of the "boy problem" in school, it is not just conservative commentators who claim that contemporary society promotes a masculine identity incompatible with the social and psychological needs of boys. Some critics fault parents and schools for linking a stereotypical masculine identity with emotional distance from adults. William Pollack (1999) argues that a "boy code" reinforced by mothers and schools leaves boys lonely and trapped behind a "mask" of masculine power and autonomy. Michael Kimmel (2008, 73) argues that the boy problem "has to do with the ways in which boys and girls experience masculinity and femininity. Again, it's about gender—about the *guy code*." Dan Kindlon and Michael Thompson (2000) agree that the problem stems from gender stereotypes that steer boys away from emotional connectedness as well as schools that are insensitive toward the special needs of elementary school-age boys. David Anderegg (2007) argues that the problem is anti-intellectualism, manifested in American culture as being against "nerds," who are always gendered as masculine. Thus, the development of masculine self-identity produces detachment from school. In short, all of these authors see the emergence of an "oppositional culture" among boys as linked to misunderstandings by parents, schools, and the broader society about the nature of masculinity during childhood and adolescence. Others elaborate this critique to explain the especially large disadvantage of African American males that is produced by the power imbalance between racially stigmatized youth and the dominant society (Lopez 2003; Noguera 2008). We revisit the important issue of masculine identity as it relates to educational outcomes in later chapters.

Our Approach

It certainly is plausible that biology plays a role in producing the educational gender gap, but our focus is sociological and empirical, and we resist explanatory frames that overly homogenize the genders or that cast the problem in a zero-sum "war against boys." Instead, we emphasize the need to study heterogeneity within genders as a basis for understanding why average differences between males and females have become so prominent. We examine the global environment that shapes gender-specific constraints, opportunities, and incentives for education. We also examine the local environments of families, peers, and schools that shape how individual girls and boys respond to the global environment. Because the society has changed over time in ways that affect the relative performance of boys and girls, we address the question of gender differences in the context of widespread social changes that have created changing opportunities for women and men to utilize their skills. Then we seek to establish how family context might affect gender gaps in academic achievement and attainment. We similarly ask whether and how school and classroom environments have an impact on the gender gap in achievement and attainment.

Our focus on local environments corresponds to our emphasis on heterogeneity of experience—including but not limited to social class, race, and ethnicity—as the best way to understand why the average gender gap has grown so large. We seek to identify both the environmental characteristics that have the biggest effects on the gender gap and the students who are most sensitive to environmental effects. The current landscape suggests a perspective that divides student populations into thirds based on their likelihood of completing four-year college. Most of those in the top third of this population are already getting a college degree. Those in the bottom third of the population of students are very unlikely to be in a position to complete college. Roughly half do not graduate from high school, while most of the rest complete high school by means of a GED. Although some students in this bottom third get some postsecondary education, their poor academic performance limits how far they can go in school. Therefore, the best potential for raising college graduation rates is found within the middle third of this population. Almost all of these students graduate from high school and attain some postsecondary education, and most assert that they expect to obtain a four-year college degree. But the majority of this middle third fails to complete four years of college, and the shortfall is significantly greater for males than females.

Whether these students would benefit from additional education and what form this education should take remain contentious issues. As noted earlier, James Rosenbaum (2001) argues that American schools need to prepare the "forgotten half"—those who do not complete college—for other careers. In contrast, Paul Attewell and David Lavin (2007) maintain that open education in the City University of New York (CUNY) system produced many more people with college degrees and benefits that included higher earnings, better marriage prospects, and enriched environments for their children. In his critique of Attewell and Lavin, Steven Brint (2008) argues that the additional education attributable to the open education policy largely resulted in a new credential, not in the enhancement of skills. Jennie Brand and Yu Xie (2010) argue that marginal students actually gain more from college graduation than do typical college graduates, while Pedro Carneiro, James Heckman, and Edward Vytlacil (2011) maintain that this would be true only for the small subset of students with a low propensity to go to college who have unobservable characteristics that greatly raise the value of college for them. (In other words, selection into college on unobservable characteristics is strong.) We do not need to resolve the question about who benefits most from additional education in order to argue for policies that raise college graduation rates for those students in the middle third who realistically could complete college but currently do not. Any such policies should be responsive to the fact that this population is predominantly male.

We synthesize the existing literature and combine it with numerous analyses we have undertaken for this book or previously published articles and conference papers in collaboration with several current and former graduate students: Jill Bowdon, Jennifer Jennings, Joscha Legewie, Anne McDaniel, Allison Mann, and Uri Shwed.[13] In examining trends in the macro environment, we employed data from the decennial censuses back to 1940, using the Integrated Public Use Microdata Samples (IPUMS), monthly data from the Current Population Surveys (CPS), annual data from the October education supplement to the Current Population Survey, annual data for the most recent decade from the American Community Survey (ACS), and administrative data from the Cooperative Institutional Research Program (CIRP) Freshman Survey, the

Integrated Postsecondary Education Data System (IPEDS), the National Assessment of Educational Progress (NAEP), the cumulative General Social Surveys (GSS), and the WebCASPAR database maintained by the National Science Foundation (NSF). Data for the international comparisons were drawn from published reports of the Organization for Economic Cooperation and Development (OECD).

We also analyzed several panel data sets, including studies in which samples of children, adolescents, or young adults are surveyed periodically over a number of years. Four of these data sets were collected by the National Center for Education Statistics (NCES) of the U.S. Department of Education, spaced about ten years apart, and focused on students in middle school, high school, or college. The National Longitudinal Survey of the High School Class of 1972 (NLSHS72) began in 1972 with interviews of a national sample of high school seniors. High School and Beyond (HSB) began in 1980 with interviews of a national sample of high school sophomores and high school seniors and followed a subset of these students through 1992. The National Education Longitudinal Study (NELS) collected data on a sample of students who were in eighth grade in 1988 and followed a subset of them until 2000. The Education Longitudinal Study (ELS) of 2002 began with a sample of high school sophomores in 2002 and will continue to survey them through their early twenties. We also used a fifth NCES panel study, the Early Child Longitudinal Study, Kindergarten Class of 1998–99 (ECLS-K), which follows a national sample of students from kindergarten through eighth grade and collects data from them, their parents, and their teachers. All of the NCES panel data sets provide rich information about the school experiences of students through designs that sample clusters of students in the same school and through supplementary surveys of school teachers or administrators as well as school-based administrative data.

In addition to the NCES panel studies, we utilized three panel studies collected under the supervision of the National Longitudinal Studies program of the U.S. Department of Labor. The National Longitudinal Survey of Youth: 1979 (NLSY79) has been collecting information about a sample of young people who were fourteen to twenty-two years old when first surveyed in 1979. Starting in 1986, the National Longitudinal Studies program began fielding supplementary surveys to follow all children of the female members of the NLSY79 sample. These children are still being surveyed. Finally, the National Longitudinal Survey of Youth: 1997 (NLSY97) follows a sample of U.S. residents born between 1980 and 1984. The National Longitudinal Studies provide particularly good information about respondents' family environments, sometimes through the collection of information from both parents and children or information on more than one sibling in the same family.

In this book, we largely focus on the United States, but we bring in international evidence when it gives a useful perspective on the American experience. The fact that women are overtaking men in educational attainment across much of the industrialized world belies the validity of any answer that rests too heavily on the cultural or social structure of any one country, including the United States. International comparisons of the school performance of girls and boys reinforce the idea of a common pattern: girls perform better in realms that emphasize verbal skills, while boys have an advantage in realms that emphasize mathematical performance. At the same time, careful studies of cross-national variation in educational performance and attainment (for example, Penner 2008; Guiso et al. 2008; McDaniel 2011) reinforce other evidence (for example, Ceci et al. 2009) pointing to important social and cultural explanations for the current gender gap in education. We specifically cite collaborative studies that we have undertaken with data from the Program for International Student Assessment (PISA), including two extensions of the PISA in Germany—the PISA-I-Plus and the PISA-E—and a panel study of elementary school students in Berlin, the ELEMENT data. This international perspective provides a fuller picture of the growing gender gap in education.

Historically, many American men have tended to work in well-paid, blue-collar jobs. Some of these jobs involved apprenticeship training as an entry into construction or a trade; others involved semiskilled factory work or truck driving. Thanks in part to the once-countervailing power of labor unions (Galbraith 1956), these jobs generally paid better than the jobs available to women without a college degree and even better than many professional jobs held by women college graduates. This world flourished in the late 1950s through the 1970s, and it gradually faded away during the 1980s and 1990s as the baby boomers worked through their prime years and had children of their own. In some respects (especially for younger Americans), this world now seems remote. But in generational terms, it is not far in the past. Now, in an era of deindustrialization, globalization, and the decline of union-supported blue-collar employment, less-educated baby boomers have increasingly struggled to achieve an acceptable standard of living. High school–educated boomers could see that the jobs in the United States that paid extremely well were mostly reserved for college graduates. But they saw no "bright line" difference between the standard of living of those who had only a high school diploma and those who had a college degree, especially a degree from a local or state college or university. When their own wages failed to keep pace, less-educated male workers often managed to forestall a decline in their household standard of living through increased work hours by their wives, even as they held out hope that their future prospects would brighten through improvements in the broader economy.

Americans have been taught to be optimistic about the future. One of us recently published a paper titled "Is This a Great Country? Upward Mobility and the Chance for Riches in Contemporary America" (DiPrete 2007). This paper analyzes survey data collected in 2003, which is more than two decades after the onset of deindustrialization and the decline of union power, the decline of real wages for high school–educated men, and the stagnation of market income for households at the median of the American income distribution (Burkhauser 2012). A generation of young people had grown up during this transformative period for the American economy. Such events should have engendered pessimism about one's future standard of living for many young Americans, especially those without a college degree. Gallup interviewers asked: "Looking ahead, how likely is it that you will ever be rich?" and the answers were surprising. Even though fewer than 30 percent of young American males would have earned a bachelor's or advanced degree by age twenty-five, 58 percent of eighteen- to twenty-nine-year-old males thought it was somewhat or very likely that they would someday be rich. The extent of men's over-optimism (quantified in DiPrete 2007) was striking especially with respect to their female counterparts. Only 43 percent of eighteen- to twenty-nine-year-old women expected to ever be rich, even though, as a group, they were better educated and had a greater chance than men of improving their standard of living through marriage (because husbands make more money on average than do wives).[14] Clearly, many young men with only a high school diploma who grew up during the decades when the wage returns to a high school diploma were falling nonetheless believed that they had a good chance of earning a lot of money in the labor market. Their optimism mirrors that of autoworkers in the 1950s who dreamed of saving enough of their earnings to start their own business (Chinoy 1955). Many of today's young men are optimistic about achieving economic success without a college degree, despite the fact that in the aftermath of the recession that began in 2007, young blue-collar workers in large manufacturing industries are paid on a shrunken scale relative to that of older workers.[15]

These poll data underscore that it can take more than one generation of durable change in the environment before parents absorb its implications and communicate them to children effectively. Why do attitudes take such a long time to catch up to reality? First, ordinary people know less about labor markets and the connection between labor markets and education than do specialists. Second, Americans know that individual outcomes can be quite variable and that they depend on many factors beyond education. Their awareness of this variance causes them to overpredict the mean, such that they are overly optimistic. Compounding this inertia is the arguably tight connection between gender stereotypes in the workplace and the process of gender socialization in the family. Many blue-collar jobs in construction, transportation, and manufacturing have a strongly masculine identity. Fathers in these jobs convey their masculinity to their sons in part through the physical aspects of their work lives. Sons internalize particular stereotypes as they develop their own masculine identity. This process can strengthen a boy's attachment to the career path of his blue-collar father and thereby slow the rate of generational adaptation to a changing labor market that has increasingly devalued blue-collar work.

This book is less concerned with the broader issue of gender identity and more focused on the question of why and how gender is linked to educational attainment. We show that making sense of this question requires that we recognize the importance of the family, not only for its ability to socialize children but also for its ability to invest resources in them. We argue that the sociocultural resources of middle-class families provide distinctive advantages to males. This does not mean that a boy must be born in a middle-class family to achieve the same potential as his sister, but rather that middle-class boys have a special advantage in light of the sex-typed culture in which children grow up. School environments and the student cultures within them also play a role. Boys are especially sensitive to their local environments, and this sensitivity may produce greater variation in their behavior. In short, the global gender gap hides substantial variations that can be found when we focus on specific class, race, school, or family environments. Understanding the sources of these local variations is important for enhancing the educational performance and attainment of males. Needless to say, we do not attempt to evaluate every explanation put forward for the growing educational gender gap. We do not attempt to assess the value of single-sex schools, though we are skeptical about their value for closing the gender gap in academic performance. We do not evaluate the extent to which schools have "feminized" cultures, though again, we are skeptical. We do, however, extend current empirical evidence and synthesize what is known in order to gain insights into the causes of the male shortfall in education and what can be done about it.

Our fundamental orientation is pro-education. We care about the gender gap and want to reduce it, not because inequality per se is bad (though we have a pro-equality bias), and certainly not because girls have unfairly gained an advantage from a "war on boys," but because greater insight into the reasons for the male shortfall can help develop policies that improve educational outcomes for both girls and boys. It is telling that, in the aggregate, neither females nor males come anywhere close to realizing the educational aspirations they express in adolescence. Rates of college graduation would need to more than double for the gap between adolescent aspirations and educational attainment to close. Skeptical observers (Murray 2009) believe that this goal would be incompatible with the distribution of IQ in the population. We believe that this goal is currently infeasible, not for genetic reasons but because of financial barriers coupled with family and school environments that do not adequately promote development of the learning skills that would enable more students to successfully complete college if they are motivated to do so.

The problem of insufficient motivation among American youth is a large one. Gender shapes motivation in ways that give girls an advantage in school because—as we show—they typically derive more intrinsic gratification from performing well on a day-to-day basis. Daily performance builds knowledge and skills and makes it easier to achieve at higher stages of the education process. If boys gained more short-term gratification from academic effort, they would also work harder; this effort would enable them to perform better and go further in school than they typically do now. Short-term gratification is especially important at younger ages, but as children enter adolescence and young adulthood, the intrinsic appeal of school must be supplemented by occupational goals that can be realized via specific courses of study. Perhaps more women than men see recognizable pathways through college to desirable jobs, or perhaps females can stay the course because they have better academic work habits than do males. These are questions to which we return to later.

The growing fraction of women completing a college degree suggests that there is not a strong cognitive constraint on the fraction of a cohort who are capable of doing college work. Thus, the study of the gender gap in college completion is important in its own right and can provide a lens for viewing the broader question of how to enhance the educational attainment of both women and men.

Outline of the Book

Chapters 2 and 3 focus on educational trends and address the reversal of the gender gap in college completion from a macro perspective. Chapter 2 provides a descriptive overview of college completion trends for males and females in the United States and other OECD countries and shows how women's share of tertiary education has risen rapidly throughout the industrialized world during the past thirty years. We then describe gender-specific trends in the completion of bachelor's degrees, master's degrees, and doctoral and professional degrees to show the full picture of women's rise over men in educational attainment. Chapter 2 next examines the pathways to college completion, including high school completion and college enrollment. We compare males' and females' rates of college enrollment and completion for whites, African Americans, and Hispanics. We also address the extent to which age-specific transition rates vary by gender.

Chapter 3 examines the broader societal context in which the reversal of the gender gap in education has occurred. Women's labor market opportunities have grown dramatically since the early part of the twentieth century. The chapter explores the implications of rapid changes in labor market opportunities and considers how these opportunities varied for men and women by race and ethnicity. It also considers how changing returns to a college degree in terms of various aspects of well-being, including earnings, standard of living, marriage, and marital dissolution, are related to trends in college completion for men and women. We also consider the potential obstacles to college completion posed by military service, incarceration, and supply constraints in the available number of places in colleges in light of what can reasonably be viewed as a competition (both between and within genders) for college admission and high college grades.

In parts II and III, we shift to a life-course perspective and seek answers to the question of why males now lag so far behind females in rates of college completion in the contemporary United States. Part II (chapters 4 to 6) considers academic performance, social and behavioral skills, and the roles of parents, peers, and adolescent culture. Chapter 4 focuses on the gap in academic performance between boys and girls in elementary school, middle school, and high school. It documents the long-standing female advantage in school grades even when accounting for gender differences in curriculum. It also documents the gradual female gains in mathematics and science test scores over the past thirty years and the dramatic gains in math and science course-taking among females; in 1972 male high school students took more math and more science courses than did females, but by 2004 females led males in the overall number of math and science courses they took as well as in enrollment in middle-level to advanced-level high school math and science courses. Chapter 4 demonstrates the strong connection between academic performance in middle and high school and the probability of college completion. Most of the gender difference in college completion rates is due to the gender gap in academic performance that emerges as early as middle school. The gender difference in grades in eighth grade is reproduced in high school and then, for the subset of high school students who enroll in college, in college grades, which in turn are strongly predictive of whether a student will earn a bachelor's degree.

The academic performance gap is the proximate cause for the gender gap in college completion, and chapters 5 and 6 examine the causes of this gap in detail. Chapter 5 reports on the research on how much of the academic performance gender gap is due to gender gaps in social and behavioral skills and effort. Social and behavioral skills include orientations to learning, attentiveness, task persistence, and self-control. In general, girls have higher levels of social and behavioral skills than boys as early as kindergarten, and this advantage grows during the early years of elementary school. Social and behavioral skills are also related to gains in reading and math competence during elementary school. Analyses of young children find that a significant component of the gender gap in reading can be explained by the female advantage in social and behavioral skills. Boys have an advantage over girls in math test scores by the middle of elementary school, but girls' advantage in social and behavioral skills reduces the size of their deficit in math tests. Social and behavioral skills play an even greater role in teacher ratings of academic outcomes, such that girls get higher teaching ratings on average. This advantage comes about primarily through the cumulative benefits provided by social and behavioral skills for the learning process rather than through conduct-based grading by teachers. Effort also matters for academic performance, and chapter 5 considers the extent of the gender gap in academic performance that can be attributed to differences in average effort expended by girls and boys.

Chapter 6 examines the impact of parents, peers, and the preadolescent and adolescent subculture. While parents' human and cultural capital is strongly related to their children's educational outcomes, we explore whether some parental characteristics are differentially related to sons' and daughters' educational outcomes. Psychologists have argued that parents have limited influence on the gender differentiation of their children and that gender differentiation occurs instead largely through interaction among peers. Our central interest is in the specific issue of gender differentiation in academic performance. We believe that two corrections to the psychological model should be made. First, the model needs to recognize that peer effects on academic performance are far from uniform. Some peer cultures value and reward academic performance, while others denigrate academic performance, especially for boys in working-class cultures. Second, the model needs to consider that parents can affect not only the academic performance of their children but also the gender gap in performance between their sons and their daughters. We demonstrate how the relationship between parental socioeconomic status and the gap in educational attainment between sons and daughters has changed dramatically over the past sixty years: at one time, boys got more education in families with less-educated parents, but now they get less education relative to girls in those families.

We argue that the educational disadvantages facing many boys today can be alleviated by family resources. Chapter 6 shows that the gender gap in educational attainment between children in the same families tends to be lower when the father is present and when he is more highly educated. We believe this to be due to the ability of higher-educated parents, and fathers in particular, to instill in sons an "adult" conception of masculinity and an understanding of the instrumental role that academic achievement plays in masculine success in adulthood. This fosters an instrumental attachment to school for sons that offsets the expressive coolness toward school that is central to common preadolescent and adolescent conceptions of masculinity.

What does all of this mean for American schools? Chapter 7 explains how school environments influence the gender gap in educational performance. Schools with strong academic climates typically shrink the size of the educational gender gap by raising the academic performance of boys without harming the academic performance of girls. We address three common propositions about schools and the gender gap. We argue against the notion that the female advantage is a consequence of biased grading that favors girls, as well as the idea that the male disadvantage has emerged because schools have created a "feminine" environment that is detrimental to boys. And there is little evidence that the educational gender gap can be attributed to coeducation or that single-sex schools and classrooms provide general educational benefits to boys. But school environments can play important roles in improving academic performance overall while reducing the typical performance disadvantage of boys. We argue that much of the male disadvantage can be traced to a peer culture that often provides status rewards for an oppositional attitude toward school, and we present evidence from the United States and Europe suggesting that academically oriented classroom climates differentially raise the academic performance of boys in elementary and secondary school.

Schools also can play a role in reducing the large remaining degree of gender segregation in fields of study even as women have come to outpace men in educational attainment. Specifically, women continue to lag behind men in engineering and physical science degrees even as they have achieved parity or advantages in other elite fields such as medicine, law, and the biological and life sciences. Chapter 8 addresses gender differences in high school intentions to major in the science, technology, engineering, and mathematics (STEM) fields and gender differences in college majors and bachelor's and post-bachelor's degrees. We report on trends in both bachelor's and advanced degrees using survey and administrative data from the National Center for Education Statistics and other sources. We also present research that addresses the dominant theories proposed to account for this gap and that shows that such gaps arise neither from gender differences in mathematical skills nor from gender differences in adolescent values concerning career and family. One important source of gender differences in fields of study is the impact of the local environment on the development of stereotypes concerning gender and STEM fields during middle and high school. College-bound girls largely form their orientations toward physical science, engineering, and mathematical fields of study by the end of high school. Girls who have signaled an intent to major in one of these fields by the end of high school are just as likely as boys to follow through on their plans and graduate from college with a degree in a STEM field. But they are much less likely than boys to transition into these college majors if they have not already declared an interest by high school. In contrast, the expressed orientations of middle school girls and boys toward the sciences are only moderately predictive of the orientations they will express at the end of high school. Thus, high school is a very important period for the formation of a science or nonscience orientation, particularly for girls. School environments differ in the extent to which they support the idea that majoring in a STEM field can be an attractive choice for women. Some schools do an especially good job of providing this support by undermining common stereotypes that link majoring in a STEM field with a masculine identity. Recent evidence suggests that schools with strong science and math curricula are particularly good at delinking STEM fields from masculine stereotypes.

The final chapter (chapter 9) recapitulates the arguments developed in the preceding chapters. As should be clear by now, we believe that the cause of the educational stagnation in the United States is environmental and that changes in the environment can spur continuing advances in rates of college completion in this country to rival those achieved in other industrialized societies. Some aspects of the environment, such as the rising cost of higher education, have created challenges for all students, male and female, who aspire to get a college degree. But other environmental conditions have created specific challenges for males. We propose strategies for tackling these environmental challenges, with the goal of increasing the educational attainment of both men and women.

Part I

Trends and the Macro Environment

Chapter 2

What Has Happened? Describing the Reversal of the Gender Gap in College Completion

T HE GENERAL outlines of the gender gap reversal in college completion are now well known.[1] This reversal occurred through a sharp
slowdown in the rise in educational attainment of men, starting
with cohorts born around 1950. The rise in educational attainment for
women also slowed around this time but only temporarily; thereafter,
women continued to make steady progress. For men, the slowdown in
the growth of college completion rates lasted longer, and when growth
did resume, it was as strong as that for women. The distinctive trends
for women and men combined to reverse the gender gap in educational
attainment in women's favor. Consider this: in 1960, 65 percent of all
bachelor's degrees were awarded to men. Women lagged behind men in
college graduation rates until 1982, when they reached parity with men.
From 1982 onward, the percentage of bachelor's degrees awarded to
women climbed steadily until, by 2010, women received 57 percent of
all bachelor's degrees (Snyder and Dillow 2012) and comprised 57 percent of all college students. By all predictions, women's advantage in
college enrollment and BA completion will continue to grow over the
next decade, albeit more slowly than in past decades (Snyder and Dillow 2012, table 283). In this chapter, we describe these trends in the
United States in detail and situate them within the broader international
context.

Educational Gender Gaps in Comparative Perspective: A Global Phenomenon

The striking reversal in the gender gap in higher education is not solely
a U.S. phenomenon. Today more women than men attain higher educa-

tion in most European countries as well as in many other parts of the world; see figure 2.1, which reports data collected by UNESCO (United Nations Educational, Scientific, and Cultural Organization 2012). Among the thirty member nations of the Organization for Economic Cooperation and Development (OECD), the once-prevalent male advantage in college completion has disappeared in all but four countries: Switzerland, Turkey, Japan, and Korea (OECD 2006). This fact is all the more striking when we consider that thirty years ago women lagged behind men in completing college degrees nearly everywhere in the world. From 1965 to 1985, women's share of higher education increased, on average, from 27 to 40 percent across a range of countries (Bradley and Ramirez 1996). But in the 1980s, women began to reach parity with men and in many cases surpassed men in the amount of education they received. Figure 2.2 shows the rise of women's share of enrollment in higher education in OECD countries between 1990 and 2008. Countries are ordered by women's share of enrollment in 2008, from women's smallest share (Korea) to their largest share (Iceland). Projections suggest that women's advantage will grow in most countries. By 2020, females are expected to comprise at least 60 percent of tertiary students in Austria, Canada, Hungary, Iceland, New Zealand, Norway, Sweden, and the United Kingdom.

Note that several OECD countries have higher female shares of tertiary enrollment than the United States. This fact is related to another noteworthy comparison in overall tertiary completion: after leading the world for much of the twentieth century, the United States has fallen behind other industrialized countries in terms of the percentage of the population attaining tertiary degrees. This fallback is readily apparent in figure 2.3, which compares the fraction of the population at different age ranges who have completed a tertiary 5A degree. By this method, the United States ranks first among the fraction of fifty-five- to sixty-four-year-olds who have a tertiary 5A degree, but only eleventh among twenty-five- to thirty-four-year-olds who have this degree.[2]

Although the United States remains in the upper middle of the distribution of countries, it has nonetheless dropped substantially in the rankings. That fact raises a question: was the American decline in tertiary completion relative to other industrialized countries largely driven by the educational problems of American males? Figure 2.4 sheds light on this question by comparing tertiary completion rates for men and women in the United States and selected OECD countries for two cohorts—those born between 1945 and 1954 and those born between 1975 and 1984. For the 1945 to 1954 birth cohort, the United States had the highest rates of completion among industrialized countries for both women and men. By the 1975 to 1984 birth cohort, the percentage of U.S. women who had attained a tertiary degree had risen dramatically, while the percentage of men who had attained a tertiary degree actually declined in the OECD statistics. The amount of progress made by U.S. males across cohorts was next to last among the thirty-four OECD countries, and American males ranked only tenth among these countries by 2009.[3] However, though young American women had a much higher rate of tertiary degree completion than did older American women, the rise in this rate in other OECD countries was even more dramatic; indeed, American women also ranked next to last among the thirty-four countries in the size of their increase in degree attainment across these cohorts. The female gains in Norway, Denmark, Finland, and Poland have been particularly impressive; today more than 40 percent of all young women in these countries have a tertiary degree, and overall, American women—like American men—now rank tenth among OECD countries. Thus, even though the United States stands out for its slow educational upgrading by successive American male cohorts, the poor showing of American males is not the cause of the American shortfall in tertiary degrees; gains are greater elsewhere in the industrialized world for both males and females.

The Pathways to College Completion in Contemporary America

The pathways that individuals take from high school to a college degree vary, but all pathways are punctuated by necessary transitions (Goldrick-Rab 2006; Pallas 2003; Mare 1981). In the United States, completing high school is the first step to gaining access to postsecondary education. Many youth are not eligible to become college students because they have not completed high school. High school graduates who decide to enroll in college must navigate several more steps, such as applying, getting admitted, and then matriculating into college, before they become college students. They then face the challenge of graduating from college. American college students, and especially males, frequently fail to attain a degree. When seeking to understand mean gender differences in college completion, it is illuminating to break these differences down into differences in rates of high school completion, the transition to college, and the conditional probability of completing a four-year degree, given college entry, for males and females. It appears that the female advantage in college completion in the United States today is due to advantages at each of these transition points. For example, young women are more likely than young men to graduate from high school (Mishel and Roy 2006; Heckman and LaFontaine 2007). Girls have lower high school dropout rates than boys, and this gender gap has been widening since the middle 1990s. In 2005 almost 11 percent of males age sixteen to twenty-four were dropouts, compared to 8 percent of females (Snyder

Figure 2.1   The Gender Gap in Tertiary Enrollment, by Country, 2012

Source: From "Women now a majority of tertiary level students in most countries," UNESCO Institute for Statistics, pp. 78–79 in *World Atlas of Gender Equality in Education* © UNESCO 2012. Reprinted with permission.

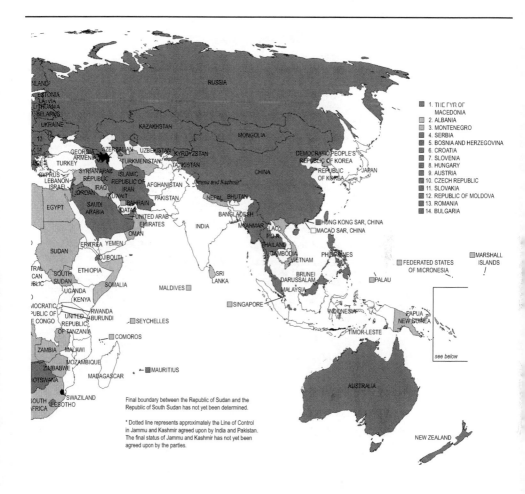

1. THE FYR OF
   MACEDONIA
2. ALBANIA
3. MONTENEGRO
4. SERBIA
5. BOSNIA AND HERZEGOVINA
6. CROATIA
7. SLOVENIA
8. HUNGARY
9. AUSTRIA
10. CZECH REPUBLIC
11. SLOVAKIA
12. REPUBLIC OF MOLDOVA
13. ROMANIA
14. BULGARIA

Final boundary between the Republic of Sudan and the
Republic of South Sudan has not yet been determined.

* Dotted line represents approximately the Line of Control
in Jammu and Kashmir agreed upon by India and Pakistan.
The final status of Jammu and Kashmir has not yet been
agreed upon by the parties.

Figure 2.2   Women's Share of Tertiary Enrollment in OECD Countries, 1990, 2008, and 2020 (Projected)

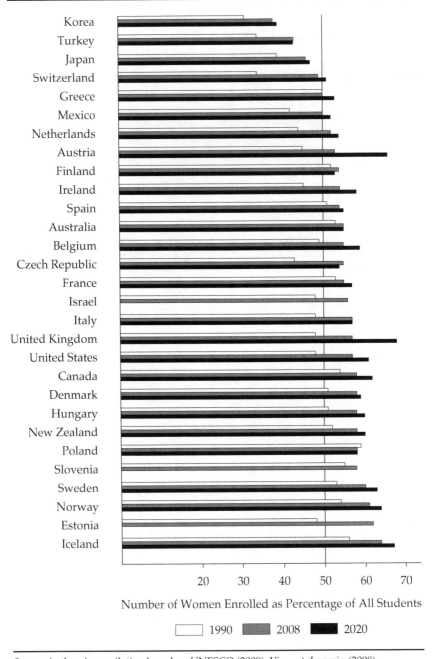

Number of Women Enrolled as Percentage of All Students

☐ 1990   ▦ 2008   ▬ 2020

Source: Authors' compilation based on UNESCO (2009); Vincent–Lancrin (2008).

Figure 2.3   Ranking of OECD Countries by Rate of Tertiary Completion

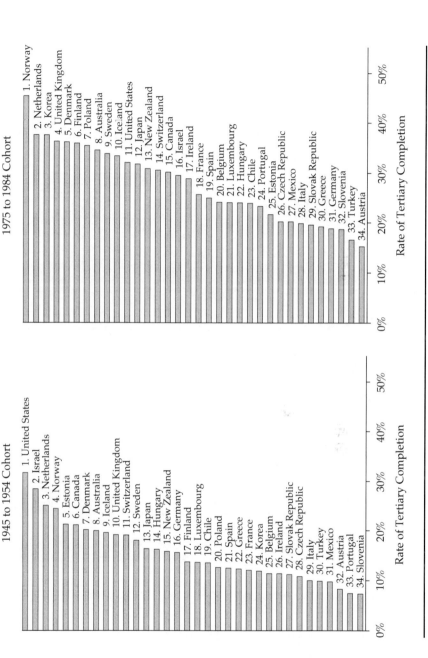

1945 to 1954 Cohort

1. United States
2. Israel
3. Netherlands
4. Norway
5. Estonia
6. Canada
7. Denmark
8. Australia
9. Iceland
10. United Kingdom
11. Switzerland
12. Sweden
13. Japan
14. Hungary
15. New Zealand
16. Germany
17. Finland
18. Luxembourg
19. Chile
20. Poland
21. Spain
22. Greece
23. France
24. Korea
25. Belgium
26. Ireland
27. Slovak Republic
28. Czech Republic
29. Italy
30. Turkey
31. Mexico
32. Austria
33. Portugal
34. Slovenia

Rate of Tertiary Completion

1975 to 1984 Cohort

1. Norway
2. Israel
2. Netherlands
3. Korea
4. United Kingdom
5. Denmark
6. Finland
7. Poland
8. Australia
9. Sweden
10. Iceland
11. United States
12. Japan
13. New Zealand
14. Switzerland
15. Canada
16. Israel
17. Ireland
18. France
19. Spain
20. Belgium
21. Luxembourg
22. Hungary
23. Chile
24. Portugal
25. Estonia
26. Czech Republic
27. Mexico
28. Italy
29. Slovak Republic
30. Greece
31. Germany
32. Slovenia
33. Turkey
34. Austria

Rate of Tertiary Completion

Source: Authors' compilation based on data from OECD (2011).

Figure 2.4   Percentage of Males and Females Who Obtained a Tertiary Type A Degree, Birth Cohorts 1945 to 1954 and 1975 to 1984, 2009

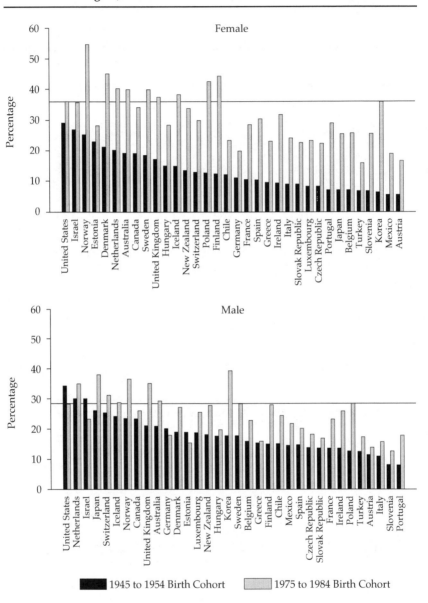

Source: Authors' compilation based on data from OECD (2011).

and Dillow 2007). The male disadvantage in terms of dropout is true for all major race and ethnic groups. In 2005 male dropout rates for whites, blacks, and Hispanics were 6 percent, 12 percent, and 26 percent, respectively, compared with 5 percent, 9 percent, and 18 percent, respectively, for females of the same groups (Snyder and Dillow 2007). Foreign-born youth are especially vulnerable to dropping out of high school for a wide variety of reasons ranging from language difficulties to lower rates of parental education and poor-quality schooling in their country of origin, among other factors (Hirschman 2001). While only 8 percent of the nation's teens are foreign-born, nearly 25 percent of high school dropouts are foreign-born, of which roughly 40 percent are recent immigrants who interrupted their schooling before coming to the United States (Fry 2005). It is unclear how foreign-born males and females compare in their dropout rates and how the factors predicting dropout for this vulnerable population vary by gender.

Among students who complete high school, more males than females acquire a General Educational Development (GED) certificate. In contrast to high school graduates who earn a traditional high school diploma, GED recipients are high school dropouts who are exam-certified as high school graduates through GED tests (Heckman and LaFontaine 2007). A GED typically indicates a lower level of college preparedness than a high school diploma. James Heckman and Paul LaFontaine (2007) note that the overall gender gap in college attendance is 10 percent, but that the gender gap given high school completion (not counting through GED) is only 5 percent. Thus, it seems that half the gender gap in college attendance is due to the lower levels of college preparedness of males.

Among those who do enroll in college, differences in the timing and pace of their enrollment have an impact on the likelihood that they will complete college. Students who enroll in college directly after high school have higher rates of overall college enrollment, persistence in college, and graduation (Bozick and DeLuca 2005; Horn et al. 1995). Although men used to be more likely than women to enroll in college directly after high school, they are now substantially more likely than women to delay enrollment in college. Of those who enrolled in college in the year 2000, 60 percent of men compared to 66 percent of women enrolled immediately after high school (Freeman 2004). The female advantage in immediate college enrollment holds regardless of socioeconomic status, but the gender gap is smaller for those of socioeconomically advantaged backgrounds (King 2000; Bozick and DeLuca 2005).

Another major reason why women earn more college degrees than men is the lower rate at which they drop out, once enrolled in college (Buchmann and DiPrete 2006). Women also earn their degrees more quickly. Catherine Freeman (2004) found that 66 percent of women who enrolled in college in 1995–1996 had completed a bachelor's degree by

2001, compared with only 59 percent of men. Men were more likely than women to have no degree or to not be enrolled, but they were also more likely than women to still be enrolled in a bachelor's degree program. Whereas 50 percent of black and Hispanic women had completed a bachelor's degree in this period, only 37 percent of black men and 43 percent of Hispanic men had done so. To put these contemporary patterns in context, it is helpful to look to the past and consider educational gender gaps over a broader time period.

U.S. Educational Gender Gaps in Historical Perspective: 1940 to the Present

All Americans became more educated over the course of the twentieth century. In 1900 most people had only primary schooling. By 1920 high school graduation had become widespread, and by 1960 most high school graduates had at least some college (Fischer and Hout 2006, 10). In the latter part of the twentieth century, college graduation supplanted high school graduation as the educational watershed. For example, while fewer than 7 percent of people born in 1915 graduated from college, 28 percent of people born in 1975 had graduated from college by the age of twenty-five (Bailey and Dynarski 2011). The rapid expansion of higher education in the United States had many sources, including a public commitment to higher education manifested through the building of state college systems and the creation of direct federal aid to students, first in the form of the GI Bill and later in grant and loan programs (Fischer and Hout 2006, 14). Of course, amid the rising educational levels of the U.S. population could be found substantial variations for different segments of the population and, most notably, for men and women.

In chapter 1, we presented trend lines in figure 1.1 for the fraction of twenty-six- to twenty-eight-year-old men and women with bachelor's degrees, by birth cohort, based on IPUMS census data for the years 1940 to 2000 and ACS data for the year 2010.[4] This figure is reproduced in this chapter as figure 2.5. In 1940 (when cohorts born in 1912 to 1914 were twenty-six to twenty-eight years old), only about 5 percent of women and 7 percent of men completed a bachelor's degree by age twenty-six to twenty-eight. By 2010, 36 percent of women and 28 percent of men in this age range had completed a bachelor's degree. How did this reversal come to pass? The gap in degrees earned between men and women was relatively small in 1940. But from 1940 onward, men earned more bachelor's degrees than women, such that by 1960 (when cohorts born in 1932 to 1934 were twenty-six to twenty-eight years old), 15 percent of men earned bachelor's degrees as compared to only 8 percent of women. Over the next decade, the rate of degree receipt continued to increase for men and women, but starting with those born around 1950, a dramatic

Figure 2.5   Proportion of Twenty-Six- to Twenty-Eight-Year-Olds with a Bachelor's Degree, Birth Cohorts 1912 to 1984, by Birth Year

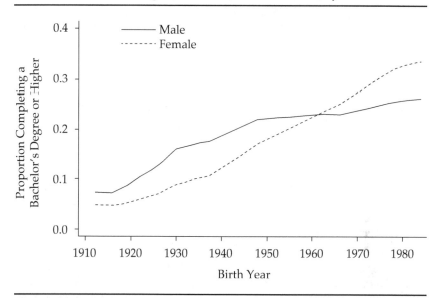

Source: Authors' compilation based on IPUMS census data, 1940 to 2000 (Ruggles et al. 2010); American Community Survey (U.S. Census Bureau 2010).

change occurred. Men's rates of BA completion began a multiyear stagnation, with the consequence that men born in the mid-1960s had virtually the same rate of BA completion as men born fifteen years earlier. This stagnation was probably due in part to the end of the Vietnam War–related draft, which had enhanced levels of college attendance among young men as a strategy to avoid military service (Freeman 1976; Card and Lemieux 2001). The timing of men's stagnating college completion rates also coincided with a decline in the wage premium to college that labor economists have attributed to the large supply of new college-educated job-seekers from the early baby boom cohorts (Freeman 1976). However, the persistence of the stagnation in men's college completion rates certainly has deeper causes than just these two events. As of 1980, the proportion of twenty-six- to twenty-eight-year-old men completing a bachelor's degree was still only 25 percent, and it would reach only 26 percent as of 2000 and 28 percent by 2010.

In contrast, women's rates of degree receipt rose steadily after the birth cohorts of 1950, even as male rates stagnated, and their steady progress erased the gender gap by the time the 1960 birth cohorts had moved through the college enrollment years. In the past thirty years, the proportion of twenty-six- to twenty-eight-year-old women earning at least a bachelor's degree has continued to increase rapidly, from 21 percent in 1980 to 30 percent in 2000 to 36 percent in 2010. In sum, the large female advantage in college completion in the United States today stems from continued steady growth in the proportion of women who earn college degrees in combination with a prolonged stagnation in the college completion rates of American men.

Women have also made impressive gains in their receipt of master's degrees relative to men. Figure A.1 displays trends in men's and women's completion of master's degrees from the 1969–1970 school year to the 2009–2010 school year. Just over three decades ago, in 1969–1970, more men than women completed master's degrees: 143,083 master's degrees were awarded to men, compared to 92,481 awarded to women (Snyder and Dillow 2012). But from 1980 onward, women's rate of master's degree completion grew more rapidly. By 2009–2010, women were awarded roughly 50 percent more master's degrees than men—417,828 versus 275,197.

Women's growth in professional and doctoral degrees has been slower than that for bachelor's or master's degrees (see figure A.2), and they have only recently reached parity with men in professional and doctoral degrees. In 1970 men completed sixteen times more professional degrees than women did. But since 1982, the number of professional degrees completed by men has declined slightly (from 40,229 in 1982 to 34,661 in 2010), while women's professional degree completion has increased almost twentyfold—from 1,534 professional degrees in 1970 to 30,289 in 2010. The gendered pattern for doctoral degrees conferred is similar to that for professional degrees: men completed almost eight times as many doctoral degrees as women in 1969–1970 (58,137 versus 6,861), but by 2009–2010, more doctoral degrees were awarded to women than men (81,953 versus 76,605). If these trends continue, the gender gap in professional and doctoral degrees may begin to resemble the female-favorable gender gap in bachelor's and master's degrees.

Figure 2.6 presents the data from figures A.1 and A.2 in terms of women's share of degrees (that is, the percentage of degree recipients who are women). In 1969–1970, women comprised almost 40 percent of all students awarded master's degrees, but they comprised only 11 percent of students awarded doctoral degrees and 6 percent of students awarded professional degrees. Women's share of master's degrees has grown over the past three decades, and women currently comprise 60 percent of students earning master's degrees. Women's share of professional and doctoral degrees has increased as well, with women now earning 47 percent of professional degrees and 52 percent of doctoral degrees. Clearly, at every level of education women have achieved equality or have surpassed men in the number of degrees earned.

Figure 2.6   Women's Share of Master's, Doctoral, and Professional Degrees Awarded, 1969–1970 to 2009–2010

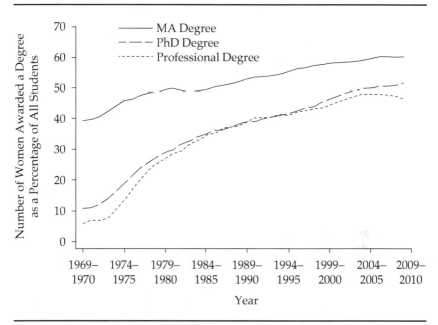

Source: Authors' compilation based on data from the National Center for Education Statistics (Snyder and Dillow 2012).

Trends by Race and Ethnicity

The female advantage in degree completion exists for all racial groups, but there are important variations by race and ethnicity in the size of the gap. It is largest for blacks, but it is also large for Hispanics and Native Americans. In 2010, 66 percent of all bachelor's degrees awarded to blacks were earned by women, as were 61 percent for Hispanics, 60 percent for Native Americans, 55 percent for Asians, and 56 percent for whites (Snyder and Dillow 2012). To get a more complete portrait of the historical trends in college completion in the United States, we consider how the trends in college completion differ for various racial and ethnic groups for much of the past century. Figure 2.7 presents the proportion of twenty-six- to twenty-eight-year-old blacks and non-Hispanic whites with at least a bachelor's degree by gender and race across the birth cohorts covered by the census and ACS data from 1940 to 2010. The trend for the two groups is clearly different. The pattern for whites is marked by a reversal of the gender gap, similar to the overall trends presented in figure 2.5, with 42 percent of twenty-six- to twenty-eight-year-old

Figure 2.7   Proportion of Twenty-Six- to Twenty-Eight-Year-Olds with a Bachelor's Degree or Higher, by Gender and Race for Blacks and Non-Hispanic Whites, Birth Cohorts 1912 to 1984, by Birth Year

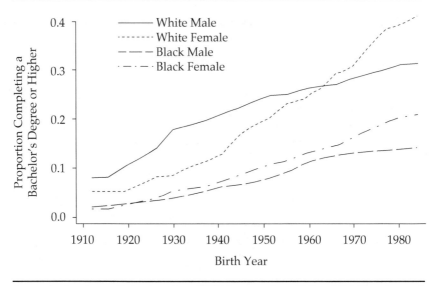

Source: Authors' compilation based on IPUMS census data, 1940 to 2000 (Ruggles et al. 2010); American Community Survey (U.S. Census Bureau 2010).

white women and 33 percent of white men earning a bachelor's degree in 2010. However, black men never led black women in rates of college completion. In 1940, only 1.3 percent of twenty-six- to twenty-eight-year-old black men earned a college degree, compared to 1.6 percent of black women.[5] By 2010, 16 percent of black men and 23 percent of black women in the twenty-six- to twenty-eight-year-old age group had completed four-year college. Blacks' rates of college completion have risen steadily over time, but more rapidly for women than for men. Black women have held a consistent advantage, albeit a small one early on, in college completion over black men for more than seventy years; among whites, women's advantage in college completion emerged in recent decades.

Trends for Asians, Hispanics, and Native Americans are more similar to those for whites than blacks. Data for these groups (presented in figure 2.8) are available only from 1970 to the present.[6] Note that Hispanics and Native Americans are placed on a different scale from Asians, whose college completion rates are higher than those of any other ethnic group. Among Hispanics, Asians, and Native Americans, women were in the process of passing men in their rate of BA completion for twenty-six- to twenty-eight-year-olds who were born in the early 1960s. By 2010 (the

**Figure 2.8   Proportion of Twenty-Six- to Twenty-Eight-Year-Olds with a
Bachelor's Degree or Higher by Gender and Hispanic, Asian, and
Native American Status, Birth Cohorts 1942 to 1984, by Birth Year**

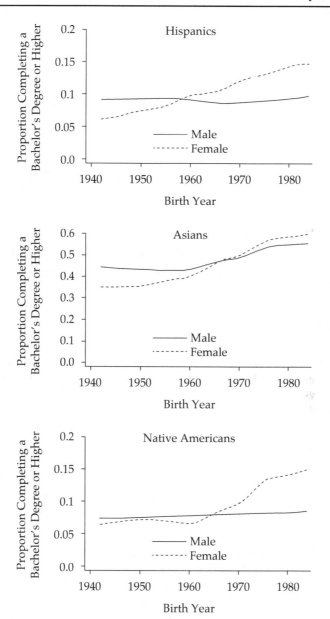

Source: Authors' compilation based on IPUMS census data, 1970 to 2000 (Ruggles et al. 2010); American Community Survey (U.S. Census Bureau 2010).

birth cohorts of the early 1980s), the female lead had grown larger in all of these racial and ethnic groups. Among Hispanics, 17 percent of women and 12 percent of men age twenty-six to twenty-eight had a college degree. Among Asians, a high 62 percent of women and 58 percent of men had a college degree, and 14 percent of Native American women had a college degree, compared to only 11 percent of Native American men. Despite the large racial and ethnic differences in the proportion of the population completing a bachelor's degree, women outperformed men within each racial and ethnic group.

Earlier we noted the declining relative position of the United States among industrialized nations in terms of college completion. The combination of lower levels of educational attainment by Hispanics and non-whites and their growing share of the American population is contributing to the current U.S. educational shortfall, but it is hardly the dominant cause. Even the 42 percent college completion rate for U.S. white females lags considerably behind female tertiary completion rates in the Netherlands, Denmark, Norway, and Finland (compare figures 2.4 and 2.7). Similarly, the 33 percent four-year college completion rate for twenty-six- to twenty-eight-year-old white U.S. males lags male tertiary completion rates in the Netherlands, Japan, Norway, the United Kingdom, and Korea.[7]

Changes in Fields of Study

In addition to gender inequalities in the quantity of education received, or what Maria Charles and Karen Bradley (2002) have termed "the vertical dimension of educational stratification," gender differences in fields of study (major) and type of institution (elite versus non-elite, public versus private) represent distinctions in the type of education received, or the horizontal dimension of stratification (for a review, see Gerber and Cheung 2008). In contrast to the rapid changes in the educational attainment of women, the gender composition of fields of study has changed far more slowly. Figure 2.9 displays changes in the dissimilarity index over the past forty years for bachelor's degree recipients, calculated by Allison Mann and Thomas DiPrete (2012). The index shows a pronounced decline in gender segregation through the mid-1990s, at which point the declining segregation trend begins to stagnate. This illustrates the continuation of the slowdown in gender integration identified over a decade ago by Jerry Jacobs (1995) and by Sarah Turner and William Bowen (1999). The education-business-other index suggests that much of the overall decline in gender segregation through the mid-1980s was situated within those areas. Changes in gender segregation within the liberal arts and sciences have been more uneven, but the overall level of segregation in the sciences has been much higher and appears to be rising. Mann and

Figure 2.9   Gender Segregation in Fields of Study, 1966 to 2009

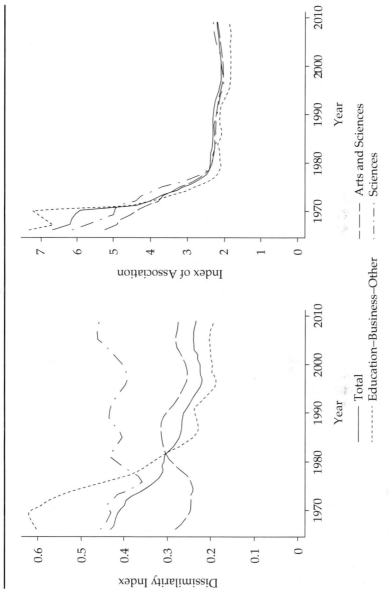

Source: Mann and DiPrete (2012), Data are from National Science Foundation, WebCASPAR database.

DiPrete (2012) also computed trends in the index of association using the National Science Foundation's WebCASPAR data (Charles and Grusky 1995). The index of association measures the factor by which women are underrepresented in the average field of study; it is not affected by changes in the share of students in particular fields, which is important because there have been substantial changes in the overall attractiveness of many STEM fields. With this measure, the gender segregation trends become more pronounced. There is a large decrease in the index for all fields (total) before 1980, dropping from more than 6 in the late 1960s to about 3 in 1980. In terms of the broad subfields, gender segregation in education-business-other majors has continued to diminish, albeit more slowly than it abated in the 1980s, but the arts and sciences (and especially the sciences) have seen rising levels of segregation in the past decade. We delve deeper into the issue of gender segregation in fields of study and its sources in chapter 8.

Age-Specific Rates and the Changing Pattern of Educational Transitions

College completion in the United States is predicated on the successful completion of a set of earlier transitions through secondary school, and from high school to college. There are normative ages at which these transitions occur. Children usually start first grade at age six, complete high school at age seventeen or eighteen, and complete college around the age of twenty-one or twenty-two. Of course, disruptions in this normative trajectory can occur for many reasons: late entry into elementary school, grade retention–related delays in completing high school, delayed entry into college, spending time in community college, going to school part-time, or exiting and reentering college, to name just a few. Here we dig deeper into the trends in the gender gap in college completion for blacks and whites shown in figure 2.7. First, we examine age-specific four-year college completion rates, and then we examine trends in the educational transitions preceding four-year college completion.

Table A.1 documents the trend over time in the gender gap for individuals by age and race by showing the proportion of respondents in the 1940 through 2000 census data who completed four years of college by race, age, gender, and census year. Table 2.1 reports the corresponding odds ratios.[8]

The pattern of white male delay is apparent throughout the cohorts covered by the 1940 to 2000 census data. In table 2.1, for the 1918 cohort, white male and female completion rates at age twenty-two are at parity, but by age twenty-eight, white females have only two-thirds the odds of completing college as do white males. The initial male disadvantage is even stronger in the 1928 cohort, but the white male catch-up is stronger

Table 2.1   Female/Male Odds Ratios for Completing Four-Year College by
Age, Year, and Race, 1940 to 2000

	Census Year/Birth Cohort						
	1940/ 1918	1950/ 1928	1960/ 1938	1970/ 1948	1980/ 1958	1990/ 1968	1996/ 1974
Whites							
Twenty-two	1.02	1.58	0.82	0.86	1.19	1.41	1.56
Twenty-three	0.85	1.18	0.71	0.81	1.08	1.38	1.57
Twenty-four	0.76	0.75	0.69	0.81	0.98	1.20	1.42
Twenty-five	0.65	0.57	0.59	0.77	0.99	1.21	1.39
Twenty-six	0.58	0.51	0.58	0.74	0.95	1.15	1.24
Twenty-seven	0.58	0.51	0.55	0.70	0.91	1.15	1.29[a]
Twenty-eight	0.63	0.48	0.52	0.69	0.89	1.12	1.25[a]
Blacks							
Twenty-two	1.70	3.15	2.63	1.41	1.79	1.34	1.67
Twenty-three	1.49	2.33	1.72	1.35	1.61	1.57	1.65
Twenty-four	1.70	1.22	1.41	1.56	1.34	1.41	1.43
Twenty-five	1.54	1.47	1.53	1.30	1.27	1.48	1.59
Twenty-six	1.14	0.92	1.12	1.17	1.24	1.40	1.39
Twenty-seven	1.55	1.66	1.36	1.32	1.27	1.42	1.61[a]
Twenty-eight	1.54	1.21	0.95	0.95	1.31	1.53	1.47[a]

Source: Authors' compilation based on IPUMS 1940–2000 (Ruggles et al. 2010).
[a]Computed based on extrapolating 1990 to 2000 results into the future.

too, such that the female odds of completing college are only half (0.48) of the male odds by age twenty-eight. The relative low point for white females occurs for the 1938 cohort; white females lag behind males at age twenty-two, and they continue to fall behind, having only slightly more than half the odds (0.52) of completing college as white males by age twenty-eight.

In the 1948 birth cohort, a strong pattern of male delay is also evident. The 1948 male birth cohort was centrally involved in the Vietnam War, and so a pattern of male delay in this cohort is not surprising: many men delayed completing college either because they were serving in the military or to avoid being drafted. Notably, the 1938 cohort (those who were twenty-two in 1960) was, for the most part, too old to be part of the Vietnam War. The major difference between the 1938 and 1948 cohorts is that the women in the 1948 cohort are more like their male counterparts in educational attainment at age twenty-two (they have 86 percent the odds of males of having completed four years of college), and they do not fall as far behind males by age twenty-eight (they have 69 percent of the male odds of completing four years of college by age twenty-eight).

By the 1958 birth cohort, white females have higher odds than white males of completing four years of college at both ages twenty-two and twenty-three. As with the older cohorts, the 1958 female birth cohort gradually falls behind males with age, but by age twenty-eight they still have 89 percent of men's odds of completing four years of college. By the 1968 cohort, females have passed males in four-year college completion in this entire age range, though their lead diminishes with age, from 41 percent greater odds of completing a BA at age twenty-two to a smaller 12 percent greater odds of completing a BA by age twenty-eight. For the most recent cohorts reported in the table (captured by the 2000 census), the white female advantage is very large: they have 56 percent greater odds of gaining a BA by age twenty-two, and 25 percent greater odds at age twenty-eight.

It is striking in table 2.1 that black women have higher odds of completing college across all time points and most ages. Like white males, black males delayed college completion relative to their female counterparts for many decades. In the 1938 birth cohort, the odds of completing college by age twenty-two for black women are 2.6 times higher than black men's odds of completing college. Black men in this 1938 birth cohort gradually reduce their education deficit, such that by ages twenty-six to twenty-eight they lag only slightly behind black women in their likelihood of finishing four years of college. The 1948 cohort of black men is similar to the 1938 cohort in being well behind black women in rates of college completion during their early twenties but achieving near-parity with black women by their late twenties. Across subsequent cohorts, however, black males, like white males, experience a growing disadvantage in educational attainment: the female/male odds ratio at age twenty-six grows from 1.12 for the 1938 birth cohort to 1.17 for the 1948 birth cohort, 1.24 for the 1958 birth cohort, and 1.40 for the 1968 birth cohort, and it remains roughly constant at this level for the 1974 birth cohort as well.

The comparisons discussed here compare genders within racial groups, but it is also illuminating to compare racial groups within genders. Figure 2.10 presents the changing odds ratio in the education of twenty-six- to twenty-eight-year-old white males to black males and of white females to black females. Racial progress has clearly been much stronger for black males than for black females. The relative odds of a white male versus a black male completing college have declined from nearly five times as high to twice as high from 1940 by 2000, with continuing strong gains until 1980 and slower gains since then. In contrast, there has been little or no trend in the relative odds of a black versus a white woman attaining a four-year college degree since about 1960. The reason for the gender difference in racial trends is largely explained by the different trajectories taken by white males and white females in the past forty years. White males have made relatively little progress in their

Figure 2.10   White Versus Black Odds of Completing a Bachelor's Degree by Age Twenty-Six to Twenty-Eight, 1940 to 2010

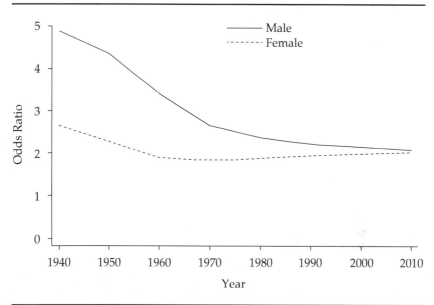

Source: Authors' compilation based on IPUMS census data, 1940 to 2000 (Ruggles et al. 2010); American Community Survey (U.S. Census Bureau 2010).

rates of college completion over these years, and it has therefore been easier for black males to reduce their disadvantage from an enormous to a merely large deficit. Black females have not been able to gain in relative terms on white females because both groups have made comparably large strides in their rates of four-year college completion. These figures demonstrate both that black males have become more like white males over time and that the racial gap for males has come to resemble the racial gap for females. To repeat, this convergence has been driven more by differing trajectories for white males and females than it has by differences in the trajectories of black males and black females.

Next, we examine gender and racial differences in the transitions that lead to college completion. The top panel of figure 2.11 shows the trend in rates of black male and female entry into postsecondary education for census respondents age twenty-six to twenty-eight, by birth year, while the bottom panel shows the same trend, conditional on completing high school via either a high school diploma or a GED.[9] Figure 2.12 shows the trend in the probability of completing four-year college, given some postsecondary education for the same samples. We see in these figures that the rising black gender gap is largely attributable to the differential in rates of entering postsecondary education. This rise in postsecondary

Figure 2.11   Probability of Blacks Age Twenty-Six to Twenty-Eight Attaining Some College, by Birth Year

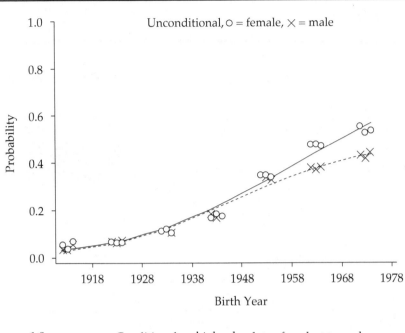

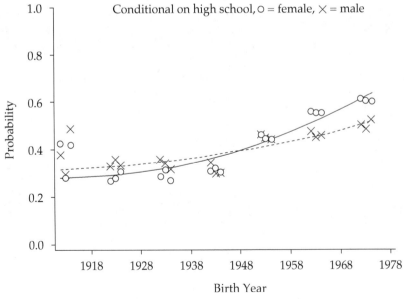

Source: McDaniel et al. (2011). Data are from IPUMS.

Figure 2.12   Probability of Blacks Age Twenty-Six to Twenty-Eight Attaining a Bachelor's Degree Given Some College, by Birth Year

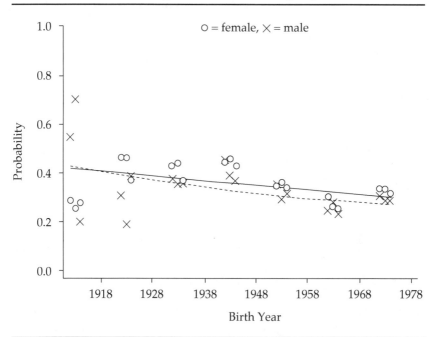

Source: McDaniel et al. (2011). Data are from IPUMS (Ruggles et al. 2010).

education involves both increased rates of enrollment in community colleges (Snyder and Dillow 2007) and a more academically diverse selective population opting to enroll in higher education. Both of these processes have probably contributed to the declining odds of completing four-year college, given college entry, for men and women. The decline in the odds of completing four-year college, given college entry, has actually been somewhat greater for black women than black men, but this greater decline has not been enough to offset the female advantage that stems from their more rapid rise in postsecondary enrollment.

Figures 2.13 and 2.14 present the corresponding graphs for whites. In qualitative terms, the story is the same for whites and blacks, with whites also experiencing rising rates of college entry. The white male rate of completing a bachelor's degree, conditional on college enrollment, has been constant or declining over the past thirty years. This pattern is similar to that for blacks and probably arises for the same reasons: the rising share of postsecondary students in community college and the broadening self-selection into postsecondary education. Just as for blacks, the

Figure 2.13   Probability of Whites Age Twenty-Six to Twenty-Eight Attaining Some College, by Birth Year

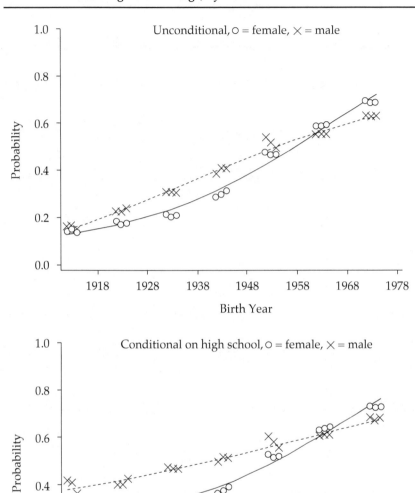

Source: McDaniel et al. (2011). Data are from IPUMS (Ruggles et al. 2010).

Figure 2.14   **Probability of Whites Age Twenty-Six to Twenty-Eight Attaining a Bachelor's Degree Given Some College, by Birth Year**

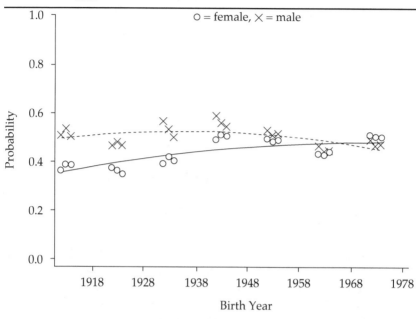

Source: McDaniel et al. (2011). Data are from IPUMS (Ruggles et al. 2010).

rising female advantage in college completion for whites is largely due to rising rates of college entry. However, the gender gap in completing college, given some postsecondary education, is larger for whites than for blacks, and whereas the black female line trends slightly downward, the white female line trends upward. In combination with the strong gender gap among whites in trends in college entry, the gender gap for whites in trends in college completion contributes to the strong female-favorable trend in the probability of completing college by age twenty-six to twenty-eight for whites.

Conclusion

American women have overtaken American men in rates of college completion, and females have matched or exceeded males in their rates of obtaining master's degrees, doctoral degrees, and professional degrees. This growth in the educational advantages of women in the United States parallels developments in many other industrialized countries, though important aspects of the trend are distinctive to the United States.

From an international perspective, the steady relative increase in mean female educational attainment occurs against a backdrop of considerable variation in both the size of the gender gap and the gender gap trend across countries. The stagnation in male college completion rates, particularly in the 1970s and 1980s, is especially prominent, but equally noteworthy is the steady decline in the relative position of the United States among other industrialized countries. Neither American men nor American women have advanced their rates of completing tertiary education to the same extent as their counterparts in several industrialized countries.

The growing female advantage in college completion in the United States stems from growing female advantages within each of the transitions that lead from high school to four-year college completion. Although the reversals in the gender gap in transitions to college and college completion are relatively recent, the pattern of male delay in completing college is long-standing and continues to the present. For this reason, the size of the gender gap depends on the age at which educational attainment is measured.

Trends for Hispanics and Asians since 1980 are generally similar to those for whites. The historical trend for blacks is distinctive in two respects. First, black females have long maintained a lead in educational attainment over black males. In percentage terms, black females have been increasing their lead, just as white females have been increasing their lead over white males. In other words, blacks' historic disadvantage relative to whites has been much greater for males than for females, but black males have made larger strides in closing the racial gap in college completion rates than have black females during the past fifty years. Racial progress, however, has slowed in recent decades for both sexes.

In contrast to the rapid changes in the educational attainment of women, the gender composition of fields of study has changed far more slowly. Gender segregation in fields of study declined through the middle 1990s, especially for majors outside of the liberal arts and sciences, but since then the level of segregation has not changed much, and the overall level of segregation in scientific fields of study has actually been rising during the past fifteen years.

Chapter 3

Changing Incentives and Opportunities for Higher Education

THE "GREAT Recession" of 2008 was unique in many ways, but one of its most striking aspects was that it had a far greater impact on men than it did on women.[1] News headlines used terms like "hecession" and "sheconomy" to get this point across. From the beginning of the recession in December 2007 until February 2010, when the job market hit bottom, the U.S. economy lost over 8.5 million jobs. About 70 percent of all job losses were to men.[2] Although it appears that men are regaining jobs at a faster rate than women (Kochhar 2011), it is also the fact that now, two years after the end of the recession, women appear to have weathered the economic downturn and weak recovery better than men.[3]

These gendered impacts of the recent recession provide just one signal of the massive changes in the U.S. labor market. At the same time, gradual but nonetheless large-scale changes in marriage and family life have also had an impact on women's and men's education decisions and trajectories. Embedded in these two central and intricately related institutions of society—the labor market and the family—are the seeds of the desire of many women to obtain more education than ever before. This chapter examines how major changes in the labor market, marriage, and family life and the incentives and opportunities arising from these changes are related to the rapid rise of women in higher education. Recall that the sources of the rise of women in higher education are located both within the structures that produce opportunities and incentives to obtain more education and within the structures that provide women with the resources to excel in school and thereby gain access to higher levels of education.

The Rise of Women in the World of Work

The tremendous technological and economic changes of the twentieth century transformed the position of women in the American labor market. In 1900, 20 percent of American women were in the labor force. By 2000, the female labor force participation rate had risen to 60 percent (Fischer and Hout 2006). The sources of this remarkable trend have been well documented elsewhere (Goldin 1990; U.S. Department of Labor 2010a) and need only be briefly summarized here. In addition to expanding opportunity for clerical jobs, women's large-scale entry into occupations that required some form of higher education—teaching, nursing, and white-collar clerical work—increased their incentives to earn a college degree. In the early decades of the twentieth century, the teaching profession became rapidly feminized, and school administrators' preference for unmarried female teachers created continual demand for new teachers; as women left the profession upon marriage, younger women stepped in to fill their ranks (Rury 2008, 110). By the early 1940s, the pervasive marriage bars that excluded the employment of married women were almost completely eliminated, and they entered the labor force in greater numbers (Goldin, Katz, and Kuziemko 2006). In the two decades after World War II, the U.S. economy enjoyed a major expansion, coupled with increases in productivity, higher standards of living, and rapid acceleration in the growth of college enrollments. This economic growth increased the demand for labor, raised women's wages, and increased the opportunity cost of remaining a full-time homemaker (Bergmann 2005). Women responded to these changing circumstances by entering the workforce in greater numbers and remaining in the workforce for longer periods. For example, before World War II most women worked only until they got married and began having children. After the war, it became far more common for women to return to work after their children were school age or older (Goldin 1990; Thistle 2006). Then, in the 1960s and 1970s, the civil rights movement and the women's rights movement brought legislation promoting equal opportunity in education and employment and created an environment that was more amenable to women getting advanced skills and working outside the home, even when they had young children.[4] In fact, the growth in the number of women with children who are employed has driven much of the increase in women's labor force participation rates from the 1970s to the present (Toossi 2002, 18). In 1950 only 18 million women (34 percent of women of working age) were in the labor force, but by 2000, 66 million women (60 percent of all women of working age) were in the labor force. The rate has remained stable in the past decade (U.S. Department of Labor 2010a). Assuming an average annual growth rate of 0.7 percent, the number of working women is projected to reach 92 million by 2050. That same year, women are expected to comprise nearly 48 percent of the workforce (U.S. Department of Labor 2010a).

The impact of these labor market developments was long muted for black Americans, because of both legal and de facto discrimination and segregation. The much lower rate of college completion for blacks than whites was due in part to the lack of educational resources devoted to blacks, especially in southern states, where the majority of blacks resided (Rury 2008). Black men in the South also benefited less from the GI Bill. Although the GI Bill was race-neutral in statutory terms, segregation in the southern states and severely limited state investment in the colleges accessible to blacks restricted the extent to which southern black veterans could use GI benefits to obtain a college degree (Turner and Bound 2003). Thus, throughout much of the middle twentieth century, college completion rates of blacks, especially black males, were constrained by lack of resources, including access to education and funding to pay for it. At the same time, it is likely that different structures of occupational opportunities for blacks and whites and for men and women created different incentive structures for each group.

To examine racial differences in the gender gap in labor market opportunity for the college-educated, McDaniel and her colleagues (2011) computed the percentage of individuals age twenty-eight to thirty-two with a bachelor's degree who were currently employed during each census year. Additionally, they measured gender and racial differences in the proportion of individuals employed in high-status occupations, such as doctors, lawyers, managers, and engineers, or in female-dominated occupations that historically required a bachelor's degree, such as teaching and nursing.

Figure 3.1 shows the proportion of black and white, male and female twenty-eight- to thirty-two-year-olds with a bachelor's degree who were employed in each of the decennial censuses from 1940 through 2000. The fact that college-educated black men had lower employment rates than college-educated white men in all decades suggests that even highly educated black males faced barriers to employment commensurate with their level of education. As John Rury (2008, 122) explains, "Even in the North, African Americans encountered great trouble in gaining employment commensurate with their credentials. Racism permeated the job market and served to dramatically counteract the benefits of schooling for African Americans."

The small but prolonged female advantage in college completion for blacks prior to 1980 may also be related to the high labor force participation rates of black educated women. Black college-educated women were far more likely than white college-educated women to be employed until the 1980s. In 1930 black women were three times more likely to work than white women. By 1970 black women worked 1.3 times more than white women (Goldin 1990). In fact, as figure 3.1 indicates, employment rates were higher for college-educated black women at all time points. Historically, black women worked more because black families had lower incomes, owing in part to black men's high unemployment

Figure 3.1   Proportion of Twenty-Eight- to Thirty-Two-Year-Olds with a Bachelor's Degree Who Are Employed, by Race, Gender, and Census Year

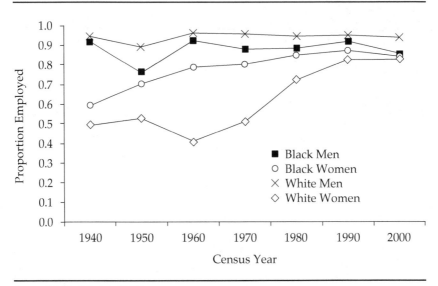

Source: McDaniel et al. (2011).

rates and low education levels. However, family and individual characteristics are not the only reasons for black women's high labor force participation. Goldin (1977) found that black women work more than white women even if they have the same education level, family income, and number of children. One legacy of slavery was that paid work carried less social stigma for black women than for white women throughout the twentieth century (Goldin 1977). As a consequence, the employment gap among college-educated women and men was much smaller for blacks than for whites. Historical differences in the labor force participation rates of black and white women arguably contributed to the higher rate of college completion of black women relative to black men.

Although large racial differences in college completion have persisted throughout the period under study, the gender trends for blacks and whites became similar because of changes in the impact of gender as well as race on labor market opportunities. In the 1980s, a large female advantage in college completion emerged for both racial groups (see figure 2.7). The stagnation in the proportion of male BA holders in the 1980s for both blacks and whites is also striking. Between 1980 and 1990, black women's BA receipt rose more slowly than did white women's BA receipt, but their rapid gains between 1990 and 2000 meant that by 2000 the gender gap in college completion among blacks (0.048) was approaching that for whites (0.063).

Table 3.1   Percentage of Employed Twenty-Eight- to Thirty-Two-Year-Olds with a
Bachelor's Degree, in Various Occupations, 1940 to 2000

	1940	1950	1960	1970	1980	1990	2000
Black women							
Doctors, dentists, or lawyers	0.0%	0.0%	0.8%	0.6%	2.0%	3.1%	3.3%
Engineers	0.0	0.0	0.0	0.0	0.9	1.5	2.1
Managers and other proprietors	0.0	0.0	0.8	0.6	5.6	9.2	10.3
Teachers	56.9	65.1	61.2	64.5	35.1	15.7	14.8
Nurses	3.5	0.0	3.7	3.3	3.6	6.5	5.1
Other	39.7	34.9	33.5	31.1	52.9	64.0	64.4
White women							
Doctors, dentists, or lawyers	0.9	2.2	1.5	1.1	2.4	4.1	3.8
Engineers	0.2	0.0	0.4	0.3	0.7	2.0	2.0
Managers and other proprietors	1.5	1.8	2.1	2.1	6.6	11.3	11.4
Teachers	53.3	33.9	45.4	50.7	33.9	17.5	19.5
Nurses	2.7	12.1	5.3	3.9	5.6	7.5	5.3
Other	41.4	50.0	45.2	41.9	50.8	57.6	58.1
Black men							
Doctors, dentists, or lawyers	5.1	5.7	5.0	2.2	4.3	4.3	3.5
Engineers	0.0	0.0	2.5	4.3	4.7	4.8	4.8
Managers and other proprietors	2.6	5.7	2.5	5.2	8.9	12.2	13.8
Teachers	35.9	28.6	31.5	29.2	12.4	7.6	10.3
Nurses	0.0	0.0	0.5	0.3	0.6	0.5	1.7
Other	56.4	60.0	58.0	58.8	69.1	70.6	65.8
White men							
Doctors, dentists, or lawyers	15.7	10.4	8.4	6.9	7.9	6.8	5.4
Engineers	7.5	11.1	12.5	11.3	6.8	9.1	1.7
Managers and other proprietors	9.4	11.6	11.3	10.5	15.4	17.7	17.6
Teachers	11.4	7.2	11.1	12.9	9.7	5.7	7.3
Nurses	0.2	0.1	0.1	0.3	0.7	0.7	0.9
Other	55.9	59.7	56.7	58.2	59.5	60.0	61.2

Source: McDaniel et al. (2011).

To understand further the changing incentives for higher education,
McDaniel and her colleagues (2011) examined differences in the types of
occupations held by race and gender groups. Table 3.1 presents the percentage of employed twenty-eight- to thirty-two-year-olds with a bachelor's degree in various occupations by gender and race for five main
occupational groups: doctors, dentists, and lawyers; engineers; managers and other proprietors; teachers; and nurses. These five occupational
categories represent some of the most prestigious and high-paying occupations that require at least a bachelor's degree as well as traditionally
female-dominated occupations that require a college degree. All other
occupations are grouped into a sixth category.

Table 3.1 makes clear that black men were largely barred from many of the high-status, male-dominated occupations that were available to white men. White men monopolized the most prestigious jobs through the first four decades reported in the table—1940 to 1980—in both the professions and the corporate world. College-educated black men, in contrast, were largely shut out of high-status occupations. In 1940 and 1950, there were almost no college-educated black male engineers, while 7.5 percent of white BA holders in 1940 and 11.1 percent in 1950 were in engineering occupations. Fewer than 8 percent of black males with a bachelor's degree worked as doctors, dentists, lawyers, or managers in 1940 (compared with 25.1 percent for white males), and fewer than 11 percent of black male degree-holders worked in these occupations in 1950 (compared with 22.0 percent for white males). Instead, black men with a four-year college degree were more likely to be working as teachers than in any other occupation, and far more likely to be doing so than corresponding white males.

The contrast between black and white educated women was strikingly different from that for men. As mentioned earlier, the lower incomes of black families, the high black male unemployment rate, and the corresponding fact that working was more socially acceptable for black women than for white women gave black women greater incentives to work compared with white women. The majority of college-educated black and white women worked as teachers from 1940 through the 1970s. Nursing was the second most common occupation for college-educated women in those years, but far less common than teaching. In the 1970s, women moved into other occupations, including management, medicine, law, and engineering. Women's access to jobs as teachers probably gave them an incentive to complete a college degree. Because black men could not gain access to the high-paying jobs that white men with college degrees held, their incentives to complete a college degree were lower. These historical differences help explain why the trend in the gender gap in college completion is so different for African Americans and whites.

Women are now represented in the workforce at a rate nearly equal to that of men, but for the most part they continue to earn less. The gender wage gap has narrowed substantially since 1960, when women earned just 60 percent of men's earnings (Blau and Kahn 2007a). Today median earnings for women are 81 percent of men's earnings among full-time, year-round workers (U.S. Department of Labor 2010a; Dougherty 2010; Gertz 2010).[5] The slow pace of convergence in women's and men's earnings since the 1990s has led some scholars to wonder whether "women have gone as far as they can" (Blau and Kahn 2007a, 7). However, other evidence points to surprising undercurrents of change in the story of gender inequalities in earnings. One recent analysis found that in 147 of the largest U.S. metropolitan areas, the median full-time salary of young women is 8 percent higher than for their male counterparts (Dougherty 2010).[6]

The fact that women and men tend to be segregated in different occupations is one long-standing reason for the continuing gender wage gap. Paradoxically, however, the greater tendency for men to work in manufacturing and construction is also a reason why women have generally fared better in the "Great Recession." The structure of job opportunities in the United States has grown increasingly polarized by social class in recent decades, with declining jobs in middle-skill white- and blue-collar occupations and increasing job opportunities in both low-skill, low-wage occupations and high-skill, high-wage occupations (Autor 2010). Importantly, because of occupational sex segregation, this job polarization has had different impacts on men and women.

> The decline of middle-skill jobs has clearly displaced males toward the tails of the occupational distribution and the net effect is an increase in the share of males in low-skill occupations compared to the share of males in high-skill occupations. Women's losses in middle-skill occupations were substantially offset by employment gains in high-skill occupations, and this is true for both high school- and some-college-educated females. (Autor 2010, 10)

Women's gains in the high-skill sectors of the economy have not solely been due to "demand shifts" favoring traditionally female occupations. Women have also gained by entering higher-status, previously male-dominated occupations in fields such as law, business, and the sciences (Goldin et al. 2006). In 2009, for the first time in history, women comprised the majority (51 percent) of workers in highly paid managerial and professional positions, even though they comprised 47 percent of the total workforce (U.S. Department of Labor 2010a, 1). Women have also gained skills and experience on the job through higher rates of labor force attachment. Conversely, the share of women in traditional female careers such as teaching and nursing has declined. The net effect of these changes is that women adapted more successfully to the shifts in demand that have eroded employment opportunities in middle-skill clerical, administrative, and production jobs (Autor 2010). These changes in the labor market experiences of women have influenced their decisions to attend and complete college and are related to women's rising rates of college enrollment and completion from the 1980s onward.

Rapid Change in Marriage and Family Life

Striking changes in women's experiences in the labor market are both forces behind and consequences of the remarkable changes in marriage and family life. As women have come to comprise half of all workers, timelines and norms for getting married and raising a family have become much more diverse. Today, in what has come to be called the "retreat from marriage," American men and women are marrying later in life, and a growing, though still relatively small, proportion are never marrying at all. The median age of first marriage has been climbing for decades, from twenty-three for men and twenty for women in 1960 to twenty-eight for men and twenty-six for women in 2008. Goldin and her colleagues (2006) show how the increase in the median age of first marriage has played a role in women's growing rates of college completion and graduate and professional education; as women marry later, they can take college more seriously and form their identities before getting married and having a family. The rising educational attainment of women likewise contributes to the increase in the median age at first marriage. Today 40 percent of women over the age of twenty-five are unmarried (Ventura 2009). A small percentage of these women will never marry. In his neoclassical microeconomic theory of family change, Gary Becker (1981) argued that the economic division of labor between men and women was the primary incentive to form stable unions. As women's and men's roles have become more similar, this incentive has been weakened and marriage has declined in importance—as evidenced by declining marriage rates, postponement of marriage during the life course, and rising rates of nonmarital cohabitation and divorce. In short, the economic emancipation of women is believed to have produced changes in family organization that have become increasingly common in contemporary industrialized societies (Mason and Jensen 1995, 2–3).

Within the institution of marriage, the traditional model of breadwinner husband and stay-at-home wife has declined to the point where only one in five American families conform to this model (Boushey 2009); dual-income couples, breadwinner wives, stay-at-home dads, and other forms of coupling have become common. As women's presence in the labor force has increased, so has their contribution to the household income. In 2008, among married couples, working women contributed 36 percent of their family's income, up from only 9 percent in 1970. Indeed, in many families dual incomes have become a necessity for maintaining a middle-class living. Even more surprising is the fact that today 27 percent of working women whose husbands also work earn more than their spouses (up from 18 percent in 1987) (U.S. Department of Labor 2010a, 2), and if we include all couples regardless of the employment status of husbands, the fraction of wives who earn more than their husbands has risen from 24 percent in 1987 to 38 percent in 2009 (Mundy 2012).

There has also been a decoupling of marriage and motherhood among American women, such that 41 percent of all children born in 2008 had an unmarried mother (Ventura 2009). Parallel to the climb in nonmarital births has been the dramatic rise in single-mother households, which rely

almost exclusively on the mother's earnings for their survival and constitute 18 percent of all American households today (Boushey 2009, 35).

Among all women, the average age at first birth rose from 21.4 in
1970 to 25 in 2006 (Mathews and Hamilton 2009). More striking is the
rapid rise of rates of first birth among older women. In 1970 only one in
one hundred first births were to women over the age of thirty-five; in
2006 about one in twelve first births were to women age thirty-five or
older (Mathews and Hamilton 2009). Although increases in the age at
first birth were more pronounced in the 1970s and 1980s, even since
1990 rates of first birth for women age thirty-five to thirty-nine have
risen 47 percent, and first birth rates for women age forty to forty-four
have risen 80 percent (Livingston and Cohn 2010) as women—especially professional women—invest in their careers and delay motherhood into their thirties and forties. Access to reliable contraception in
the form of the birth control pill has had a positive impact on women's
college attendance and a host of related factors, including their age of
first marriage, professional labor force participation, and age of first
birth (Goldin and Katz 2000; Charles and Luoh 2003; Goldin et al. 2006).
In addition to delaying childbearing, a growing segment of American
women are foregoing childbearing altogether. Today, nearly 1 in 5
women have no children, compared to only 1 in 10 in 1970 (Livingston
and Cohn 2010). The rise in childlessness is due in part to the fact that as
more women delay marriage and childbearing, their chances of a successful pregnancy decline with age (Livingston and Cohn 2010). But it is
also true that more women are choosing to not have children as public
attitudes toward childlessness have changed and many American
women have come to view childbearing as only one of several options
for having a fulfilling life.

Returns to Higher Education for Women and Men

The rapid changes in work and family life in the past half-century have
certainly affected women's decisions about how much education to attain. Human capital theory argues that education is an investment decision. Positive returns to education provide the incentive to make an educational investment. This theory implies that trends in educational
returns should produce trends in educational investments. What impact
might the extensive changes in the realms of work and family life have
had on the returns to higher education for men and women? To address
this question we examined whether differences in college completion
trends for women and men are related to changes in the returns to higher
education for women and men in terms of three critical outcomes in the
work and family realms: earnings, the probability of getting married and
staying married, and the family standard of living operationalized as

family income adjusted for family size (DiPrete and Buchmann 2006). We conducted a trend analysis of the value of higher education for each of these outcomes measured against the baseline value of a high school education using thirty-nine years of data from the Current Population Survey (CPS).

Prior research provides evidence for the beneficial effects of higher education for women's wage labor opportunities, rates of marriage, standard of living, and protection against divorce and poverty. These findings, however, do not necessarily imply gender-specific trends in these benefits of higher education. To determine whether incentives to attain higher education have been rising faster for women than men, we need to determine whether the value of higher education with respect to both labor market and family returns has been rising faster for women than men. We focus on the value of college as measured against the baseline value of a high school diploma by comparing respondents who completed a high school diploma and those who completed four or more years of college; respondents were white and African American men and women between twenty-five and thirty-four years of age. We use several distinct outcome variables to assess the value of higher education. Earned income is the sum of income from wages and salaries, self-employment, and farm income before taxes for full-time, full-year workers, defined as respondents who worked fifty or more weeks and thirty-five or more hours per week in the previous calendar year.[7] Marital status is measured at the time of the survey, regardless of the year of the marriage, so it captures the combined impact of educational differentials on the probability of getting married and on the probability of staying married. Gross family income is the sum of the total gross incomes for all family members in the previous calendar year.[8] Gross family standard of living is defined as gross family income adjusted for family size.[9] As an alternative way to measure family standard of living, we created a measure of "not income-deprived."[10] The threshold we use corresponds to a household income at roughly the twentieth percentile of the household income distribution for a single person and at roughly the fortieth percentile for a family of four. Thus, it might be loosely characterized as the threshold for a middle-class standard of living.

To analyze the returns to higher education, we combined the thirty-nine CPS annual samples and computed the difference between respondents with at least a bachelor's degree and respondents with only a high school diploma for the following outcomes: (1) the difference in the log of earned income, (2) the difference in the log of family income, and (3) the difference in the log of standard of living as defined earlier for men and women in the age groups twenty-five to twenty-nine and thirty to thirty-five. We also computed (4) the difference in the proportion married as of the time of the survey, and (5) the difference in the proportion who were "not income-deprived." Our primary goal was to determine whether there is a link in the apparent effect of education on outcomes—measured most simply as the difference between the outcomes of college- and high school–educated individuals—and gender-specific educational trends. We would expect incentive effects to arise from trends in simple associations such as those between earnings and education, marriage rates and education, or the earnings of one's spouse and one's own education, not from trends in causal effects that are only revealed through sophisticated data analysis. As a practical matter, it would hardly be surprising if trends in simple associations and in the underlying causal effects moved in the same direction, but this question is not the focus here. We are interested in trends in incentives as they might appear to adolescents and young adults who are making decisions about their education.

Income Returns to a College Degree

It would seem reasonable to expect that women's growing labor market opportunities in managerial and professional jobs would have produced relatively (to males) strong growth in the earnings return to a college degree. But prior research found no evidence of such a female-favorable trend in the wage returns to higher education (Averett and Burton 1996; Goldin and Katz 2000; Charles and Luoh 2003; DiPrete and Buchmann 2006; Cho 2007).[11] This apparent puzzle is readily resolved when we consider that while women's wage returns to higher education have indeed increased, male returns have increased as well because of the declining opportunities for high-wage, male-dominated manufacturing jobs for high school–educated workers that are a part of the phenomenon generally referred to in the economics literature as "skill-biased technological change."[12]

Marriage Returns to a College Degree

Many scholars have argued that women's motivation to attend college stems in part from the marriage returns of higher education that derive from educational assortative mating—that is, the tendency for individuals to choose spouses with similar levels of education as themselves (Mare 1991; Goldin 1992; Mickelson 1989). This tendency remains strong and may even have increased in the United States in recent decades (Schwartz and Mare 2005). Moreover, the increasing propensity of women with at least some college education to marry relative to less-educated women between 1972 and 1987 (Qian and Preston 1993) implies that the "marriage returns" to education increased during the 1970s and 1980s. Meanwhile, Jay Teachman (2002) found that the bivariate relationship between a woman's education and divorce is negative: a woman's risk of divorce drops 6 percent for each additional year of schooling. College-educated women are more likely to marry college-educated men, who have substantially lower rates of divorce than high school–educated men, perhaps because men with a college education are less likely to initiate divorce, or perhaps because women find college-educated men to be more desirable partners and thus are less inclined to initiate divorce themselves. Higher levels of education for women actually imply greater divorce risks, but Teachman found that the divorce-suppressing effects of women's higher education via marital homogamy are larger than the divorce-enhancing effects of women's education. He found no evidence of different trends in divorce by educational level. Steven Martin (2005) likewise reported similar trends of increasing divorce rates for college- and non-college-educated women through 1980, but he found that after 1980 the trends diverged: divorce rates fell among college-educated women, while they continued to rise for less-educated women. In sum, the combination of higher marriage rates and lower divorce rates for college-educated women suggests strong marital returns to higher education.

Figure 3.2 examines the association between higher education and the probability of being currently married for whites. The figure shows that, through the early 1990s, having a BA or higher degree implied a lower probability of being married at age thirty to thirty-four than having only a high school diploma. Of course, at least some of this penalty was due to the delayed timing of marriage that comes with higher education. After about 1990, the higher education marriage penalty was transformed into a higher education marriage premium for both men and women in this age range.

Standard of Living and Insurance Against Poverty

Beyond the question of returns to education via the labor market and marriage, a sound incentives theory should attend to the role of education as "insurance" against poverty, especially for women who must rely on their own labor earnings to determine their (and their dependent children's) standard of living. In fact, a college degree has probably become a more important form of insurance against living in poverty for women, simply because the risk of living in poverty for females relative to males has grown over this time. Female/male poverty ratios increased during the period between 1950 and 1980 (McLanahan, Sørensen, and Watson 1989). Among whites, women's poverty rates were 10 percent higher than men's in 1950, but almost 50 percent higher in 1980. Suzanne Bianchi (1999) reported that this upward trend in the feminization of poverty peaked in 1978; the ratio dropped during the 1980s, but women's pov-

Figure 3.2   The Effect of a Bachelor's Degree on Marriages Among Whites, 1960 to 2000

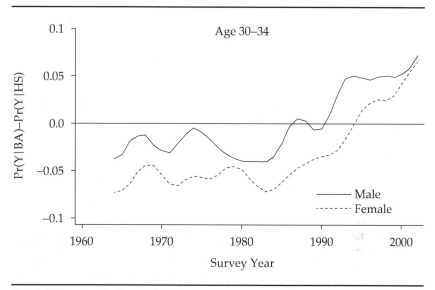

Source: DiPrete and Buchmann (2006).
Note: Pr(Y | BA) – Pr(Y | HS) = Probability of Marriage, Given BA or More Minus Probability of Marriage, Given High School Completion.

erty rates remained roughly 50 percent higher than men's poverty rates in the 1990s. In 2009 the percentage of Americans living in poverty was 15 percent, and women were 29 percent more likely to live in poverty than men (DeNavas-Walt, Proctor, and Smith 2010). Of course, one primary reason for the gender difference in poverty rates is the greater tendency for women to be single parents, owing to either divorce or nonmarital childbirth (Bianchi 1999; Cancian and Reed 2001). As already noted, nonmarital childbearing has become increasingly common: today 41 percent of births are nonmarital births. In sum, higher education provides a woman with insurance against living in poverty through three mechanisms: higher wages, lower rates of out-of-marriage childbearing, and (because of educational homogamy) lower risks of divorce. The well-documented trends in the relationship between gender and poverty may have created a growing incentive for women to pursue higher education to protect themselves against this risk.

Figures 3.3 and 3.4 show the trends in the association between education and the family standard of living and the association between education and the probability of remaining above the threshold between "income deprivation" and a "middle-class" standard of living for thirty- to thirty-four-year-old whites. Here the double benefit of marriage to

Figure 3.3   The Effect of a Bachelor's Degree on Household Standard of Living Among Whites, 1960 to 2000

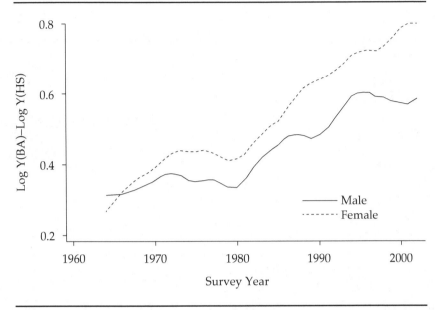

Source: DiPrete and Buchmann (2006).
Note: Log Y(BA) – Log Y(HS) = Log Household Standard of Living Given BA or More Minus Log Household Standard of Living Given High School Completion.

women (in the labor market and the marriage market) is clearly at work. Figure 3.3 shows that women gained a greater return to their standard of living from higher education than did men from 1960 through 2000; the female-favorable gain began to increase in size in the early 1980s and continued through the end of the period. Figure 3.4 shows similar benefits of higher education to the probability of remaining above the threshold between "income deprivation" and a "middle-class" standard of living. Regardless of how the returns to higher education are conceptualized, the family-level returns of higher education were trending up faster for women than for men during this time period, and especially after 1980.

It is clear that the returns to higher education for women and men extend beyond returns in the labor market and include a higher probability of marriage, a higher standard of living, and insurance against poverty. For all of the outcomes considered here, with the exception of personal earnings, women's returns to higher education appear to have risen faster than those for men. These results suggest a possible connection between the white female–specific increase in college completion rates during the 1980s and the white female–specific rise in the returns to college around the same point in time. We should note, however, that the

Figure 3.4   The Effect of a Bachelor's Degree on Whites' Probability of Not Being Income-Deprived, 1960 to 2000

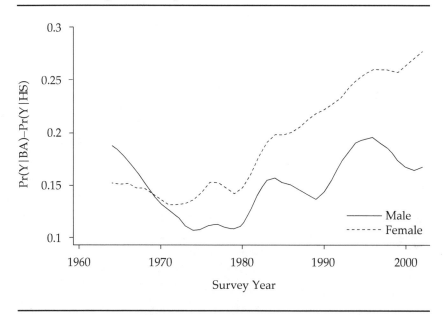

Source: DiPrete and Buchmann (2006).
Note: Pr(Y | BA) – Pr(Y | HS) = Probability of not being income-deprived given BA or more minus probability of not being income-deprived given high school completion.

increase in the standard-of-living returns to college for women was unlikely to be the only reason for the female-specific increase in college completion rates. Our calculations show that the increase in the association between college completion and the probability of being above the "income deprivation" threshold began to rise for twenty-five- to twenty-nine-year-olds around 1974 (DiPrete and Buchmann 2006). Around 1978, the return from college completion on household standard of living began to rise. The timing is similar when thirty- to thirty-four-year-olds are used as the basis for the classification. Meanwhile, according to yearly CPS data (DiPrete and Buchmann 2006), the yearly increases in rates of college completion for successive birth cohorts paused for women around the birth cohort of 1950 (who were eighteen years old in 1968) and then resumed its upward climb about five years later. It seems reasonable to assume that a gender-specific trend in the value of education would have to persist for some time before it was noticed and became the basis for educational decisions, and the rising rate of college completion for females was already well established by the time the birth cohorts of the early 1940s were moving through their high school and college years. Nonetheless, the rise in the value of higher education to women during the 1970s was a stimulus that is likely to have strengthened the female-favorable trend that led to women overtaking men in their rates of college graduation.

This discussion about incentive effects has to this point focused on white Americans. The role of incentive effects from returns to education on educational behavior is more complicated for blacks. First, broader historical forces related to the civil rights movement undoubtedly had a strong impact on educational trends. Second, lower family resources among African American families and high levels of social disorganization in the neighborhoods of many black teenagers might have inhibited them from responding to labor market and family-based incentives to the same extent as whites, both because poverty increases outcomes such as teenage pregnancy or incarceration that interfere with the possibility of completing higher education and because higher education is facilitated by family-level resources, which have been less available to black teenagers. Gains from the civil rights movement, trends in the socioeconomic standing of blacks, and trends in behaviors that interfere with college attendance doubtless have had important impacts on trends in gender-specific college completion rates for blacks in addition to specific trends in the returns to higher education.

Military Service

Because military service is predominantly undertaken by males, it is reasonable to ask whether military service competes with higher education and is therefore part of the explanation for the reversal of the educational gender gap. The U.S. military recruits about 200,000 enlisted personnel each year, almost all of whom are high school graduates. The size of the military has remained stable in the past twenty years; since 1973, it has comprised less than 1 percent of the total population (Office of the Under Secretary of Defense, Personnel, and Readiness 2012). In fiscal year 2010, active-duty personnel numbered almost 1.2 million people, 85 percent of whom were men (Office of the Under Secretary of Defense, Personnel, and Readiness 2012). The enlisted population is disproportionately young, with a median age of twenty-seven, so it is possible that military service competes with college as a destination for young adults, and especially young men. The GI Bill offset some of these potentially negative effects of military service; starting in 1944, it offered educational benefits to veterans of World War II and, later, the Korean War (Turner and Bound 2003; Stanley 2003). Marcus Stanley (2003) shows that the trend in male BAs after World War II was along the same trajectory established in the 1936 to 1940 period; this finding is consistent with an interpretation that the GI Bill offset the direct negative effect on educational attainment that would have been produced by military service during the years when some GIs otherwise would have been in college. Indeed, many of the young people who enlist after high school cite the educational benefits available to them to get a college education, either during or after their military service, as a primary motivation to enlist (Kleykamp 2006). Thus, for some, military service may have made enrolling in college possible, albeit at a later point in life, and may be one source of the observed male delay in college enrollment and completion discussed in chapter 2. Moreover, of the 20,000 officers commissioned by the armed forces each year, nearly all are college graduates, and about 40 percent received their commission through participation in a university's Reserve Officers' Training Corps (ROTC) (Segal and Segal 2004, 8). For this group, military enlistment occurs after completing college.

On the whole, men who serve in the military receive less education than those who do not serve. Among high school graduates, veterans who served during the peacetime cold war period were less likely to attain a college education than were nonveterans at all levels of socioeconomic status (MacLean 2005). This difference held even among those who reported plans to attend college. It is possible that merely delaying college enrollment reduces the likelihood of attending or completing college, perhaps owing to a sense that one has become "too old" for college, or perhaps because serious romantic involvement is more likely as one ages (Hogan 1981). It is not known whether military service reduces the likelihood of attaining a college degree or whether the military differentially selects young people who are less committed to postsecondary education (MacLean and Elder 2007). Alair MacLean's findings are at least consistent with the idea that military service competes with higher education for young men. Also consistent with this idea is research by Meredith Kleykamp (2010), who finds that the downsizing of military jobs in the 1990s was associated with substantial increases in college-going, especially among black men. To the best of our knowledge, no research has examined the relationship between military service and educational attainment for women or whether the effects of military service found in the past remain the same for military personnel today. These are important questions for future research.

Incarceration and the Gender Gap in College Completion

The IPUMS data that we have used to report education trends are representative of the entire population, including people who were in jail or prison at the time of the data collection. As a consequence, the race and gender trends shown in figures 2.7 and A.1 incorporate the sharp increase in the size of the incarcerated population that began in the late 1970s and has continued to the present day. Nevertheless, it is revealing to consider the impact of the changing size of this population on calculations of the gender gap. Incarceration rates in the United States held stable between 1925 and 1975 at roughly 100 per 100,000 of the resident population, but after 1975 the incarceration rate increased rapidly, and by 2001 it was 472 per 100,000—nearly five times its historical average (Langan 1991; Pettit and Western 2004).

It is important to distinguish between the arithmetic impact of accounting for the incarcerated population in the computation of college completion rates and the causal impact of incarceration on the size of the changing gender gap, especially for blacks. The arithmetic impact can be obtained simply by comparing the year-specific rates of college completion estimated only for the non-institutionalized population with the estimate of completion rates obtained for the total population. The Current Population Surveys are administered only to the non-institutionalized population. We obtained estimates of the number of inmates in state prisons and federal correctional facilities by race, gender, education, and age from the Surveys of Inmates in State and Federal Correctional Facilities for the years 1974, 1979, 1986, 1991, 1997, and 2004. Using these data, we interpolated the results for the intermediate years. Available information for the jail population is less complete, so we simply assumed that the jail population matches the prison population in its race, gender, education, and age composition and scaled up the size of the prison samples to correspond to the size of the combined prison and jail population in each year. Finally, we rescaled the combined prison and jail samples so that they were the same proportion of the population as the CPS samples, and we combined the data sets in order to estimate rates for the total population.

The addition of the prison and jail data to the CPS data has a noticeable effect on the computed rates of college completion for black males in particular, both because a considerable portion of the young black male population was in prison or jail in these years and because the incarcerated population had relatively low levels of education. This shows that the black gender gap is noticeably larger when the incarcerated population is taken into account.[13] Moreover, the impact of the incarceration adjustment grows larger for blacks over time because the size of the incarcerated black population grew as a fraction of the total black population over time.

It is more difficult to determine the causal effect of the rise in incarceration of young males, and especially young black males, on the growing gender gap in college completion in the 1980s and 1990s. In one respect, our (McDaniel et al. 2011) adjustment understates the magnitude of the prison experience of black males because it pertains only to individuals who were currently in prison or jail at the time of the survey. Many other individuals interviewed in the CPS in each of these years had experienced a period of incarceration in the past. The impact of incarceration spells on educational attainment—that is, on how much education these young males would have achieved if they had not spent time in jail or prison—is unknown. However, other considerations suggest that the sharp rise in the prison population has had a relatively small impact on the gender gap in educational attainment. Our analysis of the prison and jails surveys confirms that the young people who are sentenced to time in jail or prison are disproportionately high school dropouts; other evidence shows that they were performing poorly in school at the time of their arrest (Laub and Sampson 1993). In other words, if these individuals are drawn disproportionately from the bottom of the educational achievement distribution, then we can conclude that very few of these individuals would have earned a bachelor's degree or even enrolled in college if they had never been incarcerated. From this perspective, the rising rates of incarceration may have contributed relatively little to the rise in the gender gap in educational attainment. As noted earlier, the gender gap for blacks is now more similar to that for whites than it was in 1960, even as young black males' experiences with incarceration have diverged from those of young white males. Indisputably, the incarceration of young black males has a major impact on their early adulthood experiences, including work, cohabitation, and marriage, and it has probably affected their rates of high school graduation and postsecondary education. However, incarceration's direct effect on rates of college completion may be relatively small. This question is difficult to answer with certainty and clearly requires further research.

Although incarceration per se may not contribute very much to lower rates of four-year college completion, prison experience is a marker for earlier adolescent problems that may have contributed to academic difficulties and thwarted the possibility of college attendance or completion, regardless of whether the individual in question was ever arrested or incarcerated. As with the direct effect of prison on educational attainment, the impact of adolescent problem behaviors on college completion rates is an important question for future research.

The Competition for College Admission

The educational system is sometimes viewed as an arena within which students compete with each other for prizes. Students with higher grades are perceived as having out-competed students who earn low grades. Those who gain admission to elite colleges and universities or graduate and professional programs are the winners in this process. Contests by their nature have a zero-sum character, and in the American educational system the zero-sum game is most visible in the annual scramble for admission into highly selective colleges and universities. These institutions have many more applicants than they have spaces, and the level of competition for entry into the most selective institutions has been intensifying for many years.[14] Academically elite institutions have great prominence on the educational landscape, but they enroll only a small fraction of the students in four-year educational institutions. Only 14 percent of four-year colleges accept fewer than 50 percent of their applicants (Hawkins and Lautz 2007).

To what degree are constraints on the supply of admission spaces in U.S. institutions of higher education related to gender gaps in college enrollment rates today? The answer to that question depends on which sector of American higher education one focuses on. The overall gender imbalance in college enrollment favoring women primarily exists at less-selective colleges and universities, which comprise the large majority of higher education institutions in the United States. Of course, even less-selective colleges typically reject at least some of the applications they receive; only about 20 percent of four-year, nonprofit colleges and universities in the United States accept more than 85 percent of their applicants (Hawkins and Lautz 2007). Nonetheless, the process of admission to less-selective colleges and universities mainly consists of meeting some baseline standards for high school grades and course curricula imposed by the admissions officers. In fact, selectivity has fallen for colleges outside the most selective 20 percent of institutions when selectivity is measured by the mean SAT/ACT scores of matriculants (Hoxby 2009). Caroline Hoxby finds that the ratio of the number of "freshman seats" (that is, the aggregate number of first-year students in four-year colleges) to the number of twelfth-grade students who score both at the relatively low "basic" level and at the higher "proficiency" level on the National Assessment of Education Progress (NAEP) mathematics and reading tests increased moderately from 1970 to the present. This ratio is greater than unity even when potential supply is measured in terms of students at "basic" levels of proficiency. The implication of the supply ratio trends and of the selectivity statistics is that the increase in the college-going population has been matched by supply increases. Thus, it is highly unlikely that males are being denied entry to four-year colleges because of competition from female applicants at the great majority of colleges and universities today.[15]

The situation is quite different in highly selective colleges and universities. The "college squeeze" described by Sigal Alon and Marta Tienda (2007) is very real in this top 10 percent of colleges. Indeed, the colleges in this most selective tier have become substantially more selective than they were thirty to forty years ago (Alon and Tienda 2007; Hoxby 2009; Bound, Hershbein, and Long 2009). Aside from the early years of coeducation at formerly male institutions, when female quotas were in place (Karabel 2005), these highly selective institutions have asserted a preference for a roughly balanced gender mix on their campuses, which they can readily achieve from their deep pool of highly qualified applicants of both genders.[16] In the 2011 Inside Higher Ed Survey of College and University Admissions Officers, 11.1 percent of four-year colleges and universities responded that they admitted men with "lower grades and test scores than other applicants" in order to achieve gender balance, as compared with 2.7 percent that responded similarly with respect to women (Green 2011). But very few selective universities are included in this survey. Other data suggest that females' acceptance rates at highly selective colleges are lower than males' acceptance rates, but any comparison of acceptance rates cannot prove either gender-based affirmative action or discrimination; student applications are hardly submitted at random, and we do not know whether the typical male applicant to a highly selective college is "equivalent" to the typical female applicant (Heriot and Somin 2011). It is certainly plausible that qualified female applicants are at greater risk of being denied admission at highly selective institutions because of a desire by admissions offices for gender balance, but no definitive analysis of this question has yet been accomplished.

Conclusion

This chapter has examined factors in the social, economic, and cultural environments that are likely to have contributed to the closing and then the reversal of the gender gap in educational attainment. Large-scale increases in the rate of labor force participation by women across the twentieth century, especially in occupations that require some form of higher education, certainly played a role. The pattern of labor demand shaped the trajectory of educational attainment for both men and women. Because the shape of labor demand differed for whites and blacks, their trajectories of educational attainment also differed. Not only were black attainment rates much lower than those for whites, but because black males were effectively shut out of corporate white-collar jobs, black males lagged behind black females in educational attainment, even while among whites males had a clear advantage in educational attainment until the 1980s. Since the mid-1980s, women's growing advantage in college completion cannot be explained solely in terms of labor market opportunities, which have grown to a similar extent for both men and women. However, the structure of occupational gender segregation and the consequent differences in the structure of demand for male and female labor probably continue to play a role in the gender gap in educational attainment.

The returns to higher education for women and men extend beyond returns in the labor market and include a higher probability of marriage, a higher standard of living, and greater insurance against poverty. Women's standard-of-living and insurance-against-poverty returns to a college degree have risen faster than those for men. The trend lines suggest a plausible connection between the female-specific increase in college completion rates during the 1980s and the female-specific rise in returns to a college degree in terms of standard of living and insurance against poverty that were taking place around the same time.

We then examined environmental factors that may hinder college completion more for one gender than the other. Military service has been largely a male activity during the twentieth century. On the one hand, the size of the military did not grow during the decades when men were falling behind women in college completion rates, which casts doubt on the military being a major part of the explanation for the observed trends. Nonetheless, available evidence finds a negative relationship between military service and rates of college completion, and we note that some research findings suggest that military service may compete with college for at least some young males and may also contribute to men's tendency to delay completing their education longer than women. Incarceration is another factor that can negatively affect educational attainment, especially for young black males. However, incarceration is unlikely to be a major impediment to college completion for black males, if only because the segment of the black population that is most affected by the risk of incarceration had poor prospects of completing four-year college even in the absence of incarceration.

Finally, in addressing the possibility that the gender gap in educational attainment is shaped by constraints in the supply of places in four-year colleges, we determined that this is not very plausible. The female-favorable gender gap has grown largely in the less-selective colleges and universities, where the supply of college spaces appears to be large enough to meet the demand. In the smaller sphere of highly selective institutions, where demand substantially exceeds supply, supply constraints, if anything, appear to help males at the expense of females, as some admissions offices may strive to enroll a gender-balanced freshman class. Whether selective colleges are actually practicing affirmative action for males cannot be determined with available data.

Do these environmental factors by themselves account for the reversal of the gender gap in college completion? Although important, they clearly are not the whole story. Generally speaking, college completion depends on financial costs and parental resources, on opportunity, incentives, and educational aspirations, and on academic skills and preparation. For a long time, girls had lower opportunity, incentives, and aspirations to go to college. In the next chapters, we consider evidence that these lower incentives were linked with lower parental educational investment in daughters than sons. We also consider evidence that these lower incentives reduced girls' academic preparation for college compared with boys. Until recently, however, the great majority of boys were firmly oriented not toward college but toward blue-collar occupations, and especially those well-paying blue-collar occupations that never offered much opportunity to girls but that have become both less lucrative and less available to boys as well since the 1970s.

As we discuss in the next chapter, girls have long had a performance advantage over boys in school. As costs and resources have become the same for sons and daughters and as opportunity, incentives, and educational aspirations for girls have grown to the point where they equal or exceed those of boys, the end result is that young women have overtaken young men in educational attainment and particularly in the rates of college completion.

An understanding of the college completion gap requires an examination of the educational life course over the years leading up to college admission, and specifically an understanding of the character and causes of the female advantage in educational achievement. As it turns out, achievement is a major determinant of both enrollment and completion of four-year college. In the next chapters, we address the characteristics and origins of the female advantage in educational achievement and examine their impact on the gender gap in rates of college completion.

Part II

Academic Performance, Engagement, and Family Influence

Chapter 4

The Gender Gap in Academic Performance

IRLS HAVE long gotten better grades in school than boys.[1] This fact is generally not known or acknowledged in much of the academic research and popular press focused on current gender gaps in education. In fact, some commentators assume that females' better academic performance over that of males is a recent phenomenon and that boys used to perform as well as or better than girls academically. This misrepresentation of trends in the gender gap in academic performance has led to much hand-wringing over the "problem with boys." Of course, for much of the twentieth century, the female advantages in academic performance were more than offset by male advantages in educational aspirations, males' higher enrollment in college preparatory high school courses, and males' higher levels of college enrollment. In this chapter, we document and analyze the trends in academic performance and course-taking using anecdotal historical evidence as well as nationally representative data from the 1970s to the present in order to "set the record straight" about gendered patterns and changes over time in these two factors, which are centrally related to college enrollment and completion. We show that the male advantage in college preparatory courses in high school gradually diminished and essentially disappeared for cohorts born around 1964. Although male advantages in high school course-taking and transitioning to college have changed substantially since the mid-1960s, the female advantage in academic performance has changed little, if at all. As other gender differences have diminished or reversed from a male advantage to a female advantage, the long-standing performance advantage of girls has assumed greater importance. Arguably, gender differences in academic performance are the single most important factor behind the contemporary gender gap in college completion. In other words, females' better average academic performance is central to their higher level of educational attainment and in males' shortfall in attainment. Girls' academic performance advantages must also figure centrally in any predictions about future trends in educational attainment for both girls and boys.

Why have girls long earned better grades than males? Some commentators see academic performance as depending largely on academic ability. Genetic theories aside, the population distribution of measured IQ has not been constant over the past one hundred years, but rather has shifted strongly upward (the so-called Flynn effect) (Flynn 1994, 2007). The shift is so large that it calls into question whether IQ tests can accurately measure changes in population IQs over time (Wicherts et al. 2004). This upward shift in IQ scores also indicates that current generations know more than prior generations and are therefore more prepared for college than ever before. At the same time, research demonstrates that gender differences in cognitive performance are relatively small (Hedges and Nowell 1995; Hyde 2005), with girls generally having an edge in reading and boys leading in math (Maccoby and Jacklin 1974). Other studies find a greater dispersion of reading and math test scores for boys than for girls and a greater preponderance of low scores in reading and high scores in math among boys (Hedges and Nowell 1995; Machin and Pekkarinen 2008). The evidence for relatively small gender differences in measured ability, combined with historical evidence for increases in the average test scores of the general population over time (Rampey, Dion, and Donahue 2009, 56), suggests that there is no "ability constraint" preventing further increases in rates of college completion. In other words, there is no reason to believe that males' lower rates of college completion are due to cognitive limitations among the male population.[2]

Performing well in college and completing a college degree have less to do with performance on standardized tests and more to do with grades in high school courses.[3] Studies of educational attainment consistently find that students with good grades in academically rigorous high school courses are much more likely to obtain a college degree than are poorly performing students. This chapter clearly demonstrates that the proportion of high school students who take college preparatory courses has increased in recent decades and that the most academically able students have increased both the number and depth of the math and science courses they take in high school.

Although female students once lagged behind male students in the number of math and science courses they took in high school, they have made great progress and are now very similar to male students in their course-taking patterns; they also exhibit a greater propensity to convert their academic performance in college prep high school courses into college enrollment and completion. Female students remain different from male students in two principal respects: (1) their choice of college courses and major, and (2) their superior academic performance from kindergarten through high school and college (Alexander and Eckland 1974; Alexander and McDill 1976; Thomas, Alexander, and Eckland 1979; Goldin et al. 2006).

Age and Development

In the United States, most children start formal schooling at age five, but approximately 10 percent of children begin kindergarten a year later. Parents decide when their children begin school and, along with teachers, determine whether their children are promoted to the next grade. Delayed entry into kindergarten, or academic "redshirting," is more common among boys and among children from families of high socioeconomic status (Graue and DiPerna 2000). Nationally representative data from the Early Child Longitudinal Study, Kindergarten Class of 1998–99 (ECLS-K) indicate that boys comprise about 60 percent of the children whose entry into kindergarten is delayed and 66 percent of those who repeat kindergarten (Malone et al. 2006). Boys are also more likely than girls to be retained a grade or more during elementary school (Alexander, Entwisle, and Dauber 2003; Entwisle et al. 2007).

These differences in early school trajectories are important to bear in mind when comparing boys and girls in terms of their academic performance. In age-based comparisons, girls will have attained a slightly higher average grade level than boys. In the grade-based comparisons common in most research, boys will be slightly older on average than girls. The different developmental trajectories of girls and boys make the matter even more confusing: girls tend to mature more quickly than boys (Tanner 1990; Gullo and Burton 1992). One could argue that comparisons using chronological age ignore sex differences in maturational tempo and result in comparing more-mature girls to less-mature boys (Eaton and Yu 1989), yet these complexities are infrequently considered in the literature.

Test Scores

Many researchers, educators, and politicians regard academic performance as the bottom line in K-12 education. From parent-teacher association meetings to the national No Child Left Behind Act, the question "How are our children doing?" is usually addressed with data from standardized tests and other uniform assessments or grades and report cards. When the question turns to "Who is doing better, girls or boys?" the answer depends on the age of the students being compared, whether grades or test scores are used, and the academic subject.

Test scores and grades capture different elements of academic performance and ability, as is evident by the generalization that males tend to obtain higher scores on standardized tests than females, whereas females tend to get higher grades than males (Duckworth and Seligman 2006). Most of the literature on academic performance focuses on adolescents, but the recent availability of data for younger children (such as the ECLS-K) has stimulated research on performance earlier in childhood. Gender differences in test scores have been the subject of much research for many decades. Eleanor Maccoby and Carol Jacklin's important book *The Psychology of Sex Differences* (1974) provided a comprehensive analysis of more than 1,600 studies in the areas of achievement, personality, and social relations and served to stimulate much interest and new research on gender differences in achievement in particular.[4]

Results from various national and international large-scale assessments indicate that boys have higher test scores in mathematics and girls have higher test scores in reading (Baker and Jones 1993; Beller and Gafni 1996; Hedges and Nowell 1995; Gallagher and Kaufman 2005; Marks 2007), but there is considerable cross-national variation in the size of these gaps (Penner 2008; Guiso et al. 2008). There is also a life-course component to gender differences in test scores. Research consistently finds generally similar performance of girls and boys in mathematics and reading in the early grades and a growing male advantage in math scores and growing female advantage in reading scores as they move through school (Maccoby and Jacklin 1974; Willingham and Cole 1997). These gender-based performance differences persist in standardized tests that are used in college admissions, such as the SAT, although they tend be small and the distributions of male and female scores overlap substantially (Hyde 2005; Kobrin, Sathy, and Shaw 2007). Inferring gender differences in math and verbal abilities from gender differences in SAT scores is problematic because the sample of SAT test-takers is not representative of the general population and because more females than males take the SAT, so the sample of males is more highly selected (Spelke 2005). Other evidence shows test score advantages for males or females in different contexts and time periods. For example, in Great Britain, boys were slightly more likely than girls to reach the 5+ O level threshold for proceeding to sixth form between 1962 and 1967. Then, between 1968 and 1986, the difference was either zero or one to two percentage points in favor of girls (Department for Education and Skills 2007). British girls opened up a larger lead (up to ten percentage points) over boys in the years after 1986, when the criteria for achieving this threshold were broadened to include more course work (Machin and McNally 2005). When evaluation methods include essays, projects, and homework, the female-favorable gender gap is larger than when evaluation is based solely on multiple-choice-type tests. Despite the large literature in this area (for a review, see Willingham and Cole 1997), disagreement remains on several fronts, including: the point in the life course at which gender differences in math performance typically emerge (Leahy and Guo 2001); the question of whether males are more variable than females on measures of achievement (Willingham and Cole 1997); and whether gender differences in test scores have been declining over time.

Researchers have consistently found relatively small changes in the gender gap in standardized tests over the past thirty years, and there is some evidence of a small reduction in the female shortfall in math performance. Using data from six U.S. national probability samples spanning from 1960 (Project Talent) through 1992 (National Education Longitudinal Study [NELS]), Larry Hedges and Amy Nowell (1995) found a gradual reduction of the male advantage in math and science tests and no reduction in the female advantage in tests of reading and writing ability.[5] Claudia Goldin and her colleagues (2006) found female relative gains in math achievement between the seniors in the Wisconsin Longitudinal Survey in 1957 and the seniors in the National Longitudinal Study in 1992, as did Donghun Cho (2007) in his comparison of the National Longitudinal Survey of the High School Class of 1972 and the NELS. The National Assessment of Educational Progress, often called "the Nation's Report Card," shows that females have consistently scored higher in reading than male students since 1971, and the size of the gap has changed little over the past forty-five years, with girls outperforming boys by at least seven points in all age groups and all years. This trend applies to all three age groups tested: nine-year-olds, thirteen-year-olds, and seventeen-year-olds. Gender gaps in math scores tend to favor males, but they are smaller and exist only at certain ages. For example, there is no significant difference in the average mathematics scores of male and female students at age nine and age thirteen, and this has been the case for virtually all years since 1971 in which the NAEP was conducted. By age seventeen, however, a small male score advantage of roughly five points has been found in most years since 1971 (Rampey et al. 2009; see figures A.5, A.6, A.7, and A.8).

Information about academic progress for boys and girls through the early childhood years can be drawn from the ECLS-K. Figure 4.1 shows gender differences in mean reading and math scores in the ECLS-K data from the beginning of kindergarten through fifth grade, expressed in standard deviation units. The female advantage on the reading test starts at the beginning of kindergarten at about 0.15 standard deviations from the beginning of kindergarten and declines only slightly through the end of fifth grade.[6] In contrast, kindergarten boys have a slight lead over girls on the math test (0.04 standard deviations) at the start of kindergarten; this gap grows to about one-fourth of a standard deviation by the end of third grade, and then remains about the same size as of fifth grade.

Figure 4.1   Gender Differences in Math and Reading Test Scores

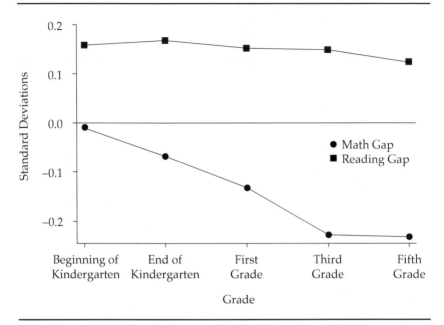

Source: Authors' compilation based on ECLS-K data (National Center for Education Statistics 2009).

Some evidence suggests that gender gaps in test scores are more pronounced among low-income children (Hinshaw 1992), but results are not definitive. For example, Doris Entwisle and her colleagues (2007) find that although girls and boys start first grade with similar reading scores, a female-favorable gap in reading emerges by fifth grade, but only for children from economically disadvantaged families; boys and girls from middle- and upper-class families have very similar reading scores. Conversely, with nationally representative data, Thomas DiPrete and Jennifer Jennings (2012) and others (Corbett et al. 2008) find that girls have higher reading scores than boys across all levels of socioeconomic status.

Figure 4.1 is concerned only with mean differences in test score performance. Gender differences can also be found in the variance of test scores and other aspects of the test score distribution. For example, Andrew Penner and Marcel Paret (2008) have recently shown that the male advantage in mathematics scores among entering kindergartners at the top of the distribution is larger among families of higher social class. This finding parallels long-standing research that shows a greater variance in math test scores for males than for females (Hedges and Nowell 1995).

Grades and Courses in School

In contrast to their generally similar levels of performance on standardized tests, boys and girls perform very differently when measured by grades in their courses in school. Because performance in courses is less standardized, there is less consensus on trends in gender differences in this measure of academic performance. Nonetheless, evidence indicates that girls have outperformed boys in school grades since the turn of the century. In the middle of the nineteenth century, girls enrolled in coeducational schools at roughly the same rate as boys, and for the most part, girls in those schools took the same classes with the same teachers as their male counterparts. Even then, girls earned higher grades than boys and were promoted to the next grade more readily (Clarke 1875; Hansot and Tyack 1988).[7] Writing in 1910, J. E. Armstrong reported that "the first three primary grades of the schools of the whole United States show that a larger number of boys than girls have to repeat grades. The census shows that the sexes are born in very nearly equal numbers and yet the boys are four per cent more numerous in the first grade" (Armstrong 1910, 347–48). It is also striking that as early as 1870, when rates of high school completion were extremely low (only 2 percent of seventeen-year-olds completed high school at that time), more girls than boys completed high school (Newcomer 1959; Solomon 1985).

Regardless of their better performance in elementary school and higher rates of high school completion, young women were barred from attending college for much of the nineteenth century. They were first allowed to enroll in college in 1837, when Oberlin College began admitting women, "ostensibly to provide ministers with intelligent, cultivated and thoroughly schooled wives" (Graham 1978, 764). When the Civil War led to a shortage of male students, more colleges became willing to enroll tuition-paying female students. By 1870, women comprised 21 percent of undergraduates in U.S. colleges and universities. Of course, this figure includes the many women who enrolled in women's colleges or the "coordinate colleges" adjacent to established men's colleges that refused to admit women students (for example, Radcliffe at Harvard, Barnard at Columbia, Evelyn at Princeton, Pembroke at Brown, and Jackson at Tufts). By 1900, however, more than twice as many women were enrolled in coeducational institutions as were enrolled in women's colleges (Solomon 1985). In the first decade of the twentieth century, the rapid rise in the number of women enrolling in coeducational institutions precipitated a new fear that women would take over colleges.

Chicago, Stanford, California, Wisconsin, Boston University, and even Oberlin had qualms; the impact on male enrollments was the central issue and complaints by some male students were noted. Academic achievement was held against females when they surpassed males in either sheer numbers or academic honors. Faculty members echoed the views of disgruntled or perhaps envious, male students and charged that women interfered with male academic performance. (Solomon 1985, 58)[8]

Fast-forward to the current era and the female advantage in academic performance at all levels of education is indisputable. As early as kindergarten, girls demonstrate more-advanced reading skills than boys (West, Denton, and Reaney 2000; Tach and Farkas 2006), and boys continue to have more problems with reading in elementary school (Trzesniewski et al. 2006). From kindergarten through high school and into college, girls get better grades than boys in all major subjects, including math and science (Perkins et al. 2004). To dig deeper into the gender gap in the grades of high school students, we analyzed data from four panel data sets derived from surveys designed to study the educational, vocational, and personal development of young people in the United States as they transition from high school into adulthood: the National Longitudinal Study of the high school class of 1972 (NLS72); the High School and Beyond (HSB) high school class of 1982 (first surveyed as sophomores in 1980); the National Education Longitudinal Study (NELS) of 1988, which surveyed the high school class of 1992; and the Education Longitudinal Study of 2002 (ELS), which surveyed the high school class of 2004.

First, we examine gender differences in academic performance by examining overall high school grade point average (GPA) for male and female high school seniors and gender gaps in GPA across the four decades represented by the surveys, with data drawn from the high school transcripts included in these data sets. Because the NLS72 does not include transcript data, we must rely on student self-reports of their overall high school GPA for the seniors in 1972.[9] Figure 4.2 reports trends in GPA over time for male and female students in the graduating cohort from each survey. Several points are noteworthy. First, the figure shows an increase in overall GPA between 1972 and 2004 for males and females of about 0.4 to 0.5 on a 4.0 GPA scale. This increase is in line with the rise in high school grades over time documented in some prior research.[10] A statistically significant female-favorable grade gap exists for each time point, and the size of these gaps remains relatively constant, ranging from about 0.24 to 0.30 over the period.[11]

In the 1950s, males had a clear advantage over females in the average rigor of their high school math and science course work. For example, using data from the state of Wisconsin, Goldin and her colleagues (2006) find that male seniors in the 1957 high school graduating class took, on average, over a semester more math than did female seniors (4.02 semesters versus 2.89 semesters) and nearly a semester more science, which was largely concentrated in physics (1.01 semesters versus 0.30 semesters).[12]

Figure 4.2   Mean Grade Point Average for High School Seniors, 1972 to 2004

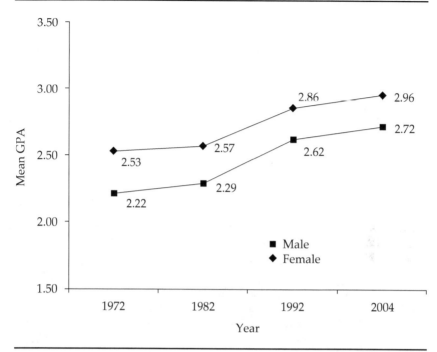

Source: Authors' compilation based on data from National Longitudinal Survey of 1972, High School & Beyond, National Educational Longitudinal Study and Educational Longitudinal Study (National Center for Education Statistics 1994, 1995, 2003, 2007).

Using the panel data sets, we compared males and females in their high school course-taking patterns over the last four decades.[13] Particularly striking in this comparison is a clear pattern of a gender reversal from a statistically significant male advantage in mean number of math and science courses taken in 1972 to a statistically significant female advantage by 2004. In 1972 males reported taking 0.29 more math courses and 0.19 more science courses than their female counterparts. This male advantage declined in 1982, and by 1992 high school transcripts revealed virtual parity in the mean number of math and science courses taken by male and female students. Over the next twelve years, the mean number of math and science courses reported on the transcripts of females exceeded the mean for males, and this gender gap was statistically significant. Moreover, a female advantage in foreign language courses has persisted and appears to have grown over time (from a 0.28 female advantage in 1972 to a 0.34 female advantage in 2004).

Our analysis also made clear that a higher percentage of students reported taking middle- to advanced-level math and science courses in

2004 than in 1972 (see figure 4.3). Algebra 2 is the entry-level advanced course in the math pipeline that leads to more advanced courses such as precalculus and calculus. In 1972, for example, fewer than 30 percent of graduating high school students took algebra 2 or chemistry, and only 17 percent completed both; by 2004, more than half of all students completed one of these courses, and more than one-third completed both. The female advantage in high school course-taking is further reflected in the fact that more female students than male students complete middle- to advanced-level course work in math and science. In 2004, 56 percent of females completed algebra 2, and 61 percent completed chemistry. Nearly 43 percent of female high school students completed both of these advanced courses. A smaller percentage of male students completed these advanced courses (52 percent, 54 percent, and 37.8 percent, respectively; see also Cho 2007).

Figure 4.4 compares the GPAs of males and females in two categories: those who complete advanced courses (algebra 2 and chemistry) and those who do not. It is striking that in both categories of students, females earn higher average GPAs than do male students and these gender gaps in GPA are quite stable over time. Among students enrolled in advanced courses, the average GPA for females is roughly 0.20 points higher than the GPA for males in 2004; for students not enrolled in advanced courses, the female-favorable GPA gap is slightly higher at 0.25. This finding underscores the stability of the female advantage in high school grades even when the rigor of the course work is held constant. In the next section, we consider how the higher average grades earned by young women compared to young men relate to the female-favorable advantage in college completion that has emerged in recent decades.

Academic Performance and College Completion Rates

Because the relative educational attainment of males and females—particularly for whites—has changed so rapidly in the past three decades, we use the most current data available to assess the contemporary impact of grades in school on college completion rates. The National Longitudinal Survey of Youth: 1997 (NLSY97) is an ongoing longitudinal study of young people who were born between the years of 1980 and 1984 and thus were twenty-two to twenty-seven years old when the most recent wave of data was gathered between October 2006 and July 2007. We estimated an individual's probability of completing college as a function of birth year, gender, race, whether enrolled in school in 1997, father's education, grades, and test scores. From these results, we computed the estimated probabilities of college completion if the respondent was in the second year of high school in 1997. This procedure gives the predicted probability of receiving a bachelor's degree seven years after finishing high school for those who make normal progress through high school.

Figure 4.3   Percentage of Female and Male High School Students Completing Advanced Courses, 1982 to 2004

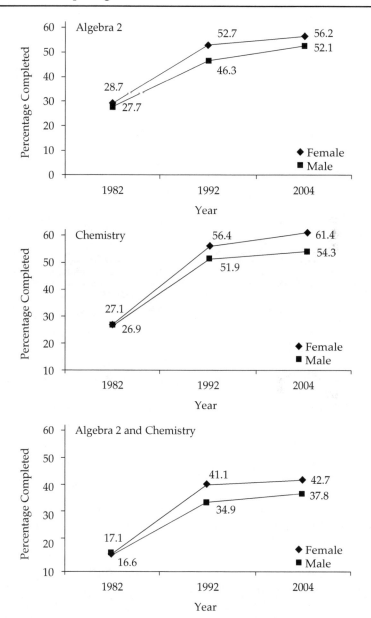

Source: Authors' compilation based on data from High School & Beyond, National Educational Longitudinal Study, and Educational Longitudinal Study (National Center for Education Statistics 1995, 2003, 2007).
Note: Data are weighted and pertain to high school seniors who subsequently graduated from high school.

Figure 4.4   Mean High School Grade Point Average, by Advanced Course-Taking and Gender, 1982 to 2004

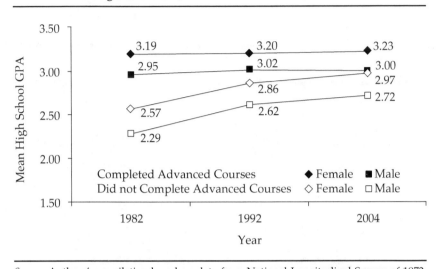

Source: Authors' compilation based on data from National Longitudinal Survey of 1972, High School & Beyond, National Educational Longitudinal Study and Educational Longitudinal Study (National Center for Education Statistics 1994, 1995, 2003, 2007).
Note: Data are weighted and pertain to high school seniors who subsequently graduated from high school. Advanced courses include algebra 2 and chemistry. All gender differences are significant at the 0.01 level.

All members of the NLSY97 cohort were given the Armed Services Vocational Aptitude Battery (ASVAB) of tests in the 1997 survey, when they were twelve to seventeen years old. The ASVAB is a military enlistment test battery consisting of twelve subtests that are administered using an adaptive testing procedure that matches the difficulty level of the individual items to the ability levels of the respondents. It has been used as a general test of aptitude in many studies. With these data, we produced a summary age-specific percentile score from four key subtests—mathematical knowledge, arithmetic reasoning, word knowledge, and paragraph comprehension. Figure 4.5 shows the distribution by gender across the combined mathematical and verbal scores. This distribution mirrors other data on test score distributions (Hedges and Nowell 1995) in showing a wider variance in performance on standardized tests for males than females. Males are nearly as likely as females to have high percentile scores, but they are also substantially more likely to have low percentile scores. Females are more likely to be in the middle and upper middle percentiles.

Not surprisingly, ASVAB scores had a strong relationship to the probability of college completion by the 2009 survey, a time when virtually

Figure 4.5   Gender Distribution Across ASVAB Quintiles, 1997

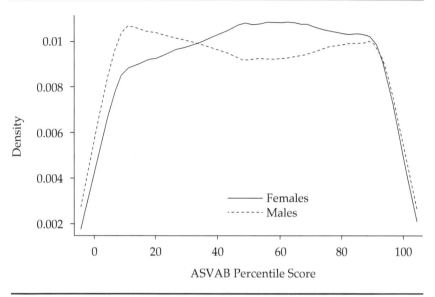

ASVAB Percentile Score

Source: Authors' compilation based on National Longitudinal Study of the High School Class of 1997 data (U.S. Department of Labor, Bureau of Labor Statistics 2012).

all NLSY97 respondents were twenty-five or older. As figure 4.6 shows, the estimated proportion of students in the top quintile who complete a bachelor's degree by age twenty-five is over 60 percent. In the fourth quintile, the proportion of females who complete a college degree is, at 50 percent, still very high relative to the overall proportion of the population that completes a college degree. In contrast, the proportion of boys who complete college and score in the fourth quintile is a much lower 35 percent. It is striking that the fraction of boys in the fourth test score quintile who complete college is not much higher than the total fraction of girls who complete college, even though these boys score in the top 40 percent of the test score distribution. If we look at the lower and middle quintiles, labeled Q2 and Q3 in the figure, gender discrepancies are also noticeable.

These data verify a strong relationship between test score performance and the likelihood of completing a college degree. They also suggest that there is no sharp cutoff in the standardized test score that is required for college completion; students in the top three and in some cases even the top four quintiles of the test distribution are able to do sufficiently well academically in order to complete a bachelor's degree if other facilitating factors are in place. Figure 4.6 also demonstrates that the gender gap in the likelihood of completing college cannot be ex-

Figure 4.6   Proportion Who Complete College, by ASVAB Score

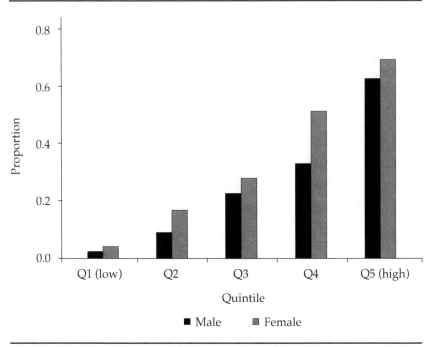

Source: Authors' compilation based on National Longitudinal Study of Youth 1997 data (U.S. Department of Labor, Bureau of Labor Statistics 2012).

plained in terms of gender differences in the test score distribution. Females have an advantage over males in completing a bachelor's degree by age twenty-five in all quintiles. This figure begs the question as to why such a consistent gender difference exists after accounting for standardized test scores. The answer to this question is found largely in the gender differences in grades and course work.

Even as early as middle school, course grades have a very strong relationship to four-year college completion.[14] Figure 4.7 shows that students who report getting mostly A's in middle school have a nearly 70 percent chance of completing college by age twenty-five. Those who report getting about half A's and half B's have about a 40 percent chance of completing college. For those who report getting mostly B's, the probability of completing college drops to about 30 percent, and fewer than one in ten students who report that they get mostly C's in middle school will complete a bachelor's degree by age twenty-five. It is possible that some of these weaker students will complete college at older ages, especially boys, who are more likely to delay the completion of education. Clearly, however, poor academic performance in middle school heavily disadvantages students who aspire to complete four years of college.

Figure 4.7   Proportion Who Complete College, by Grades in Eighth Grade

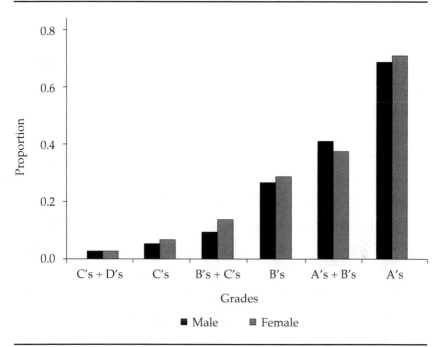

Source: Authors' compilation based on National Longitudinal Study of Youth 1997 data (U.S. Department of Labor, Bureau of Labor Statistics 2012).

Note that the relationship between academic performance and college completion is different from the relationship between academic performance and high school completion. Students getting all B's, or even B's and C's, have high probabilities of graduating from high school. Elaine Allensworth and John Easton (2007) report that almost all students with a B average or higher in ninth grade and 86 percent of students with a 2.5 GPA graduate from high school within four years. But while a student earning all B's in middle school has an excellent chance of completing high school and even a good chance of enrolling in college, he is far less likely to complete college. Paul Attewell and David Lavin (2007) report that over half of students who graduate with B averages from high school enroll in a four-year college. But lower grades are less of an impediment to enrolling in a four-year college than they are to college completion. It is relatively easy to enroll in a four-year college with average high school grades; it is more difficult to complete a college degree.

Figure 4.7 also underscores the point that course grades do a better job than standardized test scores of explaining the gender gap in college completion. Boys and girls who get either mostly A's or half A's and half B's in middle school have roughly equal chances of graduating from a

Figure 4.8   Proportion Who Complete College by Grades, in High School

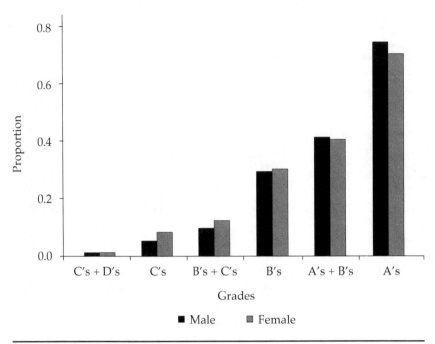

Source: Authors' compilation based on National Longitudinal Study of Youth 1997 data (U.S. Department of Labor, Bureau of Labor Statistics 2012).

four-year college by age twenty-five. This contrasts with the clear advantage that girls have over boys at every quintile of the test score distribution shown in figure 4.6.

Respondents in the NLSY97 were also asked to report their "overall" high school grades, and we graph the relationship between the last reported high school grades and the probability of completing college in figure 4.8. The general pattern is the same as that for middle school grades. Boys who report getting mostly B's, half A's and half B's, or mostly A's in high school have very similar chances to girls of graduating from college by age twenty-five.

Girls have a big advantage over boys in educational attainment, but when we control for grades, the educational attainment of girls and boys is very similar. Why is this the case? Simply stated, girls in most survey samples, including the NLSY97 used here, receive higher grades than boys in middle and high school. In particular, a much higher fraction of girls than boys earn mostly A's or half A's and half B's (see figures 4.9 for eighth grade and 4.10 for high school). In the middle of the performance distribution, the number of boys and girls is comparable, but boys pre-

Figure 4.9   Distribution of Girls and Boys, by Self-Reported Grades in Eighth Grade

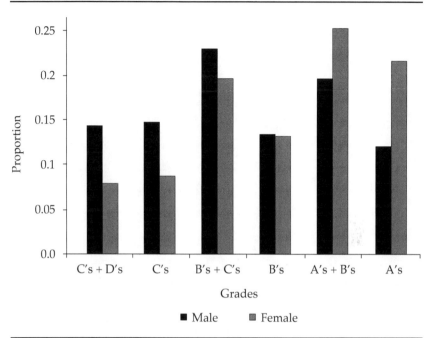

Source: Authors' compilation based on National Longitudinal Study of Youth 1997 data (U.S. Department of Labor, Bureau of Labor Statistics 2012).

dominate at the lower end of the distribution—namely, those who get mostly C's or lower. This huge female advantage in academic performance translates directly into large gender differences in educational attainment in general and into higher rates of four-year college completion in particular.

The importance of grades in accounting for the gender gap in college completion can be readily seen if we compare the educational attainment of female students with a hypothetical group of male students who are unchanged in any way except that they have earned the same course grades as females. Figure 4.11 shows three bars at each quintile of the ASVAB standardized test. The left bar in each group shows the predicted rate of four-year college completion by age twenty-five for male students. The right bar in each group shows the predicted rate of four-year college completion for female students. The middle bar shows the estimated rate of college completion for males if their reported performance in eighth grade is statistically adjusted to match that of female students. In the top quintile, the gender gap in college completion is completely accounted for by performance differences. In the other four quintiles,

Figure 4.10   Distribution of Girls and Boys, by Self-Reported Grades in High School

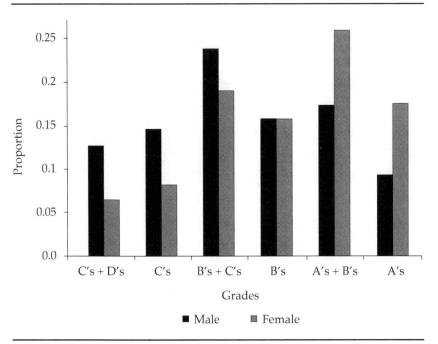

Source: Authors' compilation based on National Longitudinal Study of Youth 1997 data (U.S. Department of Labor, Bureau of Labor Statistics 2012).

middle school grades explain a considerable portion of the gender difference in college completion. At the same time, figure 4.11 shows that early performance in school is not the whole story. In particular, if we match a group of girls with a group of boys on the basis of eighth-grade performance (as we did using the National Education Longitudinal Survey; see Buchmann and DiPrete 2006), we find that the average performance of these girls is typically higher than that of the boys by the time they are high school seniors.

High school grades are not a perfect measure of preparation and capacity for college. Schools vary in the courses they offer, and students vary in the high school courses they take. High grades in academically demanding courses are better indicators of college readiness than are high grades in less-demanding courses. And students with lower grades often take less-demanding courses than students who consistently get high grades (Kelly 2004). However, even when we account for their earlier course-taking and performance in high school, we find that women typically earn higher grades than men in college courses (see Buchmann and DiPrete 2006).[15] In short, female students generally outperform male

Figure 4.11   Expected Proportion Completing College if Males Have the Same Grades in Eighth Grade as Females

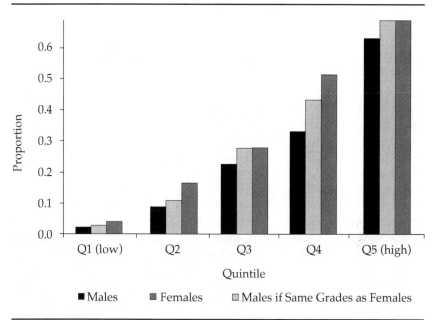

Source: Authors' compilation based on National Longitudinal Study of Youth 1997 data (U.S. Department of Labor, Bureau of Labor Statistics 2012).

students, and this advantage persists over time, even net of earlier performance advantages.[16]

Gender differences in college completion, as well as trends in these differences, involve performance differences, but as discussed in chapter 2, they also involve differences in transition rates between high school and postsecondary education, between two-year and four-year colleges, and between college entry and college completion (Buchmann and Di-Prete 2006). From a statistical perspective, the probability of graduating from a four-year college can be expressed as the probability of transitioning to postsecondary education multiplied by the probability of completing four-year college, given that one has some postsecondary education. We saw in chapter 2 that a powerful mechanism in the female overtaking has been the faster increase in the probability of making a transition to postsecondary education, given high school graduation. The fact that women's gains have largely occurred through higher rates of transition from high school to college, however, does not mean that increasing men's rates of transitioning to college is the best way to increase their college completion rates. The rate of transition to postsecondary education is already very high in the United States, but a large number of students who begin college do not complete a bachelor's degree by age twenty-six. Table 4.1, taken from our analysis of the NELS data (Buchmann and DiPrete 2006), breaks down each cohort of males and females according to the route they took through the educational system. Twenty-two percent of male high school graduates and 19 percent of female high school graduates attend a four-year college but do not complete a BA by age twenty-five or twenty-six. Focusing only on students who make the transition from high school directly to a four-year college, we find that 9 percent of males who attend only a four-year college have not completed a degree by age twenty-five or twenty-six, compared with only 7 percent of females. To put it another way, 68 percent of males and 77 percent of females who attend only a four-year college complete a BA, while only 39 percent of males and 47 percent of females who spend any time in community colleges complete a BA by age twenty-five or twenty-six. As Bowen and his colleagues (2009) have recently highlighted, the most straightforward way to increase college completion rates would be to ensure that more of the students who start four-year college—whether via a transition from a two-year college or directly from high school—successfully complete a bachelor's degree. Both men and women have a problem with starting but not completing college, but it is a greater problem for men. Moreover, this gender gap in completion rates, given a transition to four-year college, is related to educational performance.

Analysis of NELS data confirms that the primary reason for the present and growing gender gap is males' weaker academic performance (Buchmann and DiPrete 2006). For the NELS cohort, the gender gap in the probability of completing a BA by age twenty-five or twenty-six is about five percentage points (33 percent for women and 28 percent for men). As table 4.2 shows, this gap can be statistically broken down into the part due to different rates of transition into postsecondary education and the part due to different rates of completing a BA, given a particular transition into postsecondary education. Relatively little of the gap (13 percent) is due to women's higher rates of transition into two-year college, and even less is explained (6 percent) when we take account of men's higher rate of making a transition from two-year college to four-year college (because this factor advantages men). As table 4.2 shows, about nine percentage points of the 0.28 male BA completion rate (0.47 × 0.48 × 0.39) comes from students who have some two-year college. For women, the corresponding figure (0.50 × 0.46 × 0.47) is a higher eleven percentage points, which accounts for 46 percent of the overall gender gap in BA completion. Table 4.2 further shows that most of this explanatory power (0.33 of the 0.46) comes from the fact that women get better grades than men in college. Another 45 percent of the overall gender gap comes from the higher grades that women who go directly to a four-year

Table 4.1   Route Through the Educational System by Ages Twenty-Five and Twenty-Six

	HS Grads Only		All Students	
	Males	Females	Males	Females
No high school diploma	n/a	n/a	9%	8%
High school diploma, but no college	24%	21%	22%	19%
Two-year college only	24	27	22	25
Two-year plus four-year college				
BA	9	11	8	10
No BA	14	12	13	11
Four-year college only				
BA	20	22	18	20
No BA	9	7	8	6

Source: Authors' compilation of data from Buchmann and DiPrete (2006).

college receive while in college. Thus, the gender gap comes predominantly from higher educational performance and the advantages it conveys in college graduation rates as opposed to higher transition rates into college. Since 1988, when the NELS cohort was in eighth grade, women have opened up a larger lead in transition rates to postsecondary education. For more recent cohorts of young men and women, the combination of this higher rate of transition to college and females' higher educational performance accounts for the growing gender gap in the rate of BA completion.[17]

Table 4.2   Breaking Down the Gender Gap in Terms of Pathways and Performance

Probability of . . .	Men	Women	Men if They Have Women's Grades	Fraction of Total Gap
Any two-year college	47%	50%		13%
Any four-year college, conditional on some two-year college	48	46		6
BA, given both four-year and two-year college	39	47	(46)	46
Only four-year college	29	29		49
BA, given only four-year college	68	77	(76)	100

Source: Authors' compilation of data from Buchmann and DiPrete (2006).

Conclusion

This chapter has focused on the gender gap in academic performance in elementary, middle, and high school. If the academic differential between boys and girls could be taken as a stable attribute of gender, then the explanation for the widening gender gap in college completion would be relatively straightforward—namely, that girls today make greater use of their edge in average academic performance to obtain higher levels of education than they once did.

This chapter has reviewed the evidence for four facts that together predict a gender gap in college completion: (1) relatively small and offsetting gender gaps in reading and math standardized scores, where the reading gaps favoring girls have been stable and the math advantage for boys has been declining over time; (2) a large female advantage in academic performance as measured by grades; (3) a catch-up and outpacing by females relative to males in college preparatory course-taking, particularly in math and science (which may explain the small female-favorable trend in math standardized tests); and (4) the rise of women to overtake men in the proportion of each cohort that makes the transition to postsecondary education. Taken all together, these facts result in females typically overachieving relative to their performance on test scores. Given the importance of the gender gap in academic performance as a primary source of the gender gap in college completion, we examine the proximate causes of the academic performance gap in the chapters that follow.

Chapter 5

Social and Behavioral Skills and School-Related Attitudes

IN THIS chapter, we discuss three primary reasons for girls' tendency to do better in school than their test scores would predict. First, girls have an advantage relative to boys in terms of the social and behavioral skills that are valuable in producing higher levels of academic performance. Second, on average girls put forth greater effort than boys, and therefore girls gain greater average returns to their abilities than boys do, as measured by grades in school. Third, girls show greater levels of attachment to school, which may produce stronger gratification from school performance and therefore stronger immediate incentives to do well in school. These advantages reinforce each other as children become adolescents. Students who are more interested in school will work harder. Students whose behavior conforms more closely to school norms and expectations will get more out of school. Effort, interest, and conformity generally translate into higher levels of cognitive growth, as measured by test scores. Students who work harder and conform to school norms will also get higher grades, and the combination of grades and test scores is a strong predictor that a student will succeed in college and complete college.

Social and Behavioral Skills

Social and behavioral skills have assumed a central role in explaining persistent differences in school performance by socioeconomic status, race, and gender (Bowles and Gintis 1976; Farkas 2003; Rosenbaum 2001; Lareau 2003). Much research reports that boys have higher rates of aggression, antisocial behavior, attention disorders, learning disabilities, mental retardation, stuttering, delayed speech, and other related disabilities (Halpern 1997; Muter 2003; Rutter et al. 2004; Ready et al. 2005; Hyde 2005). As early as kindergarten, boys are more disruptive in class and are less positively oriented toward learning. For example, according to parent and teacher reports, twice as many boys as girls have difficulty paying attention in kindergarten, and girls more often demonstrate persistence in completing tasks and an eagerness to learn (Zill and West 2001). Several studies have demonstrated boys' stronger tendencies toward externalizing behavior (Entwisle, Alexander, and Olson 2005; Raffaelli, Crockett, and Shen 2005). Walter Gilliam (2005) reports that boys are five times as likely as girls to be expelled from prekindergarten. These gender differences persist into middle and high school. Boys are more likely to be disciplined in middle school and high school (DiPrete, Muller, and Shaeffer 1982; Arum and Roksa 2011). Adolescent males engage in more risky behaviors, such as smoking, drinking, drug use, and fighting (Byrnes, Miller, and Schafer 1999; Bachman 2002). Our own calculations from National Education Longitudinal Study (NELS) data show that high school senior males are more likely than females to skip school, to get in fights, or to get into self-reported "trouble" in school.

Table 5.1 shows differences in social and behavioral skills by gender, race, and social class during early elementary school, as reported by Thomas DiPrete and Jennifer Jennings (2012) using data from the Early Child Longitudinal Study, Kindergarten Class of 1998–99 (ECLS-K). Teachers were asked to rate student social and behavioral skills at several time points from the beginning of kindergarten through the end of fifth grade, and these ratings were grouped into several behavioral dimensions. Using factor analysis, DiPrete and Jennings (2012) combined three scales measuring approaches to learning, self-control, and interpersonal skills into a single "social and behavioral skills factor" that provides a more parsimonious description of gender differences.[1]

Girls lead boys in their social and behavioral skills by nearly 0.4 standard deviations at the start of kindergarten. From kindergarten to the end of fifth grade, boys fall further behind girls, lagging by 0.53 standard deviations by the end of fifth grade. As table 5.1 demonstrates, the gap in social and behavioral skills between boys and girls is considerably larger than the gap between children from poor families and nonpoor families or the gap between black and white children.[2]

Numerous studies find links between social and behavioral skills and educational outcomes. Kali Trzesniewski and her colleagues (2006) demonstrate that antisocial behavior and reading difficulties go hand in hand for boys; antisocial behavior leads to poor reading skills and vice versa.[3] John Coie and Gina Krehbiel (1984) found that low-achieving, socially rejected fourth-graders who were assigned to an intensive social and academic skills training intervention gained in reading, but not in math; similar results were obtained by the MTA-Cooperative-Group (1999), which focused on children with attention deficit and hyperactivity disorder (ADHD).[4] Emotional and behavioral problems early in childhood

Table 5.1   Social and Behavioral Skills, Kindergarten Through Fifth Grade

| | Social and Behavioral Skills Factor[a] | | | | | |
	Boys	Girls	Poor	Not Poor	Black	White
Beginning of kindergarten	−0.203	0.210	−0.241	0.063	−0.249	0.083
End of kindergarten	−0.199	0.205	−0.247	0.065	−0.291	0.091
First grade	−0.193	0.199	−0.203	0.055	−0.266	0.075
Third grade	−0.203	0.209	−0.281	0.082	−0.334	0.077
Fifth grade	−0.247	0.255	−0.276	0.076	−0.323	0.058

Source: Authors' compilation of data from DiPrete and Jennings (2012).
[a]Measured in standard deviation units.

also contribute to educational outcomes later in life, such as the likelihood of repeating a grade in secondary school, completing high school, and enrolling in college (Shanahan 2000; McLeod and Kaiser 2004). Given that girls and boys differ in social development and in their predilection for exhibiting behavioral problems, it is reasonable to expect that noncognitive skills will play a role in producing gender differences in academic outcomes.

Meanwhile, cultural capital researchers contend that a broad array of cultural skills affect educational attainment, primarily through their impact on the evaluation process in school. Samuel Bowles and Herbert Gintis (1976) argued that differential socialization by class (later often summarized under the rubric of "cultural capital") has played a central role in the reproduction of class over generations by affecting both school and occupational outcomes. Just as Otis Duncan, David Featherman, and Beverly Duncan (1972) argued that the content of IQ came to be those skills that are most demanded in high-status occupations, so Bowles and Gintis, and later Pierre Bourdieu (1984) and Annette Lareau (2003), argued that teachers and employers reward those whose socialization reproduces the cultural behaviors associated with the professional and upper classes. Elementary teachers frequently consider student effort, homework, and broader performance assessments than multiple-choice tests when assigning grades (McMillan, Myran, and Workman 2002; Brookhart 1993), and previous research suggests that social and behavioral skills have strong effects on teacher-rated academic achievement, especially at the start of elementary school (Ladd, Birch, and Buhs 1999; Lin, Lawrence, and Gorrell 2003). Whatever the mechanism, Farkas and his colleagues (1990) have shown that test scores and noncognitive behaviors such as student work habits, disruptiveness, and absenteeism almost completely explain differences in course grades by gender, race-ethnicity, and poverty status for middle school students.

James Rosenbaum (2001) similarly finds that the test scores and noncognitive skills of high school seniors can explain most of the differences by gender, race-ethnicity, and class in high school grades and subsequent educational attainment.

DiPrete and Jennings (2012) analyzed ECLS-K data in order to estimate the impact of the evolving gender gap in social and behavioral skills on the gender gap in academic achievement in elementary school. They used a two-dimensional representation of social and behavioral skills, because their analyses found separate effects from these dimensions. One measure was the one-factor summary of the approaches to learning, interpersonal skills, and social control scales noted earlier. The second measure was the unique part of the approaches to learning scale (hereafter the "approaches to learning factor") that was not accounted for by the social and behavioral factor.[5] They estimated the impact of social and behavioral skills on math and reading achievement at the end of kindergarten, first grade, third grade, and fifth grade, using an instrumental variables regression designed to remove spurious correlations between the social and behavioral measures and the cognitive outcomes. Both the social and behavioral factor and the approaches to learning factor have a strong relationship to reading and math performance at the beginning of kindergarten, net of background variables. Table 5.2 shows that both the social and behavioral factor and the approaches to learning factor affect reading and math performance in subsequent waves as well. The significant effects are notable given that the models control for lagged measures of social and behavioral skills and lagged reading and math scores as well as other background factors.

Next, DiPrete and Jennings (2012) addressed the total contribution of social and behavioral skills to the gender gaps in math and reading between fifth grade and the beginning of kindergarten, the end of first grade, and the end of third grade, respectively. From their regression models, they obtained as a point estimate that the female advantage in social development at the end of kindergarten accounts for 34 percent of the female advantage in reading at the end of fifth grade, and that the male-favorable math gap would be 21 percent larger but for the female advantage in social and behavioral skills.

Measures of social and behavioral skills are strongly related to other outcomes besides test scores, and in statistical terms they account for a considerable portion of gender differences on these outcomes. Sixteen percent of boys versus 12 percent of girls have been retained by the start of fifth grade—with particularly large gender differences in retention for kindergarten and first grade (see table 5.3)—and that low social and behavioral skills strongly predict retention. Net of social and behavioral skills and academic measures, girls are significantly less likely to be retained in kindergarten than boys. At the end of first grade, however, the

Table 5.2   Estimated Effects of the Social and Behavioral Skills Factor and the Approaches to Learning Factor on Reading and Math Test Scores

School Year	Reading	Math
End of kindergarten		
Social and behavioral skills factor	0.044*	0.106***
Approaches to learning factor	0.038	0.099***
End of first grade		
Social and behavioral skills factor	0.057	0.106**
Approaches to learning factor	0.174**	0.228***
End of third grade		
Social and behavioral skills factor	0.119***	0.047
Approaches to learning factor	0.107*	0.135*
End of fifth grade		
Social and behavioral skills factor	0.026*	0.032**
Approaches to learning factor	0.043	0.094*

Source: Authors' compilation of data from DiPrete and Jennings (2012).
* $p < 0.05$; ** $p < 0.01$; *** $p < 0.001$.

gender difference in retention is entirely explained by gender differences in social and behavioral skills and in reading skills. By the end of third grade, the male disadvantage in retention has disappeared, but social and behavioral skills continue to strongly predict the probability of retention.

The ECLS-K data contain a second set of academic outcome measures—academic rating scales (ARS), which are teachers' ratings of students' progress in language and literacy, general knowledge in science and social studies, and mathematical thinking. The academic rating scales are indirect cognitive assessments that differ in two principal respects from the direct cognitive assessments provided by the tests. First, the ARS measures both the process and the products of children's learn-

Table 5.3   Proportion Retained (Conditional on Not Having Previously Been Retained), by Grade and Gender

	Male		Female	
Kindergarten	0.054	(0.008)	0.024	(0.006)
First grade	0.088	(0.011)	0.065	(0.008)
Third grade	0.035	(0.005)	0.043	(0.013)

Source: Authors' compilation of data from DiPrete and Jennings (2012).

ing in school, where the process includes "the strategies they used to read, solve math problems, or investigate a scientific phenomenon" (Westat and Educational Testing Service 1998, 3–15). In contrast, the tests measure only the products of learning. Second, while the tests are constrained by a standardized testing format, the ARS is intended to "reflect a broader sampling of the most recent national curriculum standards and guidelines" and a broader curriculum content (Westat and Educational Testing Service 1998, 3–15). They differ in a third obvious respect in that they are teacher ratings of academic progress as opposed to measures from standardized tests.

Unlike with reading scores, the gender gap in reading ARS scores continues to grow between kindergarten and fifth grade (from 0.22 to 0.32 standard deviations). As with math test scores, the math ARS trend favors boys, though it only brings them from a deficit of 0.15 standard deviations in kindergarten to parity in fifth grade. Although fifth-grade teacher evaluations are not the same as formal grades, DiPrete and Jennings's (2012) results mirror other findings (Entwisle et al. 1997, 2007) that show that the gender gaps in teacher evaluations of reading and math achievement favor girls by a larger amount than do the gender gaps in reading and math test scores. Table 5.4 reports the predicted fifth-grade math and reading evaluations that boys would have received had they received the same average third-grade social and behavioral ratings as girls. It shows that the gender gap in social and behavioral skills is large enough to explain almost the entire additional gender gap in teacher reading evaluations beyond that revealed in reading test scores. It also explains most of the difference between the considerable male advantage in math test scores and the virtual gender tie on teacher evaluations of mathematics performance.[6]

Homework and Time Use

Related to the issue of social and behavioral skills is students' engagement with the learning process. Engagement and effort are not the same thing, although greater engagement generally implies greater effort, so it is important to investigate direct measures of effort. Research on children's time use shows significant differences by parental socioeconomic status. Children of highly educated parents study and read more and watch less television (Hofferth and Sandberg 2001; Bianchi and Robinson 1997; Bianchi, Robinson, and Milkie 2006). There are also significant trends over time in children's time use. The amount of time children spend in school increased by about two hours per week between 1981 and 1997. Sandra Hofferth and John Sandberg (2001) also find some convergence between girls and boys in their time use. Even though in 1981 girls were more likely to study than boys, in 1997 boys and girls were similar. This was due to a decline in the proportion of girls who reported

Table 5.4   Mean Differences Between Girls and Boys on Fifth-Grade Academic Outcomes and Third-Grade Social and Behavioral Outcomes

Variable	Females		Males		Male-Female
Fifth-grade math test scores	−0.118	(0.041)	0.114	(0.036)	0.232
Fifth-grade reading test scores	0.063	(0.039)	−0.061	(0.038)	−0.124
Fifth-grade teacher math evaluations	0.002	(0.035)	−0.002	(0.032)	−0.004
Fifth-grade teacher reading evaluations	0.160	(0.036)	−0.115	(0.033)	−0.275
Third-grade social and behavioral skills factor	0.209	(0.034)	−0.203	(0.030)	−0.412
Third-grade approaches to learning factor	0.133	(0.031)	−0.129	(0.033)	−0.262
Fifth-grade predicted math evaluation					
Males with own means on social and behavioral variables	0.104		0.106		0.002
Males with female means on social and behavioral variables			0.243		0.139
Fifth-grade predicted reading evaluation					
Males with own means on social and behavioral variables	0.242		−0.052		−0.294
Males with female means on social and behavioral variables			0.129		-0.113

Source: DiPrete and Jennings (2012)
Note: Standard errors are in parentheses.

they were studying, while the time boys spent studying was stable across the two surveys. The amount of time spent on homework is also directly related to learning. The NLSY97 collected data about homework for respondents between the ages of twelve and fourteen. Ranking students within grades based on how much homework they reported doing per week, we report in figure 5.1 the fraction of girls and boys in each of the five homework quintiles. The figure shows quite clearly that girls report doing more homework than do boys.[7]

We would expect that students who study more get better grades, and

Figure 5.1   Proportion of Girls and Boys in Each Quintile of Grade-Specifc Time Spent on Homework, NLSY97

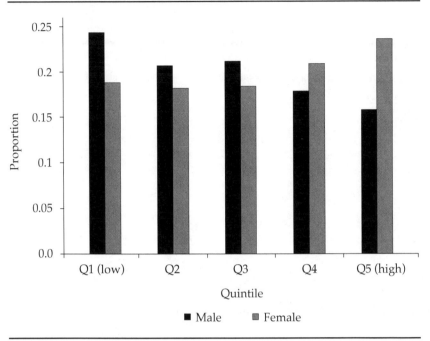

Source: Authors' compilation based on National Longitudinal Study of Youth 1997 data (U.S. Department of Labor, Bureau of Labor Statistics 2012).

like other researchers (Keith, Diamond-Hallam, and Fine 2004), we find that self-reported time spent on homework by twelve- to fourteen-year-olds has a significant effect on high school grades, even net of ASVAB test scores and other background factors. However, the effect is not large in magnitude. Consequently, the inclusion of homework in a regression model explains only a small portion of the female performance advantage. We suspect that the explanatory power of homework is weak partly because the NLSY97 measure is not a very reliable measure of actual effort expended by students during high school, and partly because self-reported high school grades also contain measurement error. More importantly, educational achievement is the outcome of a cumulative process. Two students of similar abilities who differ in terms of their long-term intensity in academic effort bring a different level of knowledge and discipline to the study of any high school subject. Their performance difference would largely be independent of the difference in their level of studying in a typical week of that semester. A similar explanation would apply to gender differences in performance during high school.

Beyond the patterns of course-taking shown in chapter 4, girls have other advantages that stem from the way they use their time. Girls are more involved in extracurricular activities, with the notable exception of participation on athletic teams (Bae et al. 2000). Female students also participate in more cultural activities within and outside of school (Dumais 2002). All these advantages are related to academic success in school, the likelihood of enrolling in college, and ultimate educational attainment.

Educational Expectations

The role of expectations as a causal mechanism in educational attainment has been a matter of great controversy for several decades. The Wisconsin model of status attainment gave a central causal role to educational expectations as shaped by the expectations of significant others, specifically parents, teachers, and peers (Sewell et al. 1969; Sewell and Hauser 1975). This "social psychological model" of status attainment drew its power from the strong statistical association between: (1) the expectations of others and family background, (2) the expectations of others and one's own expectations, and (3) one's own expectations and educational attainment. However, critics of this model asserted, raising the educational expectations of disadvantaged children would not alone have a strong impact on their educational attainment. Bourdieu (1973) argued that educational expectations are determined by the structural conditions that define a student's educational possibilities, not the other way around. Stephen Morgan (1998) argues that educational aspirations are not causal, but rather are students' "predictions" of their likely educational attainment (see also Morgan 2005). Morgan points to the tendency for black students to have especially high educational aspirations, relative to their actual educational attainment, as evidence that structural factors tied to race make it more difficult for them to accurately predict their educational futures.

For some scholars, the excessively high "aspirations as predictions" of educational attainment suggest that students are expressing their desire for the future rather than realistically assessing the possibilities (Adelman 2006, 223). This position is consistent with recent findings from the Consortium on Chicago School Research project: fewer than three-fourths of the high school seniors who report that they plan to get a four-year degree also plan to attend a four-year college in the fall after their senior year, and only 82 percent of these students have actually applied to a four-year college (Roderick et al. 2008).[8] However, both Melissa Roderick and her colleagues (2008), in their study of Chicago schools, and Andrea Venezia, Michael Kirst, and Anthony Antonio (2003), in their study of California schools, view the gap between aspirations and attainment as evidence of a failure of the educational system to provide students with an accurate means to assess their likelihood of completing four-year college given their current level of performance. Alan Kerckhoff (1977) even argued that the educational system itself affects a student's ability to predict his or her educational outcomes accurately and thus leads to systematic differences across nations in the extent to which adolescents overestimate their eventual educational attainment. Similarly, other scholars have found that students have more realistic educational expectations in countries with differentiated educational systems (Buchmann and Dalton 2002; Buchmann and Park 2009; McDaniel 2009).

Using ECLS-K data, we examined the educational expectations of male and female eighth-grade students. Consistent with other data sources (Schneider and Stevenson 2000), eighth-grade students in the ECLS-K have unrealistically high expectations for their own educational attainment. Fully 65 percent of boys in eighth grade expect that they will get at least a bachelor's degree, and 27 percent expect to get a master's or doctoral degree. Girls have educational expectations that are even higher, and the higher the degree in question, the more the gender gap in educational expectations grows. Seventy-five percent of girls expect to get a bachelor's degree, relative to 65 percent of boys. Fully 42 percent of girls expect to get a master's degree or higher, which is nearly 50 percent higher than for boys. At the doctoral level, the gender gap is enormous. While 11 percent of boys expect to get a PhD, MD, or other doctoral-level degree, 20 percent of girls expect to attain this level of education. Thus, the percentage of girls who expect to get a doctoral-level degree is nearly 80 percent higher than the corresponding percentage for boys.

Trends in gender-specific educational expectations have paralleled gender-specific trends in educational attainment. Indeed, the size of the female lead in educational expectations approximates the contemporaneous size of the gender gap in college completion. The current gender gap in educational aspirations may have little to do in a causal sense with the current gender gap in educational attainment, though surely Pierre Bourdieu's (1973) critique of the Wisconsin model—that educational opportunities are determined by class and this inequality is merely reflected in student expectations—is not persuasive for the case of gender, because boys and girls are equally distributed across class and racial backgrounds. At the same time, the fact that boys now have lower educational expectations than girls may support Morgan's (2005) argument about the theoretical status of educational aspirations as a prediction rather than a cause of educational attainment. Since girls have better average grades than boys do, and since both boys and girls generally understand that grades are related to educational attainment, it stands to reason that girls' average predictions of their own educational attainment would exceed the average predictions of boys. But whether boys are collectively predicting that they cannot go as far in school as girls because of their worse grades, or whether they are expressing an on-average-lower interest in higher education and the occupations that require it is a question that cannot be answered from data on educational expectations.

The dramatically overstated educational expectations of eighth-graders in the ECLS-K suggest that many boys and girls in middle school do not have accurate knowledge about their educational futures. In particular, the high educational expectations among so many students (mainly boys) with poor grades indicate that they do not understand the American educational attainment process. Becky Francis (2000) has argued that the poor performance of boys reflects a lack of understanding of the world of work, because otherwise they would recognize the labor market value of education and put more effort into their schoolwork. This is true at some level, but the ECLS-K data show that many students also do not understand the world of school and the connections between early academic success and educational attainment and, more fundamentally, between educational effort and educational attainment.

Rosenbaum (2001) has documented this disconnect, but he points more clearly to the fact that students who do not plan to go to college may correctly perceive that grades do not matter very much for their labor market chances. Although important, this is a different issue than the question of whether middle and high school students understand the connection between grades and educational attainment. Rosenbaum has also noted that students do not see low grades as an impediment to enrolling in or completing college. Whether this impediment stems from the direct connection between effort and grades or from students' perceptions of the weak connection between mediocre college performance and labor market outcomes is an open question. But the ECLS-K data demonstrate that middle school students lack this understanding, and that this lack of understanding may be a greater problem for boys since boys put forth less effort and, in turn, receive lower grades.

Attachment to School

Attachment to school is an equally powerful motivator for educational performance. Despite common perceptions, students do not generally disparage academic engagement, so long as it is accompanied by other desirable behaviors like being popular, dressing stylishly, being athletic, and otherwise participating in extracurricular activities. John Bishop and his colleagues (2003, 161) report that 81 percent of middle and high school students who were surveyed in 1998–1999 disagreed with the statement that "it's not cool to frequently volunteer answers or comments in class," 85 percent disagreed with the statement that "it's not cool to study real hard for tests and quizzes," and 73 percent disagreed with the statement that "it's not cool to be enthusiastic about what you are learning in school." Apparently, students begin to cross the "not cool" line when they exhibit overt competitiveness about grades (51 percent said that this is not cool, but still 49 percent disagreed), but students generally appreciate that high levels of educational achievement and educational attainment are valuable in today's world.

At the same time, it is also clear from the data that girls express stronger allegiance to educational values than do boys. We examined a series of questions that were asked of eighth-grade students in the ECLS-K about their orientation toward school and their expectations for future educational attainment. Students were asked how important grades were to them and how important they perceived grades to be to their parents. As other studies have shown, students in the ECLS-K place much less emphasis on good grades than they attribute to their parents. Almost 99 percent of the ECLS-K eighth-graders reported that good grades are "important" to their parents, and 80 percent reported that good grades are "very important" to their parents, with essentially no variation in these proportions by gender, parental education, or parents' educational expectations for their child. In contrast, 90 percent of eighth-grade boys responded that good grades are "important," but only 50 percent reported that good grades are "very important." Girls expressed a valuation of academic success that was closer to what they attributed to their parents than was the case for boys; 95 percent of girls reported that good grades are important to them, and 62 percent said that good grades are "very important." The 62 percent figure for "very important" is far below the 80 percent that girls reported for their parents, but it is higher than the 50 percent of eighth-grade boys who reported that they consider good grades very important. Clearly, boys place greater distance between their own values and the values they attribute to their parents than do girls.

This greater gender gap between self-reported values and the perception of parental values persists even when the sample is limited to students who are getting A's in middle school (see table 5.5). Seventy-one percent of girls getting mostly A's reported that grades are "very important" to them, while only 60 percent of boys getting mostly A's made a similar assertion. At the other extreme, only 2 percent of girls getting mostly A's responded that grades are only "somewhat important" or "not important," which contrasts to the 6 percent of high-achieving boys who attach relatively little importance to grades.

Students who report high educational aspirations and assert that grades are important are clearly articulating an attachment to school. However, attachment can take multiple forms. Students whose main interest in school stems from their belief that school success is necessary

Table 5.5   Eighth-Grade Student Reports on the Importance of Grades to
Them (Proportions), by Their Own Grades, 2007

	Males		Females	
	Mostly A's	Other	Mostly A's	Other
Very important	0.60	0.43	0.71	0.51
Important	0.34	0.44	0.26	0.39
Somewhat important	0.06	0.11	0.02	0.09
Not important	0.01	0.02	0.00	0.01

Source: Authors' compilation based on ECLS-K data (National Center for Education Statistics 2009).

for a well-paying job might have only an "instrumental attachment" to school. For them, school is an instrument that they use to obtain a desired goal. Alternatively, students may be attached to school because they are emotionally invested in school, or receive daily gratification from it, especially when they do well and receive positive feedback from teachers. These students experience an "expressive attachment" to school. Instrumental and expressive attachment are idealized constructs in that most students might experience both types of attachment in varying degrees, but the distinction is nonetheless useful for making sense of the patterns of attitudes and behaviors visible in the data.

Eighth-grade students answered a set of questions in the ECLS-K survey that capture their expressive attachment to school in terms of whether they enjoy school, like their teachers, and feel that they "fit in" at school. Table 5.6 shows boys' and girls' responses to these questions and suggests that girls typically have a stronger expressive attachment to school than boys do. Eighth-grade girls and boys responded similarly when asked how often they feel that they "fit in" at school. However, girls had an eight-percentage-point advantage over boys in the proportion who reported that they "often" or "always" feel close to teachers and that they enjoy school.

Table 5.6   Proportion of Eighth-Grade Students Reporting That They Fit in
at School and Enjoy School, by Gender, 2007

	Fit In		Close to Teachers		Enjoy School	
	Females	Males	Females	Males	Females	Males
Never	0.02	0.02	0.05	0.10	0.04	0.07
Sometimes	0.13	0.12	0.39	0.42	0.29	0.34
Often	0.33	0.36	0.37	0.34	0.42	0.37
Always	0.53	0.50	0.19	0.14	0.25	0.22

Source: Authors' compilation based on ECLS-K data (National Center for Education Statistics 2009).

It is difficult to distinguish empirically the extent to which high educational aspirations and a strong emphasis on good grades represent an
instrumental attachment connected to long-term educational goals versus a shorter-term expressive attachment linked to day-to-day gratification from the school experience. The data presented here make clear,
however, that girls express stronger support than boys for long-term academic achievement, as expressed by their higher aspirations, and for
immediate academic success, as expressed by the greater importance
they give to grades and their stronger expressive attachment to school.
To put it another way, girls may well have more "grit" than boys, which
Angela Duckworth and her colleagues (2007) have defined as more perseverance and passion for long-term educational goals. But girls' higher
long-term educational success could also be attributed to their greater
enjoyment of school and the stronger immediate gratification they get
from better performance. These two forces could of course be working in
tandem. We do not try to quantify the extent to which expressions of attachment are causes as opposed to consequences of educational performance, but we think that they play a causal role in girls' greater effort
and higher grades. We return to the issue of attachment as it relates to
family of origin in chapter 6 and to the issue of school effects on attachment in chapter 7.

Conclusion

Social and behavioral skills are important resources for success in elementary school, as measured by cognitive tests and, even more so, by
teacher evaluations. In general, girls have a considerable lead over boys
in these skills as early as kindergarten, and they extend this lead further
over the first six years of schooling. Social and behavioral skills are predictive of gains in reading and math competence during elementary
school as well as teacher ratings of academic outcomes. This female advantage in social and behavioral skills accounts for an important component of the female advantage in academic performance in elementary
school. Girls and boys also expend different average levels of effort in
schoolwork, and these differences are related to the gender gap in academic performance, particularly in middle school and high school. The
female advantage in academic performance continues in middle school,
high school, and college, and it may be the single most important factor
underlying the significant lead that women have over men in rates of
college completion (Buchmann and DiPrete 2006). Thus, although social
and behavioral skills once functioned like other skills in creating lifelong
advantages for children born to upper-middle-class households, they
now have a double effect: they preserve advantages for the upper-middle
class even as they allow another historically disadvantaged group—

women—to overtake men in the acquisition of the single most important resource in the stratification system of a modern industrial country: education.

American adolescents have unrealistically high educational expectations; far more expect to obtain a bachelor's degree than actually do. The dramatically overstated educational expectations of eighth-graders suggest that many boys and girls in middle school do not have accurate knowledge about their educational futures. In particular, the fact that so many students, especially male students, expect to complete college despite their poor grades in middle and high school suggests that they do not understand the process of educational attainment. How this lack of understanding may affect the gender gap in educational attainment is a question that we return to later in this book.

Chapter 6

The Family and the Gender Gap

THIS CHAPTER examines the thesis that families play an important role in producing a gender gap in educational performance and attainment. First, we review evidence that parental education at one time assisted daughters in getting the same level of education as their brothers and that this relationship has been reversed in the past sixty years, such that today boys are especially disadvantaged when their parents are less educated or when their father is absent. Then we address the question of how the relative academic performances of sons and daughters may depend on family characteristics. The mechanisms connecting parental resources to different educational outcomes for girls and boys are subtle. We consider the evidence that parental characteristics operate both directly on children's behaviors and academic orientations and indirectly by shaping children's peer environment and the influence of that environment on their behaviors, academic orientation, and educational performance.

The family has long played a central role in theories of education and status attainment. But the family's impact on differences in the educational attainment of sons and daughters has not been a central question for most scholarship, even though in popular culture it has been almost universally recognized that parents treat sons and daughters differently. Consider the example from the famous 1945 musical *Carousel:*

> Billy. I wonder what he'll think of me.... I bet that he'll turn out to be the spittin' image of his dad. But he'll have more common sense than his puddin-headed father ever had. I'll teach him to wrestle and dive through a wave when we go in the mornin's for our swim. His mother can teach him the way to behave but she won't make a sissy out o' him. Not him! Not my boy! Not Bill! ...
>
> I don't give a hang what he does as long as he does what he likes! He

can sit on his tail or work on a rail with a hammer, hammering spikes! . . .
and you won't see nobody dare to try to boss him or toss him around!

Wait a minute! Could it be? What the hell! What if he is a girl? What
would I do with her? What could I do for her? A bum with no money! You
can have fun with a son but you gotta be a father to a girl. . . .

My little girl pink and white as peaches and cream is she. . . . My little
girl is half again as bright as girls are meant to be! . . .

I-I got to get ready before she comes! I got to make certain that she
won't be dragged up in slums with a lot o' bums like me. She's got to be
sheltered in a fair hand dressed in the best that money can buy! I never
knew how to get money, but, I'll try, I'll try! I'll try! I'll go out and make it
or steal it or take it or die!

—"Soliloquy" (also known as "My Boy Bill") from *Carousel*, lyrics by
  Oscar Hammerstein II (1945)

When scholars eventually became interested in female disadvantages
in education and the labor market, their explanations alternatively emphasized biology, cultural differences in adult gender roles, or family
investment strategies that were "rational" reactions to the gendered
roles for men and women in the family and labor market. Now that girls
have surpassed boys in educational performance and attainment, family-
based theories continue to explore the ways in which families differently
socialize boys and girls.

The family, of course, has undergone profound changes in the years
since *Carousel* was written. When girls look to their mothers as role models, they have presumably been influenced by the rising education and
labor market success of women. When boys look to their fathers as role
models, many have been influenced by less-educated fathers whose
earnings have declined with changes in the labor market. Other boys
have no stable father figure in the household. Changes in the educational
and labor market positions of both mothers and fathers could well have
fueled the female-favorable trend in educational attainment through
patterns of parents' investment and socialization of children and through
children's role modeling of parents.

Some psychologists have argued against the idea that parents substantially influence the gender differentiation of their children. Eleanor
Maccoby and Carol Jacklin (1974, 301) began their chapter on the "differential socialization of boys and girls" by quoting Billy's fantasy from
Carousel as a caricatured example of the "way mothers and fathers feel
about the two sexes." They went on to write

it is widely assumed that these parental attitudes and feelings must translate themselves into differential behavior on the part of parents toward

sons and daughters. Parents, it is thought, must bring to bear direct or indirect pressure to make their children fit sex stereotypes. The theory that sex typing in children's behavior is brought about through direct "shaping" by socialization agents is probably the most pervasive point of view in writings on the subject. (p. 301)

In their review of the literature as of 1974, Maccoby and Jacklin found evidence that boys experience greater pressure to avoid sex-inappropriate behavior than girls do, but they had little information on the parenting practices of fathers because most of the research had focused on maternal parenting practices. In general, they concluded that the socialization of boys and girls is similar and cannot account for sex-typed behavior during childhood. Maccoby (1998) later amplified but largely reinforced these conclusions, even as she noted that fathers in particular appear to put more pressure on boys to be masculine and girls to be feminine, that the cultural context influences the particular gender-typed content of children's play (for example, Indian girls pretend to make chapatis and Mexican girls pretend to make tortillas), and that children use cues from their environment to decide how to sex-type unfamiliar activities. The sex-typing of activities and the reinforcement of these sex types, she argued, come largely from peer groups, which are the major carriers of social change.

An extensive body of research supports Maccoby's conclusion that young boys and girls play differently. Although preferences for some types of play are gender-neutral, others are strongly sex-typed (Berenbaum et al. 2007), even as considerable heterogeneity exists within the genders on the pattern of play and interpersonal behavior (Golombok et al. 2008). Maccoby (1998) focuses on three specific interactional patterns of boys and girls during development. The first concerns the preadolescent tendency to prefer same-sex playmates. The second involves what Maccoby calls a "differentiation of interaction styles"—namely, the tendency for boys to be more group-oriented and rough and to be more engaged in fantasy hero–oriented play as well as hierarchy-based play. The third difference is what Maccoby calls "asymmetry": boys are more vigilant about patrolling gender boundaries and less oriented to the world of adults than are girls.

Barrie Thorne's (1993) research supports Maccoby's finding of asymmetry in the ways in which boys and girls maintain gender boundaries. Thorne argues that young elementary school children will sometimes mingle across gender boundaries, but that most play is segregated: either boys and girls play separate games in different parts of the playground or they play "boys against girls/girls against boys" games, typically involving chasing one another and ideas of pollution, such as kissing or "cooties." Thorne emphasizes that typically girls are the polluting group and that boys sometimes treat objects associated with girls as polluting (Thorne 1993). When boys enter the girls' space in the playground, it is frequently as invaders with the intent to disrupt the girls' games. Thorne emphasizes two key components of what she calls gender "border work": first, an emphasis on gender as an "oppositional dualism" that defines boys and girls as "rival teams"; and second, an "exaggeration of gender difference and disregard for the presence of crosscutting variation and sources of commonality." These aspects of gender difference—dualism, gender exaggeration, and a view of girls and objects associated with girls as polluting—put greater pressure on boys to guard their emerging masculine identity against those behaviors and associations that might threaten this identity.

Although most scholars agree about average gender differences in behavior, there is more disagreement about the source of these average differences and the extent of within-gender heterogeneity in behavior. Maccoby (1998) argues that these differences are highly typical of boys and girls, meaning that the behavior variance among boys and among girls is small enough to be discounted in favor of her focus on central tendencies. Thorne (1993), in contrast, argues that this "two cultures" approach to gender differences—boys focusing on position and hierarchy and girls focusing on intimacy and connection—confuses what she terms "symbolic experience" with actual experience. In her view, binary descriptions of boy and girl culture are stereotypes that ignore the considerable variation among girls and boys.

A second dispute concerns the origins of gender differences in play behavior during childhood. Psychologists generally argue that gender differences in interactional styles arise from the interplay of biological, psychological, social, and cognitive mechanisms beginning in early fetal development (Ruble and Martin 2006; Berenbaum et al. 2007). They see sex-typed behavior increasing with age and remaining fairly stable over time. Susan Golombok and her colleagues (2008) measured this stability from ages two and a half through age eight. They argue that variation in fetal androgen exposure may explain early variation in sex-typed behavior, which then becomes reinforced by environmental selection processes involving peer interaction and the sex composition of peer groups (Maccoby 1998; Martin and Fabes 2001; Berenbaum et al. 2007). Maccoby argues that gender differences emerge not from personality differences between boys and girls but rather through interaction with peers, and that this interactional pattern enlarges the difference between boys and girls beyond that predicted by differences in stable personality attributes.

Maccoby does not ignore the role of parents; she observes that fathers appear to be particularly concerned in strengthening the masculine identity of their sons, which may contribute to what she calls the asymmetry between boys and girls. However, Maccoby argues, parents have limited ability to modify these interactional differences between the genders. Other psychologists agree with her assessment (Berenbaum et al. 2007). In this view, parents have little impact on typical patterns of gender development or on the variation in development patterns across children.

These multiple aspects of gender differentiation are not our central interest. Rather, we are interested in the specific issue of gender differentiation in academic performance and educational attainment. Although scholars may be correct in their assertions that parents have little impact on gender-typed interactional behavior, this need not mean that parents have no influence on mean gender differences in academic performance and educational attainment. Academic performance differs from other gender-typed behavior in several respects. Most notably, there is high variance in academic performance among both boys and girls, especially when compared to the other behaviors on which Maccoby and others are focused. This variance, moreover, is clearly related to parental characteristics. Since at least the time of the Coleman (1960) report, it has been known that variation in academic performance is more strongly predicted by parental socioeconomic status than by any other single variable. Recent research has further demonstrated that the predictive power of parental socioeconomic status with respect to educational performance and attainment persists even when genetic factors are controlled (Nisbett 2009).[1]

There is substantial overlap in the distribution of educational performance for boys and girls. The fact of large overlap and high within-gender variation implies that any gender-typing of academic performance is relatively weak in comparison with the strong gender-typing of the behaviors studied by Maccoby. The combination of weak gender typing and strong parental influence allows for the possibility that gender-typing on academic performance is subject to greater influence by parents—and, as we shall discuss in the next chapter, by schools—than are other gender-typed behaviors.

Consistent with Thorne's (1993) perspective on childhood play, researchers have long reported on the multiple variants of adolescent culture—including male adolescent culture—and the ways in which these cultures are associated with social class. James Coleman (1961) argued that the symbolic value of particular traits in the adolescent culture is malleable. In some schools, members of the "leading crowd" are not particularly good students, but in other schools they typically get good grades; Coleman argued that this association between status and academic performance increases the value of grades for other students.

More recently, John Bishop and his colleagues (2003) have reported that academic achievement, when combined with participation in extracurricular activities such as student government, can put a student into the "preps" group, which, along with the "jocks" and the "populars," is one of the high-status groups in school. Other researchers have found that even when the dominant student culture favors athletics over academics, students who value academic success over athletics or popularity can find peer groups within their school that support these values (Brown 1990; Brown et al. 1993). Pedro Noguera (2008) has argued against the "oppositional identity" thesis of Signithia Fordham and John Ogbu (1986) on the grounds that some high-achieving minority males avoid ostracism by adopting multiple identities. The fact of variance in peer cultures and in student responses to peer cultures points to the family as an obvious determinant of both the character of the local peer environment that children face and their response to this environment. Simply put, we need to understand the influence of families in order to understand the influence of peers on the educational orientation and performance of both boys and girls.

Parents and Educational Attainment

There are three reasons why we might expect families to play a role in the gender gap in educational achievement. The first reason is the absolutely central role played by families—and particularly by their socioeconomic and cultural resources—in children's educational attainment. The second is that mothers and fathers parent their sons and daughters differently, and some aspects of gendered parenting may produce educational differences between sons and daughters. The third reason is that parents influence the character of their children's local environments, including peer groups, neighborhoods, and schools, and parents may differ in how they manipulate these environments to mitigate or enhance their effects on educational outcomes.

Family economy perspectives view educational attainment as a rational product of parental investments. It was long argued that "rational" parents would invest in their children in light of the biologically based comparative advantage of women in child-rearing and the gender-specific value of education in labor markets and marriage markets, which together could lead to greater parental investment in the education of sons (Becker 1981; Papanek 1985; Rosenzweig and Schultz 1982). In contrast, feminist theories attribute to patriarchal culture the historical tendency for American parents to favor sons over daughters in labor market–relevant investments (Epstein 1970; Hess and Ferree 1987; Walby 1986). Both of these perspectives suggest that parental effects are shaped by the broader environment. It follows that changes in this environment, especially changes in the perceived desirability of education for women, could have stimulated a new pattern of parental investment that led to the reversal of the historic male advantage in educational attainment. Other perspectives assert that socialization and investment patterns depend on a family's socioeconomic and demographic characteristics. Changes over time in socioeconomic composition or in the demographic structure of families could have played an important role in producing the observed reversal from a male advantage to the current female advantage in college completion.

Parents who are better educated tend to hold more egalitarian values and may strive to ensure that sons and daughters receive equal levels of schooling. Many studies document more egalitarian gender role attitudes among highly educated adults both in the United States (Cherlin and Walters 1981; Thornton et al. 1983; Thornton and Freedman 1979) and in European countries (Alwin et al. 1992; Dryler 1998). Research also suggests that gender role orientations have shifted gradually from a traditional to a more egalitarian tendency over the past few decades, but considerable heterogeneity still exists in the American population (Axinn and Thornton 2000; Brewster and Padavic 2000; McHugh and Frieze 1997; Twenge 1997). If the "rate of return" to parents' education is higher for girls than for boys, then the combination of a stable higher rate of return to parents' education for girls and historically rising levels of parents' education could lead to a closing of the gender gap in higher education that traditionally favored men. The gender-egalitarian approach to educational investment could have spread not only as a result of rising parental education levels but also as a result of less-educated parents emulating highly educated parents.

The gender role socialization perspective stresses the importance of gender-specific role modeling and argues that girls look to their mothers and boys to their fathers as they develop their educational and occupational aspirations (Downey and Powell 1993; Powell and Downey 1997; Rosen and Aneshensel 1978). A "family structure" version of the gender role socialization hypothesis predicts that because of fathers' importance as role models for sons, boys differentially suffer from the absence of a father in the household (see, for example, Powell and Parcel 1997; Sommers 2001). Thus, the rising proportion of households headed by women in recent decades, attributable to rising rates of divorce and nonmarital childbearing (Cancian and Reed 2001), could result in a trend in education attainment that advantages females over males. A female-favorable trend in higher education could also result from upward trends in parents' educational or occupational status to the extent that maternal trends are stronger than paternal trends, or to the extent that the female-specific advantage from mothers is greater than the male-specific advantage from fathers.

To determine whether the relationship between gender differences in college completion and core family characteristics has been changing, we analyzed data from the cumulative cross-sectional General Social Surveys (GSS) from 1972 through 2008.[2] The twenty-seven annual General Social Surveys administered during this period provide information on the educational attainment of respondents and their fathers and mothers, the socioeconomic status of the fathers, and several other measures of family background. We restricted the analysis of college completion to white respondents between the ages of twenty-five and thirty-four who were born between 1938 and 1977. (The black GSS sample was too small to support a similar trend analysis.) The dependent variable, college completion, was operationalized as the completion of at least sixteen years of education.[3]

We examined the relationship between parents' education, fathers' absence, and rates of male and female college completion for two specific historical periods. The first period covers birth cohorts born between 1938 and 1965 and includes people who grew up before the point at which women overtook men in their rates of college completion. The second period covers birth cohorts between 1966 and 1981 and includes those who grew up during the time when women began to overtake men in their college graduation rates. These results are presented in table 6.1.

Table 6.1 shows that for cohorts born in 1965 or earlier, males were more likely than females to have completed college in all except one of the family types displayed. Only when both parents had at least some college education were women as likely as men to have completed college. When either fathers or mothers had a high school education or less, sons were more likely to complete college than daughters. If no father was in the household when the youth were sixteen years old, sons still were more likely to complete college than daughters. This pattern is consistent with the gender-egalitarian perspective. It provides little support for the gender role socialization perspective, which predicts higher graduation rates for daughters of educated mothers. In fact, the female disadvantage is greater for families in which the mother has some college and the father has a high school education or less (39 − 26 percent = 13 percent) than it is for families in which the father has some college and the mother has a high school education or less (44 − 36 percent = 9 percent).

Showing a different pattern for the 1966 to 1977 birth cohorts, table 6.1 suggests the emergence of a strong gender-role socialization effect. In cases involving parents who both had at least some college education, the completion rates for males and females look very similar to those of the earlier cohorts. But in all other cells, the changes in graduation rates are quite large, and generally to the advantage of females. Where fathers had a high school education or less, daughters increased their rates of

Table 6.1 Rates of U.S. College Completion for Males and Females, Age Twenty-Five to Thirty-Four, by Parents' Education, Presence of Father, and Birth Cohort

| | | Father's Education | | | | Father Not Present | |
| | | High School or Less | | Some College or More | | | |
		Male	Female	Male	Female	Male	Female
1938 to 1965 birth cohorts							
Mother's education							
High school or less		20%	15%	44%	36%	21%	15%
	N	1,341	1,639	325	363	193	277
Some college or more		39%	26%	62%	66%	37%	31%
	N	182	238	373	427	77	70
1966 to 1981 birth cohorts							
Mother's education							
High school or less		15%	20%	50%	40%	11%	14%
	N	349	416	155	171	109	130
Some college or more		34%	42%	67%	66%	32%	42%
	N	104	135	301	320	77	89

Source: Authors' compilation based on Cumulative General Social Surveys, 1972 to 2008 (Smith et al. 2010).

college completion, whereas the graduation rates of sons dropped, regardless of the mothers' level of education. The graduation rates of sons who had no father present at the age of sixteen years also dropped considerably. Only in families in which fathers had some college and mothers had a high school education or less did males maintain a considerable advantage over females. In contrast, daughters had a strong advantage in college completion over sons in families with mothers who had some college and fathers who had a high school education or less. A shift appears to have taken place between these two periods such that the mother's level of education became more important for daughters and the father's level of education became more important for sons.

In the absence of a structural shift, the gender egalitarianism observed during the first period would have created a female-favorable trend in college completion. In other words, in the earlier period the most gender-egalitarian families were those with the most-educated parents. As overall education rose, this pattern would have spread, representing a change in the composition of American families. However, this change alone would be insufficient to account for the gender reversal in educational attainment. The extent of change attributable to this type of compositional shift can be demonstrated via a simulation based on a logistic regression model for educational outcomes as a function of cohort, parental education and father present in the household, and interactions between parental variables and cohort. If nothing had changed between the two sets of cohorts shown in table 6.1 except the distribution of families with a father present and the distribution of parental education, the male advantage would have narrowed, but males would still have been attaining higher levels of education than females. The gender egalitarianism mechanism cannot by itself produce a reversal of the gender gap.

Instead, the emergence of a female advantage in education is attributable at least in part to a reversal in the gender-specific effects of father status. Even as the gender egalitarianism of college-educated parents remained essentially stable across the postwar decades covered by the GSS data, the disadvantage for sons of high school–educated fathers grew relative to that for daughters. This growing disadvantage constituted a reversal from the pattern at midcentury, when the rate of return to father's college education was higher for daughters than for sons, to the pattern of the current period, when the rate of return to father's college education is higher for sons than for daughters. The shift implies a growing vulnerability of boys in families with low-educated or absent fathers and a corresponding growing advantage for sons of highly educated fathers.[4]

Back in 1940, many high school–educated parents were first- or second-generation immigrants who had a strong mobility orientation for their sons (Hirschman 1983) and perhaps more traditional attitudes toward their daughters. Gender-traditional attitudes toward educational investment have declined in tandem with the growing opportunities for college-educated women in the workforce, and while Jeremy Freese and Brian Powell (1999) and Dalton Conley (2000) have found that parents still are more likely to invest money in sons' education than in daughters' education, any such pattern is likely to have weakened across the cohorts analyzed here. But these trends do not by themselves explain how or why the contemporary gender gap in educational attainment varies by parental education.[5] To address this issue, we turn to the related question of how gender differences in academic performance are related to family characteristics.

Parents and Academic Performance

Overwhelming evidence indicates that parents shape their children's intellectual development. Part of this effect is genetic inheritance, but family environment also has a major impact, whether alone or in combination with a child's genetic endowment. Nisbett (2009) estimates that parents of high versus low socioeconomic status can make a difference of between 0.8 and 1.2 standard deviations (12 and 18 points) in their child's IQ, net of genetic effects.[6] We know from the evidence that boys test as well as girls on IQ tests; their shortfall is in social and behavioral skills, effort, and expressive attachment to school, which is reflected in poorer performance in reading, lower levels of engagement and interest in school, lower educational expectations, a greater tendency to be disengaged from the process of setting educational plans, and poorer grades, especially relative to what we would predict based on test scores. Although some of the gender difference might be biological in nature, it also seems likely that parents play an important role in producing the gender gap in school performance.

Several scholars have implicated gender-based family socialization processes in the production of the gender gap in achievement. It is widely argued that parents treat their young sons differently from their young daughters in ways that affect child development (Entwisle et al. 1997; Raley and Bianchi 2006). For example, Doris Entwisle and her colleagues (1994, 2007) argue that families typically give young boys more independence than young girls, which creates gender differences in the amount of time that children spend playing in the neighborhood. They argue that the time boys spend in playing in the neighborhood with other boys in complex and spatially demanding games could be a source of the male mathematics advantage. Nancy Lopez's (2003) ethnographic study of low-income, second-generation immigrants similarly found evidence that parents give more independence to boys and exert more social control over girls. Interaction with other children outside the nu-

Figure 6.1   Distribution of Sister-Brother Differences on the ASVAB Across Families

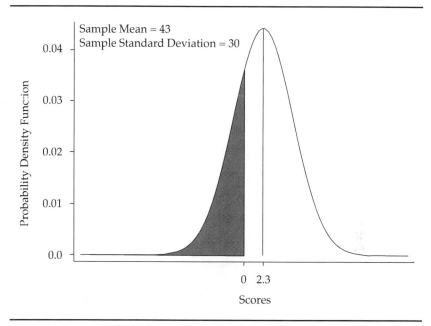

Source: Authors' compilation based on National Longitudinal Study of Youth 1997 data (U.S. Department of Labor, Bureau of Labor Statistics 2012).
Note: Shaded area is the part of the distribution where brothers outperformed sisters.

clear family may strengthen alternative norms for male behavior that are at odds with adult behavior standards and therefore seen by parents and teachers as undesirable.

In focusing on what they see as the dominant pattern of parents producing typical gender-specific behavior patterns in children, these studies parallel those by Maccoby and her associates, who also emphasize modal patterns of behavior even as they express skepticism about the importance of parents in producing these patterns. Our interest, in contrast, is in determining whether different parental investment strategies, parenting styles, or other aspects of parental involvement have distinctive consequences for the gender gap. It is possible to estimate the extent to which the gender advantage in academic performance varies within families with National Longitudinal Survey of Youth: 1997 (NLSY97) data because these data were collected from siblings. Figure 6.1 shows the estimated variation in girls' advantage on the Armed Services Vocational Aptitude Battery (ASVAB) of tests in the NLSY97. In the subsample of NLSY97 families that contained both boys and girls, girls averaged a 2.3 point advantage on this test, which was calculated as a

Figure 6.2   Distribution of Sister-Brother Differences on Self-Reported GPA Across Families

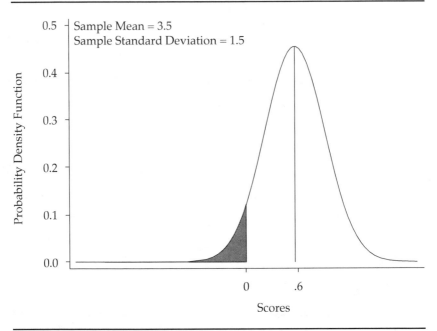

Source: Authors' compilation based on National Longitudinal Study of Youth 1997 data (U.S. Department of Labor, Bureau of Labor Statistics 2012).
Note: Shaded area is the part of the distribution where brothers outperformed sisters.

percentile score from 0 to 99. This gap was statistically significant, as it is in the overall NLSY97 sample. Moreover, the size of this gap varied more than would be expected by chance alone. Some families had larger gender gaps, while others had small gaps or even a male advantage.

Similarly, we compared the self-reported grades on the NLSY97 in eighth grade. Figure 6.2 shows a statistically significant difference of about 0.6 points in GPA between girls and boys. As with test scores, however, the within-family variation in this difference was larger than expected on the basis of chance alone. In some families the GPA difference was larger than 0.6, while in other families it was smaller, with a minority of families having estimated differences in favor of sons rather than daughters. These results support the idea that families can make a difference in how well their sons perform relative to their daughters.

The distinctive roles of fathers and mothers in child-rearing and the possibility of gender-specific effects of paternal and maternal characteristics are obvious possible sources of the variation in gender differences in academic outcomes across families. Using retrospective data provided by adult respondents born before the 1960s, Maithijs Kalmijn (1994, 272) assessed whether the status of mothers and fathers influences the educational attainment of sons and daughters equally and whether the influence of mothers' status has changed over time and concluded that "the process of educational attainment is much the same for men and women," but he studied a period before the female-favorable gap in higher education had emerged. More recent studies make use of twins and sibling data to attempt a more precise estimate of the causal effects. Some researchers find that the net effects of mother's education are larger than the effects of father's education (Björklund, Lindahl, and Plug 2006), while others find that the net effects of father's education are larger than the effects of mother's education (Behrman and Rosenzweig 2002; Ermisch and Pronzato 2009). Estimates of the relative size of mother's and father's education effects are sensitive to the sophistication with which they are computed. Thus, twin and sibling studies show both that intergenerational transmission involves considerably more than the educational level of the parents (Björklund, Lindahl, and Lindquist 2008; Ermisch and Pronzato 2009) and that ordinary least squares (OLS) regression methods overestimate the true causal effect of parental education because of education's correlation with other resources (including genetic endowments and prenatal development) that are poorly measured or omitted in standard models. Both Behrman and Rosenzweig (2002) and Ermisch and Pronzato (2009) find that father's education has a stronger effect on children's educational outcomes than mother's education, though the reasons for this imbalance are not clear.[7] Given their lack of agreement on the relative importance of mother's and father's education effects, it is not surprising that these studies provide no clear picture about potentially unequal consequences of parental characteristics for sons and daughters.

Other research has focused on the ways in which fathers and mothers treat sons and daughters differently and on the implications of such differences. Fathers in stable families are more involved in child-rearing than they used to be (Yeung, Duncan, and Hill 2000; Yeung et al. 2001; Bianchi et al. 2006). At the same time, children increasingly spend part of their childhood in a household without a father. The effects of living apart from the biological father on the cognitive and emotional development of children are clearly negative (McLanahan and Sandefur 1994; McLanahan and Percheski 2008), and there is long-standing speculation and recent evidence that father absence may be more negative for sons than for daughters (Morgan, Lye, and Condran 1988; Hetherington and Kelly 2003). Working against this interpretation is evidence that maternal employment is more likely to have negative effects on sons than daughters (Baydar and Brooks-Gunn 1991; Crouter, McHale, and Bartko 1993; Bogenschneider and Steinberg 1994; Desai, Chase-Lansdale, and Michael 1989). Perhaps boys are especially vulnerable to the absence of a

Table 6.2   **Effects of Parental Characteristics and Family Structure on Math and Reading Test Scores**

	Math		Reading	
	OLS	Fixed Effects	OLS	Fixed Effects
Average family income (logged)	1.62***		1.30***	
Mother's age at childbirth	0.18***		−0.055	
Female	0.030	−0.10	1.58**	1.70***
Black	−6.70***		−5.54***	
Hispanic	−4.44***		−2.66***	
Mother high school (less than high school is baseline)	2.64***		3.40***	
Mother some college	4.27***		5.01***	
Mother BA or higher	8.04***		7.12***	
Mother BA or higher* female	−0.92	−0.22	0.021	0.42
Live-in nonspouse	−5.6*		−5.38	
Live-in spouse	−4.8		−4.41	
Father/partner missing on education	0.43		1.102	
Father/partner less than high school	3.26		2.90	
Father/partner high school	4.68		4.31	
Father/partner some college	6.33*		5.13	
Father/partner BA or higher	8.78***		7.99*	
Father/partner BA or higher* female	−0.91	−1.76*	−0.70	−1.70*
Child lives with biological father	0.0337	0.065	1.31	−0.136
Lives with father* female	−0.581	−0.89	−0.24	−0.19
N	21,982	19,869	21,017	18,967

Source: DiPrete and McDaniel (2011). Data are from NLSY79 (U.S. Census Bureau 2010).
* $p < .05$; ** $p < .01$; *** $p < .001$

parent because they generally suffer more from disadvantaged environments than do girls.

DiPrete and McDaniel (2011) recently explored the question of whether family structure and parental socioeconomic characteristics differently affect the educational performance of boys and girls. Using data from the children of the NLSY79, they estimated ordinary regression models and also models that allowed them to compare siblings of the same mothers at the point in time when the siblings were in the same two-year age range. Table 6.2 reports the results from both modeling strategies for two outcome variables: Peabody Individual Achievement Test (PIAT) math scores and PIAT reading scores.[8] Table 6.2 shows that mother's education and, to a lesser extent, her partner's education had a strong effect on both math and reading scores.[9] The fixed-effects models in particular suggest that boys gained a relative advantage on math and

Table 6.3   **Effects of Parental Characteristics and Family Structure on Armed Services Vocational Aptitude Battery**

	OLS	Random Effects
Female	2.8***	3.1**
Biological father's education[a]		
Less than high school	−4.7***	−4.2
High school	3.2**	5.4**
Some college	8.8***	11.1***
BA or higher	16.7***	22.5***
Biological mother's education[a]		
Less than high school	−9.5***	−9.2**
High school	1.2	−0.91
Some college	4.9**	2.9
BA or higher	13.7***	8.1*
Female* father has BA or higher	−2.7	−6.1*
Hispanic	9.0***	13.5***
Nonblack/non-Hispanic	18.5***	22.5***
Constant	26.7	
N	7,005	1,705

Source: DiPrete and McDaniel (2011). Data are from NLSY97 (U.S. Department of Labor, Bureau of Labor Statistics 2012).
[a]Missing is the reference category.
* $p < .05$; ** $p < .01$; *** $p < .001$

made up much of their reading deficit when the partner/spouse had a college degree or higher. The effects of gender-specific interactions with the father are not particularly large (around 0.1 of a standard deviation). But girls' advantage in reading is only about 0.2 of a standard deviation, and so even effects of the size found here are potentially important in accounting for the size of the gender gap in these measures.

The NLSY97 and the Early Child Longitudinal Study, Kindergarten Class of 1998–99 (ECLS-K) provide additional evidence about the extent to which family resources reduce gender disparities in educational outcomes in middle and high school. DiPrete and McDaniel (2011) used the NLSY97 data to compare the outcomes for males and females on middle school grades, high school grades, and scores on the ASVAB. Table 6.3 shows regressions of the ASVAB in the first wave of the NLSY97 on the biological father's education (with the baseline category being missing education, including missing education because the biological father is absent), the biological mother's education, measures of being black or being Hispanic, gender, and an interaction between gender and whether the biological father had a bachelor's degree. Column 1 reports results from ordinary least squares regression on the NLSY97 sample, while column 2 reports results for the sample of respondents with siblings in the data, using a random effect for each set of siblings. DiPrete and McDaniel conducted a similar set of analyses using self-reported grades in eighth grade and high school.

The effect of being female on the ASVAB is positive and statistically significant. Not surprisingly, respondents with more highly educated parents scored higher on the ASVAB. However, the interaction between being female and father's education is statistically significant at the 0.10 level for the OLS regression and at the 0.02 level for the sibling analysis. In both cases, the advantage of being female disappears when the father is highly educated.

Next, DiPrete and McDaniel (2011) analyzed the impact of father's education on grades in middle school using data from the NLSY97. As shown in table 6.4, girls led boys by 0.75 points on a GPA-type (4.0 scale) measure of grades, net of race and the education of the biological mother and father.[10] Girls lose 40 percent of their advantage on a GPA-type grades measure when they focused the comparison on girls and boys of highly educated fathers. When a control for scores on the ASVAB was added (a cubic spline was used in table 6.4) alongside controls for race and the educational level of father and mother, girls still had a strong advantage of 0.72 points over boys in course grades. However, this advantage was reduced by an estimated 28 percent when the comparison involved boys and girls with college-educated fathers (see table 6.4).

DiPrete and McDaniel (2011) then measured the gender-specific impact of having a highly educated father on test scores and grades in eighth grade using ECLS-K data. The ECLS-K math and reading tests use item response theory to place students on a common scale for mathematics and reading. On average, girls perform better on reading tests than boys in all grades. They found that, net of other factors, girls performed somewhat better (about 0.04 of a standard deviation) than boys on the eighth-grade reading test, and that this difference was statistically significant. However, nearly all of this difference was eliminated when comparing girls and boys of college-educated fathers (see table A.2). Consistent with other data sources such as the National Assessment of Educational Progress (NAEP), girls performed worse than boys on the ECLS-K math test in every grade past kindergarten (DiPrete and Jennings 2012). Importantly, DiPrete and McDaniel found that the male advantage in math in eighth grade was larger when the father was college educated.

Recent studies using data from other countries give a mixed picture of the gender-specific effects of maternal or paternal characteristics. An innovative study of an educational reform that exogenously raised the education of low-educated parents in Denmark found that sons in particular suffer from low-educated parents, though the benefit of additional education is not statistically different when it accrues to the

Table 6.4   Effects of Parental Characteristics and Family Structure on Self-
Reported Eighth-Grade Grades

	OLS		Random Effects
	Model 1	Model 2	
Female	0.75***	0.72***	0.60***
Biological father's education[a]			
Less than high school	0.28**	–0.15	–0.066
High school	0.18*	0.07	0.25*
Some college	0.49***	0.24*	0.46***
BA or higher	1.1***	0.56***	0.93***
Biological mother's education[a]			
Less than high school	–0.49***	–0.17	–0.24
High school	–0.18	0.14	–0.10
Some college	–0.01	–0.19	0.06
BA or higher	0.39**	–0.13	0.32
Female* father has BA or higher	–0.30**	–0.20	–0.25
Hispanic	0.41***	0.02	0.34**
Nonblack/non-Hispanic	0.46***	–0.17*	0.57***
Constant	4.6	3.7	2.7
ASVAB—spline 1		0.03***	
ASVAB—spline 2		–0.015	
ASVAB—spline 3		0.05	
N	6,853	5,720	2,093

Source: DiPrete and McDaniel (2011). Data are from NLSY97 (U.S. Department of Labor, Bureau of Labor Statistics 2012).
[a] Missing is the reference category.
$* p < .05; ** p < .01; *** p < .001$

mother or to the father (Bingley, Jensen, and Romani 2009). Meanwhile, Ermisch and Pronzato (2009) found that Norwegian daughters benefit to the same extent as do Norwegian sons from more highly educated fathers, while they gain a larger benefit from having more educated mothers than do their brothers. Thus, although the trend of greater female relative gains in educational attainment is universal, country-level differences in relative attainment may arise from cultural differences associated with upbringing as well as institutional differences in the structure of school systems.

Parental Influence on Children's Noncognitive Behaviors

Many studies have established that family structure and parental socioeconomic status are linked with a variety of risky behaviors in children (for example, McLanahan and Sandefur 1994; Haveman and Wolfe 1995), but only a fraction of these studies have addressed the extent to which parental effects differ according to the gender of the child. Kathleen Mul-

Ian Harris and her colleagues (1998) found small but consistent effects of high father involvement with children on educational attainment, and increasing closeness between fathers and children protected them to a small extent from delinquent behaviors and emotional distress. However, the protective effects existed about equally for sons and daughters. Using data from the children of the NLSY79 for ten- to fourteen-year-olds, Marcia J. Carlson (2006) supported earlier literature in showing that both boys and girls have higher rates of behavior problems when they do not live with both biological parents. Carlson further found that the child's reports on the quality of interaction between the father and child mediate the relationship between family structure and various behavioral problems.[11] Carlson found tentative evidence that the effects of father involvement are greater for sons than for daughters, but the point estimates did not achieve conventional significance levels (see also Cooksey and Fondell 1996; Heard 2007).

DiPrete and McDaniel (2011) elaborated Carlson's analysis and used the data on the NLSY79 children to investigate whether the connection between family structure and socioeconomic characteristics had a different impact on behavior problems for boys than for girls in the seven- to fourteen-year-old age range. The Behavior Problems Index (BPI), developed by James Peterson and Nicholas Zill (1986), includes twenty-eight mother-reported measures of behavioral problems that a child may have exhibited in the previous three months.[12] DiPrete and McDaniel's OLS regression results (see table 6.5) show that mother's education and family income had strong effects on problem behaviors and that having a highly educated partner reduced behavior problems relative to having no partner or a low-educated partner.[13] The results further suggest that living with the biological father reduced the level of children's behavioral problems, but this effect held mainly for boys. The fixed-effects regression results provide a clearer indication that boys benefited differently from having a highly educated mother and from having the biological father living in the household.

The positive relationship between social and behavioral skills and educational performance, combined with the higher rates at which boys exhibit behavior problems than girls, raises the question of whether more effective parental social controls of these behaviors would especially help boys. Various measures of family-level social control have been proposed, including classifications of parenting styles as authoritarian, authoritative, indulgent, and permissive (Baumrind 1968; Maccoby and Martin 1983) or as "effective" or not (Gottfredson and Hirschi 1990). Several studies find that parental monitoring and an authoritative parenting style are related to positive social, behavioral, and cognitive outcomes (Fan and Chen 2001; Amato and Fowler 2002; Hoff-Ginsberg and Tardif 2002; Spera 2005; Mandara 2006; Bronte-Tinkew, Moore, and

Table 6.5   Behavior Problems in Children

	OLS	Fixed Effects
Average family income (logged)	−1.77***	
Mother's age at childbirth	0.35***	
Female	−3.35***	−3.8***
Black	−1.21*	
Hispanic	−1.68**	
Mother high school (less than high school is baseline)	−1.85**	
Mother some college	−1.81*	
Mother BA or higher	−3.66***	
Mother BA or higher* female	1.17	1.76*
Live-in nonspouse	−8.77*	
Live-in spouse	−9.84*	
Father/partner missing on education	8.51*	
Father/partner less than high school	10.5**	
Father/partner high school	8.58*	
Father/partner some college	8.38*	
Father/partner BA or higher	7.42	
Father/partner BA or higher* female	2.26*	0.005
Child lives with biological father	−2.17**	−1.319*
Lives with father* female	0.7	1.29*
N	22,582	20,349

Source: DiPrete and McDaniel (2011). Data are from NLSY79 (U.S. Department of Labor, Bureau of Labor Statistics 2012).
Note: A higher score indicates greater behavioral problems.
* $p < .05$; ** $p < .01$; *** $p < .001$.

Carrano 2006). However, as Greg Eirich (2010) recently pointed out, much of this literature does not control for possible confounding variables related to the family's socioeconomic status, which makes the interpretation of these studies unclear. Eirich's study with the NLSY97 data found no significant difference in the effects of alternative parenting styles (as reported by the adolescent respondents) on either high school graduation or college completion once a more extensive set of controls for socioeconomic status were included. It is not clear whether the lack of significant results reflects a true lack of effect of parenting style, or whether the current indicators contain too much measurement error to be useful. Instead, we focus on two other parental characteristics—parental religiosity and rule-setting for children—that may offer insight into the effects of parental social control on the gender gap in non-academic behavior.

A large literature reports that adolescent religiosity, measured by the frequency of attending worship services, is negatively associated with the prevalence of risky behaviors in adolescence, including age at first sexual intercourse (Studer and Thornton 1987; Thornton and Camburn 1987; Cochran and Beeghley 1991; Zaleski and Schiaffino 2000; Rostosky et al. 2004), drug use (Bahr et al. 1998), and delinquent behaviors. Moreover, Eirich (2010) has found an independent effect of parental religiosity on adolescent behavior even after adolescent religiosity is controlled. Net of a variety of control variables, parents who regularly attend religious services have children who are more likely to graduate from high school, attend college, and graduate from college. The impact of parental religiosity on children's educational attainment operates partially through the suppressing effect on risky behaviors, though most of the effect remains even after these behaviors are controlled. These findings suggest that parental religiosity may be a good proxy for parenting practices that for a variety of reasons promote academic achievement and educational attainment.

We examined this possibility using data from the NLSY97 to estimate the effect of parental religiosity on middle school and high school grades. Having religious parents had no effect on test scores, but like Eirich, we found that parental religiosity increased the odds of getting grades of B or better in eighth grade, net of standardized test scores and parental education. Even though boys got lower grades than girls, the improvement in grades coming from having strict parents did not differentially benefit boys. Next we examined the gender-specific effect of having religious parents on high school completion and college graduation. Our results agreed with Eirich's in showing rather strong effects of parental religious participation on the odds of graduating from high school or college, net of control variables. Again, we found no evidence that parental religiosity had larger effects on boys than girls. In short, religious parents enhance performance in academic courses, and parental religiosity appears to suppress the risky behaviors that boys are more likely engage in, but parental religiosity does not appear to reduce the size of the gender gap in educational performance or attainment.

A second form of parental control involves rules about children's time use. As noted in chapter 5, numerous studies document that children spend large amounts of time watching television and that children who watch relatively more television tend to have lower grades. Buchmann and DiPrete (2006) found that hours of weekday television watched is negatively related to both four-year college enrollment and college GPA. In analyses of the NLSY97 data, we found that homework had a positive effect on standardized test scores, while the effect of television watching was small and insignificant. But net of test scores and parental education, more time spent doing homework per week had a strong positive effect on the probability of getting B's or better in middle school, while more time spent watching television per week had a strong negative effect.

Television-watching is associated with socioeconomic status, with parental religiosity, and—as noted in chapter 5—with gender.[14] We found that children of highly educated parents watched many fewer hours of television a week in the NLSY97 data, just as they did more homework than the children of less-educated parents. Relative to having a high school–educated father, children of fathers with a BA watched on average three fewer hours of television a week, and they watched an additional 2.5 fewer hours if they had a mother with a BA relative to a high school–educated mother. The social controls exerted by religious parents also affected television-watching: net of parental education, children of parents who went to church on a weekly basis watched 1.3 fewer hours of television a week. Parental religiosity differed from parental education, however, in its effects on homework. Although the children of religious parents watched less television, they did not do more homework once parental education was taken into account.

The fact that parental religiosity had a negative effect on television-watching, no effect on standardized test scores, but a positive effect on middle school grades suggests that religiosity's positive effect on academic performance somehow occurs through the impact of religiosity-associated parental controls on the child's effort and orientation to learning. This impact is apparently gender-neutral. Our NLSY97 analyses showed that, net of parental religiosity, girls continued to watch less television and do more homework than boys. And they earned higher grades in middle school and high school than boys.

To examine the impact of parental rule-making we next used the ECLS-K data, which contain measures of whether and how much control parents exercised over television-watching on weekdays in third and fifth grade. We found that parental reported rules about weekday television-watching had a very weak relationship to academic outcomes in eighth grade in the ECLS-K data, and these rules had no obvious connection to the gender difference in academic performance.

Highly educated parents and religious parents both appear to offer children educational benefits. The benefits of having religious parents appear to operate in part through social control of the children's behavior, while the benefits of highly educated parents operate more directly through academic outcomes. However, these two types of parents produce different patterns of gender-specific effects. The advantages of having religious parents appear to be gender-neutral. In contrast, the benefits of having a father who lives in the house and who has at least a bachelor's degree appear to be larger for boys than for girls.

Parental Influence on Children's Orientation Toward School

Patterns

Parents express widespread agreement about the value of academic achievement, though they differ when asked about the trade-offs they would prefer between academic achievement and social or athletic success. A 1996 Phi Delta Kappa/Gallup poll asked parents: "Which one of the following would you prefer of an oldest child—that the child get A grades or that he or she make average grades and be active in extracurricular activities?" Thirty-three percent of parents responded, "Get A grades," and another 9 percent volunteered, "Both." This still left a majority (56 percent) who responded that they preferred for their oldest child to get average grades and be active in extracurricular activities. Although some might take this to indicate weak support for academic achievement, the question wording implied a trade-off between grades and other forms of school achievement and may have suggested to some parents that academic success has the side effect of social marginalization. The question about parental values in the eighth grade ECLS-K survey wave is not framed in terms of trade-offs, and the answers to this question indicate much stronger parental support for academic success. As can be seen in table 6.6, parents strongly preferred that their child be a brilliant student, and they gave the two most superficially important status markers of adolescent culture (athletics and popularity) less weight. Interestingly, parents preferred "nerdy" values more for sons than for daughters. Even more tellingly (as can be seen in figure 6.3), the preference for having a child be a "brilliant student" was even higher among less-educated parents, who are sometimes suspected of devaluing academic achievement for their children. One interpretation of figure 6.3 is that highly educated parents understand better than less-educated parents that leadership qualities and the social capital they imply are

Table 6.6   Parental Values for Children: "If your child could be only one of the following in high school, which would be most important to you?"

	Sons	Daughters
A brilliant student	63%	59%
A leader in school activities	31	35
An athletic star	5	4
The most popular	2	1

Source: Authors' compilation based on ECLS-K data (National Center for Education Statistics 2009).

Figure 6.3   Most Valued Attribute, by Gender and Responding Parent's Education

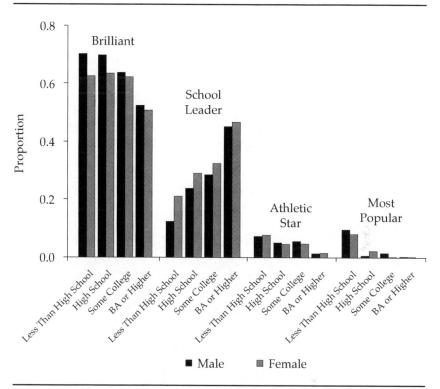

Source: Authors' compilation based on ECLS-K data (National Center for Education Statistics 2009).

precursors for success in the professions and business. Whatever the explanation, it seems evident that less-educated parents do not overtly support the antischolastic values typically attributed to adolescent culture. Based on her ethnographic research, Annette Lareau (2000) similarly reported that working-class parents were as focused as middle-class parents on good grades; indeed, the children in the ECLS-K showed no social class differences in their reporting of parental expectations that they get good grades.

Despite the relatively small variation in parents' desire for their children's high educational achievement, social class background crucially shapes children's educational experiences, including the development of a positive attachment to school. Generally speaking, children of highly educated parents report more positive attitudes toward school than do children of less-educated parents, largely because children of highly ed-

Figure 6.4   Proportion Reporting That Grades Were "Very Important" and That They "Always" Enjoyed School or Were "Always" Close to Teachers, by Gender and Father's Education

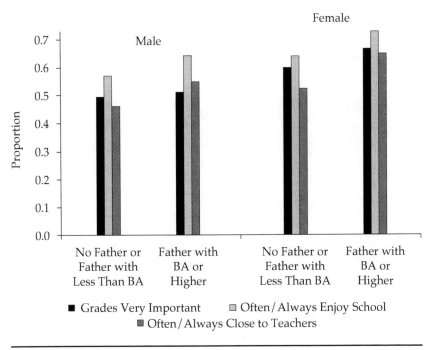

Source: Authors' compilation based on ECLS-K data (National Center for Education Statistics 2009).

ucated parents perform better in school. Nonetheless, even boys of highly educated parents and those who perform well in school resist expressing emotional attachment to school. Indeed, as figure 6.4 shows, attachment to school, expressed as the self-reported importance of grades, was quite similar for boys whose fathers had a college degree and boys whose fathers were less educated. Overall, boys' expressed attachment to school lagged considerably behind that of girls. In contrast, the academic *performance* of boys of highly educated fathers closely resembled that of similarly situated girls, while the academic performance of children of less-educated fathers lagged considerably the performance of children of highly educated parents.

The fact that expressive attachment to school differs so markedly by gender even for middle schoolers with similar academic performance suggests that these attitude differences are tied to gender identity. This conjecture is reinforced by the fact that father's education played an important role in closing the *academic* gap between boys and girls, but had less impact on closing the *values* gap between boys and girls. These apparently inconsistent effects of father's education make sense when we consider the cultural environment in which young boys grow up, which—as supported by many qualitative studies—emphasizes action-oriented, emotionally reserved behavior and identifies male power with physical prowess and mass appeal. The emotionally appealing icons for many young and adolescent boys are fantasy superheroes or sports heroes who are confident, socially and physically dominant, action-oriented, and sexually attractive, as well as sexually dominant music and movie stars who appear to lead fantasy lives and who portray fantasy characters in films or on stage (Paley 1984; Thorne 1993; Jordan 1995; Davies 2003; Maccoby 2003).[15] Young boys understand that money is another central medium of power in the world, but male fantasy heroes, sports heroes, and rock and movie stars are either wealthy or have such power that they are beyond the need for wealth. They are similarly beyond the need for books, good grades, or college degrees (except maybe to get into professional sports leagues).

To be sure, adolescent male heroes typically act intelligent, clever, crafty, and street-smart, and these are cognitive traits that are not automatically associated with academic achievement. Fantasy heroes such as James Bond, Batman, Peter Parker, Sherlock Holmes, and Ethan Hunt are also (explicitly or implicitly) well educated.[16] Yet their success does not *derive* from their education. Such men hardly mention their school-leaving credentials in the course of their adventures. It is almost preposterous to argue that excellent grades in middle school are the best route to the glamorous or heroic lifestyle of a James Bond, an Ethan Hunt, or a Batman. The collegiate route to success for sports heroes is assumed to have almost nothing to do with academic skill. For sports heroes, school is primarily a route to good coaches, competitive conferences in college intercollegiate play, and the big money of professional sports leagues. Everyone knows that a top athlete will have his pick of colleges, will not have to pay for college, and will rarely flunk out during his period of athletic eligibility even as he ignores his studies in favor of practice and games.

In the workaday real world inhabited by adults, of course, the successful and powerful men are those with the money and status that come from good jobs and that allow them to enjoy a middle- or upper-middle-class lifestyle, especially when they partner with women who also have good jobs. These men largely attain their success through education. The juxtaposition between the masculine cultures of adolescence and adulthood underscores that there are two sources of masculine power in Western society, and that they are sometimes reinforcing (being physically athletic as well as rich makes one seem even more masculine) but, in the case of educational motivation, sometimes work in opposition to each other. Each of these dimensions is a source of social dominance, which is a fundamental idealized attribute of masculinity in Western society. Most primitively, dominance comes from physical power, and strength and athletic prowess remain a source of dominance in childhood and adolescent culture (Thorne 1993; Best 1983; Schofield 1982; Sluckin 1981). In modern society, of course, the ultimate source of dominance comes from money, social prestige, organizational authority, and workplace autonomy. It is not a coincidence that childhood male heroes have power along both the physical and the status dimensions. Male heroes command deference, and they can successfully resist others' efforts to dominate them.[17] For adults, however, physical power plays a small role in the production of dominance compared to the status rewards that derive from educational advantages and the jobs that are accessible only to the highly educated. Furthermore, the very skills that produce high academic performance are those required to compete for and secure these positions.

Ethnographic research supports survey data to the effect that at least certain aspects of the adolescent masculine culture devalue academic engagement. Edward Morris (2008) reports that "nerdy" boys, defined as those who put substantial effort into school and who participate in school activities such as band, are more likely to be labeled as "gay" or "pussies."[18] A female informant at the rural white high school that he studied expressed such concerns about a "Tom Jackson," who played flute in the band and had the highest grades in the class. Another (male) informant reported that,

> I mean in this school—it's all about football. Football, football, football. Not band. Band's gay! . . . The guys [in the band] act different too. They act kinda gay. So that's why they're picked on. But the girls [in the band] ain't really said nothin' to. (Morris 2008, 738)

In contrast to intellectual activities like reading or cultural activities like performing in band, working-class boys in Morris's ethnography perceived the activities of their fathers (such as woodwork or construction) as more manly, even relative to professional and office work, which these boys recognized as being more lucrative. Similarly, Michael Kimmel (2008, 49) reported that his male informants used "*any* taste in art and music" as an example of "stereotypically effeminate behavior." Working-class fathers may subtly reinforce this conception of school as feminizing because it was never a source of masculine power for them. In their world, masculinity is not derived through status rewards linked to educational success, but rather from physical prowess and appropriate acting out of masculine roles in childhood and adolescence. Too close an attachment to school and academic work is suspect.

Not all boys act this way, of course. Masculinity takes different forms, and boys enact masculinity in different ways (see, for example, Connell 2005; Pascoe 2006; Morris 2008; Schrock and Schwalbe 2009).[19] As noted earlier, Thorne (1993) argues that the "two cultures" approach to gender differences, where boys focus on position and hierarchy and girls focus on intimacy and connection, confuses "symbolic experience" with actual experience. Binary descriptions of "boy culture" and "girl culture" are stereotypes that ignore the considerable variation among girls and boys. Not all boys engaged in the most aggressive defenses of gender boundaries in Thorne's study of elementary school children. Not all boys, in other words, maximally distance themselves from stereotypically "unmasculine" activities such as music, art, dance, and foreign language instruction. This is consistent with the argument of Becky Francis (2000, 124) that

> boys construct masculinity in different ways, and some may not attempt to construct themselves as particularly masculine at all. For some boys, a construction of masculinity may involve a rejection of school values, whereas others may use aspects of those very values (for instance a competitive approach to learning and achievement) to construct their masculinity.

Boys who pursue these interests may experience sanctions for such normative "violations." However, the extent of sanctioning no doubt varies across local environments, and the impact of potential sanctions on behavior no doubt varies across boys even in the same environment.

Data for eighth-graders from the ECLS-K (see table 6.7) highlight the fact that, although there are clear gender differences in the proportion of adolescents who engage in high-culture activities, girls and boys differ in their orientation to high-culture activities even when their parents are highly educated. But if the adolescent culture is multifaceted and boys as well as girls can choose from competing schemas, we must ask whether the choice of schema affects academic achievement or the other way around. It is certainly no accident that working-class boys are more likely than middle-class boys to develop a culture of opposition to school (Skelton 1997; Martino 1999; Bishop et al. 2003; MacLeod 2008). The relationship between culture and achievement is likely to be reciprocal; working-class boys are more likely to construct oppositional cultures, but any individual working-class boy (or for that matter, middle-class boy) lives in an environment that is not wholly of his making, and this environment affects his academic orientation and achievement. We return to this issue in chapter 7.

Data from the ECLS-K suggest that boys who disengage from the stereotypically hegemonic early-adolescent male culture and pursue cultural interests such as art, music, dance, and foreign language, which are

Table 6.7   Proportion of Eighth-Graders Who Work on High-Culture Skills, by Gender and Father's Education

	Less Than BA		BA or Higher	
	Females	Males	Females	Males
Rarely/never	0.66	0.80	0.53	0.71
Less than once a week	0.09	0.08	0.10	0.06
Once or twice a week	0.16	0.06	0.23	0.18
Almost or every day	0.09	0.05	0.14	0.05

Source: Authors' compilation based on ECLS-K data (National Center for Education Statistics 2009).
Note: Father's education is measured as the education of the biological or household father as of first grade. High-culture skills refers to taking music, art, foreign language, or dance classes outside of school in eighth grade, as measured in the ECLS-K.

all putatively devalued by this culture, express a level of attachment to academic values that is more similar to girls than boys. Figure 6.5 shows the proportion of eighth-graders who said that good grades were "very important" to them, again broken down by father's education, but it also shows the effects of getting good grades and participating in high-culture activities. Part of girls' stronger attachment comes from the fact that students who get good grades are more likely to say that good grades are very important to them. Girls' greater attachment to school also comes from the fact that students who participate in high-culture activities are significantly more likely than other adolescents to report that good grades are important to them. The net impact of high-culture participation on attachment to academic values can be further highlighted by estimating the predicted attachment for boys if they all took music or arts lessons at least occasionally (in other words, if no boys responded "rarely or never" to the high-culture participation question). Under this counterfactual, boys who participated in high-culture activities would express nearly the same level of academic attachment as girls.

A similar result was obtained when we used a measure of "strong integration" with the school as the dependent variable and the same predictor variables. We operationalized "strong integration" as existing when the student reported "often" or "always" enjoying being at school and "often" or "always" feeling close to teachers at school. As before, figure 6.6 is broken down according to whether the father had a BA degree or higher. Father's education and presence in the family was clearly more influential for strong integration than it was for attachment to school. About 53 percent of daughters of highly educated fathers felt strongly integrated; the sons of highly educated fathers lagged about ten percentage points behind this figure. About 40 percent of girls of less-educated fathers or absent fathers also reported that they were strongly integrated, as opposed to only 33 percent of boys. Grades and participa-

Figure 6.5   Proportion of Eighth-Graders Who Said That Good Grades Were "Very Important," by Father's Education, Academic Performance, and Participation in the Arts

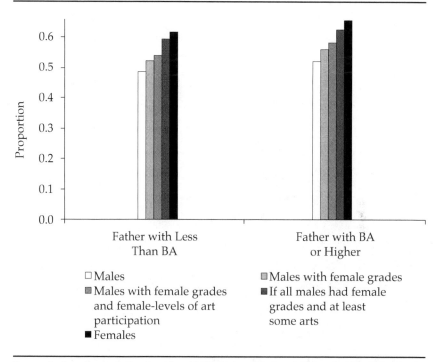

□ Males

▨ Males with female grades and female-levels of art participation

■ Females

▨ Males with female grades

■ If all males had female grades and at least some arts

Source: Authors' compilation based on ECLS-K data (National Center for Education Statistics 2009).
Note: "Arts" is the response to "How often do you spend time taking music, art, foreign language, or dance classes outside of school?" with responses "rarely or never," "less than once a week," "once or twice a week," or "every day or nearly every day." "If all males had female grades and at least some arts" is the predicted response to the "good grades" question under the hypothetical that boys get A's in the same proportion as girls and that boys responded at least "less than once a week" to this question.

tion in high-culture activities close the gender gap in attachment to school, and we can eliminate it completely through the thought experiment of giving all boys at least a minimal participation in high-culture activities.

In additional analyses of the ECLS-K, we found that engaging in these high-culture activities was associated with higher self-reported grades in eighth-grade English and higher parent-reported grades in general, net of other covariates. Of course, not all children of highly educated parents participated in high-culture activities. Recall from table 6.7 that the great majority of ECLS-K eighth-grade boys who had highly educated fathers "rarely or never" did any of these activities, even as they managed to close the gender gap in grades in middle school as well as in

Figure 6.6   Proportion of Eighth-Graders Who Expressed Strong Integration with School, by Father's Education, Academic Performance, and Participation in the Arts

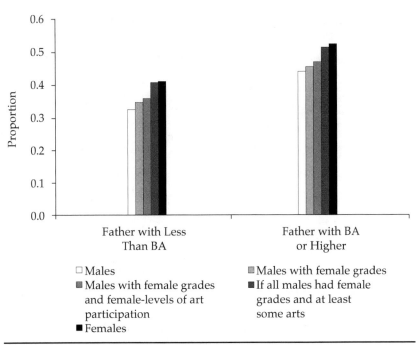

Source: Authors' compilation based on ECLS-K data (National Center for Education Statistics 2009).
Note: Strong integration is operationalized as "often" or "always" enjoying being at school and "often" or "always" feeling close to teachers at your school. "If all males had female grades and at least some arts" is the predicted response to the "good grades" question under the hypothetical that boys get A's in the same proportion as girls and that boys responded at least "less than once a week" to this question.

reading test scores, the academic dimension on which boys lag the furthest behind girls. To recapitulate, having a highly educated father is associated with closing the performance gap between boys and girls, while involvement in high-culture activities is associated with closing the gender gap in expressive attachment to school, which may be a key factor behind girls' superior academic performance. Other research by Paul DiMaggio (1982), Grace Kao (1995), and Vincent Roscigno and James Ainsworth-Darnell (1999) has found that participating in high-culture activities, such as going to museums, and learning cultural skills such as music, dance, acting, and a foreign language are associated with school success.[20] DiMaggio (1982) further found in his analysis of Project Talent data on eleventh-graders in 1960 that the associations between his measure of participation in high-culture activities (drawing, acting, attending concerts, and reading) were notably different for males and females. For girls, the effects of cultural capital on academic outcomes were strongest when they came from high-status families. For boys, the pattern was different: positive effects were restricted to male students from lower- and middle-status households, while the sons of college-educated fathers experienced no statistical benefit from participation in these activities. In other words, the boys from family backgrounds most frequently associated with oppositional adolescent masculine cultures were more likely to get high grades if they exhibited distance from stereotypical adolescent male values, and the boys with highly educated fathers received no such benefit.

Implications

The relationships between participation in high-culture activities, attachment to school, and parental (especially paternal) human capital reported in this chapter provide insights into alternative routes by which boys might narrow the gender gap in academic performance. One plausible route to higher academic performance for boys is attending a school where the dominant masculine culture *values and promotes academic achievement,* or at least where there is no hegemonic masculine culture that opposes academic achievement—perhaps because the culture allows for multiple expressions of masculine identity with minimal or no negative sanctions from peers. A second route is *detachment* from the hegemonic masculine culture when this culture opposes academic values. This second route is exemplified by boys who engage in the high-culture activities that are linked to stronger expressions of school attachment and academic values. Participation in these activities per se does not necessarily produce higher academic performance. Rather, it is likely that a stronger orientation toward learning stems from the detachment from oppositional attitudes.

The results discussed in this chapter also suggest a third route, one that involves *accommodating* the hegemonic masculine culture while maintaining an instrumental attachment to school as an eventual source of the human capital and credentials that correlate with fulfilling the more "real-world" adult version of masculine identity. Sons of highly educated fathers may be more prone to follow this route by performing well in school but reporting a weaker attachment to school and its academic values than do similarly situated girls. In other words, the distinction between an expressive attachment to school and an instrumental attachment to school can help make sense of the performance gap between adolescent boys and girls. Expressive attachment is about emotional responses to school and a student's willingness to acknowledge them. High expressive attachment occurs when a student asserts that he likes school, feels close to his teachers, and behaves in ways that readily demonstrate this positive emotional connection to teachers, peers, and parents. High expressive attachment presumably provides motivation for putting effort into school work because the student receives gratification from good performance as well as from the positive feedback from teachers, parents, and, possibly, peers. Instrumental attachment, in contrast, occurs when the student invests in school work to achieve longer-term goals and *acts as if* he has a strong emotional attachment to school even if he does not readily acknowledge this fact to himself or others. Instrumental attachment allows for accommodation to the local hegemonic masculine cultures that negatively sanction excessive striving for academic achievement. Thus, it provides a way for students to avoid negative sanctions from peers while investing effort in school work that can lead to strong academic performance.

This frame also implies two distinct routes to academic failure for adolescent boys whose peer cultures do not strongly value academic investment and achievement. The first route—which is the basic story contained in books like *Learning to Labor* (Willis 1981) and *Ain't No Makin' It* (MacLeod 2008) about the obstacles to academic success for working- or lower-class boys—is to identify with and participate in an oppositional culture that magnifies already existing difficulties with academics. The second arises from what might be termed "accommodation failure." Accommodation failure is the failure to invest enough attention and effort in school to achieve one's educational goals when the peer culture does not value academic achievement or provide immediate gratification for academic success. It can also be described as the failure to develop an instrumental attachment to school when expressive attachment is negatively sanctioned. If a student fails to navigate the competing pressures of doing well in school and maintaining positive relationships with the peer group, his academic performance is likely to suffer.

These navigational difficulties can arise for both informational and emotional reasons. For some boys, the problem is their failure to understand the level of performance necessary to achieve the benefits of an instrumental attachment to school. Their underinvestment occurs not as a conscious strategy but rather as a prediction error about the return in terms of grades that arises from a specific level of studying or about the consequences of delaying serious investment in school work until a later point. For other boys, the problem is rooted in the emotional difficulty of accommodating. Simply put, it is easier to invest time and energy in academics when the peer culture values academic achievement or when one has detached from the oppositional culture. Accommodation strategies may work well for confident adolescents who can strategically align with an oppositional peer culture and simultaneously invest enough effort in school work to achieve their educational goals. Strategic role-playing, however, does not come naturally to all adolescents, and accommodation can produce anxiety about how strongly one must express allegiance to a culture that emphasizes non-academic pursuits in order to avoid sanctions. Anxiety about playing these dual roles can undermine performance in either of them, and in particular it can reduce a student's level of investment in school work.

Multiple measures could be developed to identify information deficits and emotional signals that signal accommodation failure, including:

- Overestimation by students with marginal grades in middle or high school of the probability of completing four-year college, and in particular of the difference in the probability of entering four-year college and the probability of completing four-year college
- Overestimation by students with marginal grades in middle or high school of their personal probability of completing four-year college compared with other students getting the same grades
- Underestimation of the effect of educational attainment on adult earnings and overestimation of the impact of non-academic factors
- Overprediction of expected grades in current courses
- Rationalization of the low grades of current performance as less than deserved rather than earned because of insufficient effort
- Rationalization of current performance by expressing an intention to work harder at school in the future (next semester, next year, in high school, in college) rather than in the present
- The anxiety and stress connected with a student's social standing among peers
- The anxiety and stress connected with mediocre academic performance for students who express high educational goals but whose peer culture does not (sufficiently) positively value academic achievement.

The accommodation failure frame also provides an additional perspective on the role of parents, especially fathers, in producing students' strong instrumental (if not expressive) school attachment. Parents with resources can search out schools where the peer culture positively values academic achievement and where it is emotionally safe for adolescent boys to develop an expressive attachment to school and gratification from academic investment. Educationally oriented parents can directly increase immediate gratification for their children because they are central suppliers of emotional rewards to their children. In addition, parents and particularly fathers with high socioeconomic resources can provide alternative adult models of masculinity and strategies to enhance boys' willingness and ability to either detach from the oppositional culture or navigate oppositional culture among peers while remaining attached to school. Finally, culturally well-endowed parents and particularly fathers may reduce the likelihood that their children will experience accommodation failure from lack of information because they know better than less-educated parents the amount of discipline and effort it takes to achieve the level of academic performance required for successful college completion.

Not everyone who expresses high educational ambitions is necessarily invested in achieving these goals. And not everyone who expresses high educational ambitions would *remain* invested in achieving these goals if they knew the true level of effort required to achieve them. The same is probably true for many students who decide to try out for the high school track team and in the process have to set personal goals that are consistent with both their level of ability and the level of effort they wish to expend to achieve any particular performance level. In fact, our interpretation for the role of fathers in furthering the education of boys argues that the investment levels are not uniform even among those adolescents who have the same educational expectations. Thus, children of highly educated parents, and specifically sons of highly educated fathers, may typically have more strongly internalized the adult conception of masculinity as linked to labor market success. As a result, they may be more invested in educational achievement because it is linked with the realization of their own identity, including the gendered character of this identity. The trick is to facilitate effective strategies across a broader segment of adolescent males. We argue that policies should be designed to both increase students' development of more adult conceptions of masculine identity that are not tied to opposition toward school and provide students with better information about how effort, education, and the labor market are related so that they may better align their efforts with their goals.[21]

Minority Status

Black and Hispanic students may face greater challenges in developing expressive attachment to school or an accommodation strategy that allows effective instrumental attachment to school, even after socioeconomic factors are taken into account. Data from the ECLS-K reveal that black and Hispanic adolescents expressed a strong commitment to academic achievement. Indeed, figure 6.7 shows that black adolescents were actually more likely than whites to say that good grades were "very important" to them, while Hispanic adolescents were equally likely as whites to agree about the importance of good grades. However, minority adolescents had a high probability of feeling alienated from school even as they affirmed its importance. As can be seen in figure 6.8, black and

Figure 6.7   Proportion of Eighth-Graders Who Said That Good Grades Were "Very Important," by Race and Gender

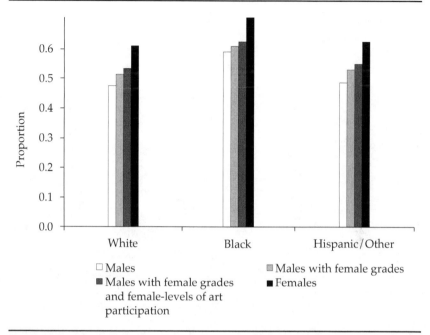

Source: Authors' compilation based on ECLS-K data (National Center for Education Statistics 2009).
Note: "Arts" is the response to "How often do you spend time taking music, art, foreign language, or dance classes outside of school?" with responses "rarely or never," "less than once a week," "once or twice a week," or "every day or nearly every day."

Hispanic youth were much *less* likely than white youth to report that they often enjoyed school and often felt close to their teachers even as they were more likely to assert the importance of good grades. This combination of allegiance to the goals of school with disaffection from the day-to-day school experience may have produced a significant handicap in actually achieving the goals implied by their high valuation of academic achievement.

Just as for whites, black and Hispanic males lagged behind black and Hispanic females in their expressed attachment to academic goals. However, blacks' tendency to value school achievement is so strong that black males actually expressed the same level of attachment as white females, even though their academic performance lagged far behind that of white females. The situation was far different, however, when it came to expressions of enjoying school or closeness to teachers. The combination of the black disadvantage and the male disadvantage on feelings of integration left black males far behind the subjective position of white fe-

Figure 6.8   Proportion of Eighth-Graders Who Expressed Strong Integration with School, by Race

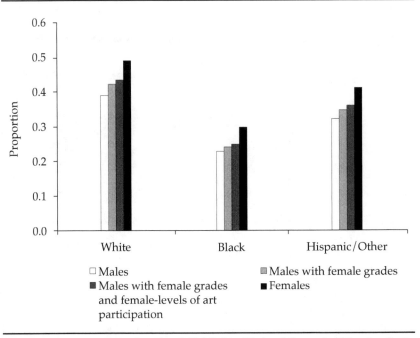

Source: Authors' compilation based on ECLS-K data (National Center for Education Statistics 2009).
Note: Strong integration is operationalized as "often" or "always" enjoying being at school and "often" or "always" feeling close to teachers at school.

males. Thus, while African American boys were just as likely as white girls to report that good grades were very important to them, they were only half as likely (25 percent versus 50 percent) to report that they enjoyed school and felt close to their teachers.

The different levels of integration for white and minority adolescents imply a much greater risk of accommodation failure for minority adolescents. Such low levels of expressive attachment imply lower levels of immediate gratification. It may be that the peer environments of minority male adolescents are more likely to be oppositional, but the ECLS-K data suggest strong attachment deficits for minority girls as well, so not all the blame can be assigned to racial differences in hegemonic masculine cultures. It may also be the case that minority students are in school environments that are objectively less enjoyable because they are more disorderly, have fewer resources, have teachers who are less talented or more stressed, and so forth. Such factors may also make it more difficult for minority adolescents to develop successful accommodation strategies. Coming from homes where parents have fewer resources and where the father is more likely to be absent, minority children probably receive less help from their parents in generating positive expressive or instrumental attachments to school. These parents are also less able to provide their children with accurate information about the amount of investment necessary to achieve their expressed academic goals. Although the prescriptions suggested earlier apply to minority as well as white adolescents, these results suggest that even more change is required in the environments of black and Hispanic adolescents. We address the issue of school environments and their connection to educational gender gaps at length in the next chapter.

Conclusion

It is well known that parents' human and cultural capital is strongly related to their children's educational outcomes, and this chapter has considered the question of whether family characteristics are differentially related to the educational outcomes of girls and boys. It finds clear support for the idea that parents' behaviors influence gender gaps in educational achievement and attainment. We have demonstrated how the relationship between parental socioeconomic status and the gender gap in educational attainment of sons and daughters has changed dramatically over the past sixty years, from boys in families with less-educated parents having a larger advantage over girls to boys' deficits being greater when the parents are not college-educated. We suspect that the shifting effects of parental background have been stronger for educational attainment than for educational performance, but there is no good trend data on performance to test this hypothesis.

Data for the contemporary period show that gender gaps within families are variable, and that the variation is larger than expected by chance alone. At least some of this variation appears to be associated with family structure and parental education. Boys' educational attainment appears to be more sensitive to the level of resources in the family than is girls' educational attainment. In particular, the gender gap in cognitive skills appears to be sensitive to parental education and especially the education of the father, while the gender gap in behavioral skills appears to be sensitive to the presence of the father in the household.

This chapter corrects a standard model from psychology, which maintains that interactions with peers shape children's gender differentiation with little influence from parents. The sociological ethnographic literature, in contrast, emphasizes the class-based as well as gender-based character of oppositional culture, which implies both that peer effects are far from uniform and that parents must to some extent be implicated in peer effects because social class derives from one's parents. The relationship is not simple, however. Even low-educated parents value academic achievement for their children, and regardless of social class, adolescents overwhelmingly report that good grades are important to their parents. Our interpretation of the parental effect on the gender gap focuses on their ability to shape the environment of their children and to influence how their children interact with and accommodate to this environment. We argue from both survey data and the ethnographic literature that boys often experience pressure—especially from peers—to adopt masculine identities that interfere with the development of emotional attachment to school. This pressure appears to be particularly strong for children from working- or lower-class families and for non-Asian minority children. Parents can aid in the development of alternative conceptions of masculinity that are more compatible with a positive orientation toward school, provide more concrete reasons for what we have called an instrumental attachment to school, and provide information and support that allow a more successful accommodation to the conflicting pressures experienced by adolescents and especially by adolescent boys. We argue that highly educated parents—especially highly educated fathers—may be able to narrow the gender gap in achievement, both because of their greater resources and knowledge of the educational process and because they provide a concrete role model for the type of masculine identity that links educational achievement with masculine accomplishment.

Part III

The Role of Schools

Chapter 7

Schools, Classrooms, and Peers

I N THE preceding chapters, we documented two salient facts about the connection between gender and educational performance. First, girls generally do better in school than boys. Second, a wider variance exists in the math performance of boys, such that more boys than girls score in the upper tail of the performance distribution. This is true in kindergarten (Penner and Paret 2008) and remains true in secondary schools, where the gender disparity grows with the sensitivity of the test to extreme performance in mathematics (Ellison and Swanson 2010). The male achievement deficit contributes to the gender gap in educational attainment, while the female deficit in the upper tail of math performance affects the gender distribution of college majors. In this chapter, we examine the connection between schools and the gender gap in overall educational performance. Then, in chapter 8, we turn our attention to the gender gap in mathematics and science and its implications for gender segregation in college majors.

How might school-based policies help improve the educational performance of boys? First, better schools could improve the performance of students in general, which would help boys in particular even if such policies did not close the gender gap. Second, school improvements could target underperforming students. Because boys underperform relative to girls, boys would differentially benefit from any programs that improve students' underperformance. Third, schools could devise programs that directly benefit boys in particular, regardless of their level of achievement. Boys face particular challenges stemming from the dual nature of masculine identity during adolescence. In schools with cultures that treat academic success as compatible with a respectable status within the adolescent culture, boys are more likely to perform on a par with girls. In other words, we expect the male shortfall to be relatively small in high-quality schools.

Much of the literature on school effects from the Coleman report (1966) forward determined that school effects were relatively small in comparison with family effects and therefore that "schools are not an effective agent for the redistribution of societal resources" (Hallinan 1988, 255; see also Hanushek 1981, 1989). This pessimistic view of schools began to change with the rise of the accountability and standards movements, which focused renewed attention on improving schools in order to improve learning (United States and National Commission on Excellence in Education 1983; Murphy 1991; Schneider and Keesler 2007). Three promising arenas of school policy intervention have the potential to improve student outcomes: teachers, student culture, and instructional and evaluation techniques. A growing literature suggests that teacher quality affects academic performance (Rockoff 2004; Rivkin, Hanushek, and Kain 2005; Clotfelter, Ladd, and Vigdor 2006), and some recent reports suggest that good teachers have long-lasting effects (Chetty et al. 2011). Scholars also increasingly recognize that, along with cognitive skills, social and behavioral skills affect academic achievement and later success in the labor market (Rosenbaum 2001; Heckman, Stixrud, and Urzua 2006) and that teachers differ in their ability to promote these skills (Jennings and DiPrete 2010). Beyond teachers, other support staff, such as guidance counselors, may play an important role in students' educational outcomes and their transition to work (Rosenbaum 2001). The second promising arena of policy change, student culture and peer effects, has been a focus since the publication of *The Adolescent Society* (Coleman 1961). Instructional effects are the most difficult of the three school policy interventions to study, partly because instructional curricula are not readily quantifiable. Considerable research suggests that small class sizes are better than large ones (Krueger and Whitmore 2001), that tracking is generally detrimental to poorly performing students (Gamoran and Mare 1989), and that grade retention and tough academic standards for high school graduation do not boost educational achievement for poorly performing students (Dee and Jacob 2006; Reardon et al. 2009). These policy arenas clearly overlap with each other; for example, teachers can contribute to student climate, better instructional techniques may improve teacher quality, and academically oriented student cultures may improve both the effectiveness of some teachers and the impact of some instructional techniques.

The original focus on "school effects" developed out of a concern for equality of educational opportunity by social class and race. Now that a female advantage in educational attainment has emerged, it is natural to ask whether and how schools affect gender inequality as well. We need to consider whether school policies that help one gender also help the other, or whether the interests of boys and girls are incompatible, such that policies designed to help boys compete with those designed to help girls. Our perspective on the potential for schools to ameliorate the gender gap in achievement is parallel to our perspective on families. In

chapter 6, we argued that boys differentially benefit from family resources. Specifically, we believe that boys' academic achievement rises
when they can develop an adult conception of masculinity that fosters
an instrumental orientation toward school as a route to labor market
success. Similarly, we believe that schools with strong academic climates
can reduce the gender gap by raising boys' performance without harming girls' performance. First, we address alternative perspectives on
schools, and then we discuss evidence in support of this key argument.

Are Schools and Teachers Gender-Biased?

Ever since the gender composition of teachers became predominantly
female, scholars have expressed concern that the "feminization" of
schools could put boys at a disadvantage (Sexton 1969; Rury 2008). Others have discounted the possibility that boys' academic difficulties are
linked to the gender of their teachers (Lahaderne 1976). Nonetheless,
there is an irony in the assertion that schools are biased against boys, in
that not long ago scholars argued that schools and teachers favored boys
over girls (Dweck et al. 1978; Simpson and Erickson 1983; Morse and
Handley 1985; Eccles 1987, 1989; Bussey and Bandura 1999; Spender 1982;
Stanworth 1984; Howe 1997; Pickering 1997; Francis 2000).

Some scholars took teachers' greater frequency of interaction with
boys as evidence of their bias in favor of boys. Others argued that while
teachers interact more with boys, they have more learning-related interactions with girls (see, for example, Younger, Warrington, and Williams
1999). Moreover, teachers' interactions with boys tend to be disciplinary
in nature (Wilkinson and Marrett 1985; Salomone 2003). As it became
clear that girls were gaining a large lead in educational attainment,
some scholars grew concerned that teachers were creating an overly
"feminine" climate in the schools and intensifying their favoring of girls
over boys (Entwisle et al. 2007; Pollack 1999; Sommers 2001; Cook 2006;
Gurian and Stevens 2007), even as other scholars (for example, Epstein
et al. 1998; Cohen 1998; Francis 2000) expressed skepticism about such
claims of teacher and school bias. From a social constructivist perspective, differences in measured social and behavioral skills arise from
family and school environments that express different expectations for
girls and boys, and perhaps for African American and socioeconomically disadvantaged boys in particular (Jackson and Moore 2008;
Entwisle et al. 2007). Doris Entwisle and her colleagues (2007, 134) argue
that girls have better social and behavioral ratings from teachers less
because of differences in maturation rates than because girls "find the
student role more compatible than boys do." As further evidence of this
bias, they report that boys are more likely than girls to get poor conduct
grades and that boys with poor conduct grades are more likely to be

retained in first grade compared to girls with poor conduct grades.[1] Their finding parallels that of George Farkas and his colleagues (1990), who found that boys are given lower course grades for being more disruptive than girls are.

The charge of gender bias has been particularly strong in the case of African American students (Holland 1992; Watson and Smitherman 1991; Noguera 2003). Pedro Noguera (2008, xvii) argues that black males are stereotyped by the schools and experience stereotype threat by virtue of their higher rates of punishment, being labeled as "special education" students ("often," he writes, "without an apparent disability") and experiencing academic failure. He notes that this pattern does not mean that black males are "innocent victims of unfair treatment," but it creates the appearance of a normal pattern rather than serving as an indicator that schools need to improve. Noguera sees the problem as partly one of "lowered expectations" on the part of teachers and schools, which reinforce stereotypes rather than ameliorate deficits. Similar to William Pollack (1999), Dan Kindlon and Michael Thompson (2000), and Michael Kimmel (2008), Noguera (2008, xxi) argues that "the trouble with black boys is that too often they are placed in schools where their needs for nurturing, support, and loving discipline are not met."

The social constructivist perspective is coherent, but measurement problems make a full evaluation of its validity difficult. For example, the findings of Entwisle and her colleagues (2007) support the conclusion that teachers evaluate girls more favorably than boys because of gender bias, but their findings are equally consistent with the contrary hypothesis that parents and teachers accurately observe gender differences in behavior, which affect both learning and production of the materials—like homework, reports, and presentations—that teachers consider in the academic evaluation process. Based on the analyses of the ECLS-K data discussed in chapter 5, DiPrete and Jennings (2012) are skeptical of the social constructivist stance that social and behavioral skill differences constitute evidence of teacher bias. They find that only about 5 percent of the variance in rated social and behavioral skills exists between the genders. Gender, race-ethnicity, and poverty status together account for 10 percent or less of the variance in social and behavioral skills. Moreover, they find that the effects of social and behavioral skills on teacher ratings are statistically indistinguishable in the ECLS-K between boys and girls and between children in poverty and nonpoor children (DiPrete and Jennings 2012). In other words, students with higher social and behavioral skills than others of their same gender, class, and race generally score higher on achievement tests and receive higher teacher academic evaluations. Social and behavioral skills are not simply a proxy for gender, class, or race differences, even if the school environment itself is shaped in part by cultural forces related to gender, class, and race.

Even within class, gender, and race groups, students who find the socially constructed student role highly "compatible" seem to be in a more advantageous position to learn relative to their peers.

Teachers evaluate students on broader criteria than their standardized test performance. In this respect, elementary school teachers are no different from evaluators later in life in the world of work. Even in a production job on an assembly line, workers are more productive when they show up for work on time, are not disruptive, and obey the instructions of supervisors. More complex and cognitively demanding jobs involve teamwork and typically have an interpersonal component. Effective communication skills are enhanced by a variety of other skills, including organizational, writing, and oral presentation skills and interpersonal skills. Therefore, it is not surprising that teachers consider such skills in evaluating students. The social and behavioral skills that produce a more effective presentation of one's ideas have an immediate effect on performance evaluation. Moreover, the effective use of these skills improves them. To practice is to get better.

The findings of DiPrete and Jennings (2012) imply that it is important to distinguish analytically between three distinct aspects of the educational evaluation process:

1. *Conduct-dependent grading:* Conduct-dependent grading would occur when teachers give better grades to students whose behavior conforms to their expectations, net of academic performance. This corresponds to what other scholars have termed "teacher bias" (Alexander et al. 1987; Farkas et al. 1990).

2. *"Well-rounded" academic evaluation criteria:* Well-rounded criteria involve academic evaluation that gives greater credit for homework that is turned in on time and neatly completed, to class participation, and to other aspects of performance that may be differentially enhanced through better social and behavioral skills. Narrow evaluation, in contrast, gives greater weight to test performance.

3. *A socially enhanced (as opposed to socially neutral) learning environment:* A socially enhanced learning environment is one where the classroom is organized such that learning is enhanced for students whose behavior is most compatible with the institutionalized student role. In such environments, teachers may pay more attention to students who display greater eagerness to learn, greater affection for the teacher, or a greater willingness to obey classroom rules. Or it could also involve group-learning environments where students' willingness to participate actively or be engaged in the group enhances learning.

All three of these aspects of the education and evaluation process—conduct-dependent grading, the breadth of the academic evaluation criteria, and the nature of the learning environment—strengthen the correlation between student conduct and student grades. Moreover, all three aspects can involve feedback loops. When the feedback runs from teacher bias to lowered self-evaluation, reduced effort, and subsequent lower academic performance, the loop involves what Farkas and his colleagues (1990) termed a "self-fulfilling prophecy," which in the more recent literature has been termed a "stereotype threat." When the feedback runs through a heightened ability to perform in a "socially enhanced learning environment" that uses "well-rounded" academic evaluation criteria, the mechanism is a kind of cumulative advantage process (DiPrete and Eirich 2006). All three of these aspects factor into what Farkas and his colleagues referred to as the "double reward" for school attendance and work habits: social and behavioral skills can factor directly into the evaluation process, because grading is conduct-dependent, and indirectly, because teachers grade on "well-rounded" criteria and because the typical classroom learning environment produces higher learning for students who have requisite conduct and work habits.

Teacher academic ratings are even more strongly affected by social and behavioral skills than are test scores. Because social and behavioral skills are also "evaluated" by teachers, it is possible that the teachers' evaluations of academic achievement are biased upward for students whom they evaluate as well adjusted to school. However, it is equally possible that educationally engaged and well-behaved students are advantaged by the use of "well-rounded" evaluation criteria and by the better fit of their skills with the classroom learning environment.

This advantage can readily be seen in the criteria that teachers are asked to use when constructing their academic rating in the ECLS-K. Fifth-grade teachers were asked to rate reading achievement on criteria such as: the presentation of oral reports using logically organized outlines; use of vocal inflection; facial expression and appropriate pacing to increase listener interest; use of multiple sources to gain information; the taking of good notes when collecting information for reports; the writing of well-organized reports; and the revising of writing to improve organization, increase clarity, and correct errors. Students who have higher levels of commitment to learning, better organization, stronger interpersonal skills, and better ability to accept feedback should be able to produce these behaviors most consistently. The literature on grading in elementary school makes clear that teachers typically consider student effort, homework, and other broad types of assessment beyond test scores when assigning grades (McMillan et al. 2002; Brookhart 1993).

The "pure bias" explanation was more plausible when the conduct penalty centered on boys of lower socioeconomic status. But in the ECLS-K data, social class plays a comparatively minor role in explaining the link between gender, social and behavioral skills, and academic outcomes. Instead, the gender gap in performance is readily apparent for both middle-class and disadvantaged children. The ECLS-K data also reveal a social and behavioral skill gap between Asians and other students and between students whose language at home was not English and other students, net of other factors. The parsimonious story that middle-class female teachers tend to favor students like themselves (that is, middle-class girls) does not carry over well to the pattern of differences in rated social and behavioral skills found in the ECLS-K data. Instead, the results suggest that the link between social and behavioral skills and academic outcomes (particularly teacher academic evaluations) is flowing largely through a direct connection between social and behavioral skills and learning, the production of homework, and other classroom exercises that factor into teachers' evaluations. Girls' superior social and behavioral skills therefore produce a stronger female advantage in course grades determined through the use of "well-rounded" academic evaluative criteria.

Should teachers use "well-rounded" as opposed to "narrow" criteria when they evaluate students? In some historical contexts, evaluative criteria have clearly been manipulated in order to produce an intended result; thus, Harvard, Yale, and Princeton modified their admissions criteria early in the twentieth century to favor "well-rounded" applicants in order to reduce the number of Jewish and other ethnic students who would otherwise have gained admission (Karabel 2005). Evaluation criteria may be shaped instead to match anticipated skill demands on students in their future roles. Thus, Otis Dudley Duncan, David Featherman, and Beverly Duncan (1972) argued that the content of IQ tests was designed to closely approximate the cognitive skills needed to perform well in high-status occupations. Specialized (and highly gendered) evaluation criteria may have been applied in sex-segregated high school classes such as cooking or home economics early in the twentieth century. Indeed, to the extent that teachers believe that teaching social and behavioral skills—especially in the early elementary grades—is an important part of their job, then they would evaluate students' social and behavior skills as part of their overall evaluation. These considerations suggest that the impact of social and behavioral skills on academic performance as well as on the size of the gender gap in academic performance is historically variable and a product of the particular institutional environment of the time. This does not mean that the connections between social and behavioral skills and academics are any less real, but does point to the importance of better understanding how and why these connections exist.

Single-Sex Schools, Teacher Gender, and the Gender Composition of Classrooms

Many writers argue that boys and girls have different "educational styles" and that teachers should use different styles for teaching boys and girls (Sax 2005). The idea that boys and girls learn differently is one of the central justifications for single-sex schools (Salomone, Riordan, and Weinman 1999; Salomone 2003, 2006; Morse 1998). Some critics maintain that coeducational schools are "feminized" and provide an unsuitable learning environment for boys regardless of whether teachers are overtly "biased" against boys (Cook 2006; Tyre 2009). Others claim that students—especially male students—learn better when segregated from the other sex (Pollack 1999; Salomone 2003; Tyre 2009). The case that boys learn better when they are in single-sex classrooms is most clearly made by Rosemary Salomone (2003, 242), who argues that coeducation is hostile to boys who have strong academic orientations: "The all-boys environment provides a protective space where boys can pursue their own paths to self-fulfillment free from the distraction of girls." In Salomone's view, it is more difficult in single-sex schools to gender-type behaviors such as playing violin, making costumes for the school play, singing operetta, working for the school newspaper, or tutoring younger children. Salomone further argues that same-sex schools would generally increase boys' exposure to male teachers in subjects that are sometimes viewed as feminine, such as foreign languages, music, and art. Moreover, single-sex elementary schools can better attend to differences in the rate of development of boys and girls. Finally, she acknowledges that students have varying needs and single-sex schools should be a choice available for those students who would most benefit from this option. Similarly, William Pollack (1999) argues that boys have unique learning styles, and the need to act "manly" makes them especially vulnerable in the presence of girls, especially when they reach adolescence. Boys feel less competitive and vulnerable in all-boy classrooms, where they can bond with their teachers and readily support one another in learning.

The empirical debate about the benefits of single-sex education traces at least back to the early 1960s, when James Coleman (1961) proposed single-sex schools as a possible antidote to the negative effects of adolescent culture on students' academic orientations. Reginald Dale (1969) argued instead that teachers and students prefer coeducation and argued that boys in particular gain academic advantages in coeducational environments. Studies from the 1980s onward (Lee and Bryk 1989; Lee and Marks 1990; Lee 1995) also have argued that coeducational schools produce better results for boys than do single-sex schools. These studies all suffered from potential biases stemming from nonrandom assignment of students to classrooms, but more recent studies using experimental and quasi-experimental variation in student assignment also conclude that both boys and girls benefit from classrooms that are more heavily female. Caroline Hoxby (2000) used exogenous variation in classroom composition from the Tennessee Project STAR data to obtain a plausible estimate of the impact of gender classroom composition on student achievement. She found that both males and females have small but systematic advantages in math and reading in classrooms that are more heavily female. Furthermore, the gains appear to hold net of students' ability. Diane Whitmore (2005) obtained similar findings with the same data. In a study of Israeli schools, Victor Lavy and Analía Schlosser (2007) used random variation in the fraction of classrooms that are female in order to estimate the impact of gender composition on school outcomes. Like previous studies, they found higher cognitive outcomes in classes with a higher fraction of girls. They concluded that higher fractions of girls raise the intermediate factors that, as shown in chapter 6, tend to be associated with girls—namely, lower levels of classroom disruption, better relationships between students and teachers and among students, a higher overall level of satisfaction with school, and less teacher fatigue. Given that students have differing needs, some boys would probably be better served by single-sex schools. In general, however, existing evidence suggests that boys would not be helped by sex-segregated classrooms.

Aside from being important in their own right, these results from Hoxby, Whitmore, and Lavy and Schlosser strengthen the argument that the association between social and behavioral skills and educational performance in elementary school is evidence of a real learning effect rather than a product of "teacher bias." If the greater social and behavioral skills of girls produce spillover effects on standardized tests for both girls and boys, it would seem that the academic gains of students of either gender with high social and behavioral skills are something more than pure bias in teacher evaluations.

Related to the issue of classroom gender composition is that of teacher gender. Many scholars have speculated that boys might benefit by having more male teachers, especially in elementary and middle school, where teachers are predominantly female. To date, however, there is little hard evidence supporting this conjecture. Ronald Ehrenberg, Daniel Goldhaber, and Dominic Brewer (1995) found no evidence that the achievement gains between eighth and tenth grade are associated with the gender match between teacher and student, while Thomas Dee (2006), who reanalyzed these same data, provided suggestive evidence that the gender of the teacher may affect test score gains of opposite-sex students. Neither study could rule out the possibility that students nonrandomly select into classes based on teacher gender. These studies pro-

vide stronger evidence that gender matching affects teachers' evaluations of students (in contrast to student performance on standardized
tests). Helena Holmlund and Krister Sund (2008), who examined upper
secondary students' gains in natural science and social science in Sweden over three years, were able to control for unmeasured student and
school characteristics using fixed effects. They found no effect of gender
matching on performance as measured by grades. Marcel Helbig (2010)
similarly found no relationship between the percentage of teachers who
are female and sixth-grade boys' reading or mathematics competence in
Germany.[2] This study used data from the Progress in International Reading Literacy Study (PIRLS), which allows a stronger test of the same-sex
teacher effect because it contains data on teacher gender and individual
achievement data for all students in the class. Moreover, in Germany the
process of student assignment to classrooms largely rules out the possibility of nonrandom selection of teachers. Using these data and a variety
of modeling strategies, Martin Neugebauer, Marcel Helbig, and Andreas
Landmann (2010) found no evidence that student achievement is affected by whether the teacher is the same gender or a different gender.
Bruce Carrington and his colleagues (2007) took a different approach by
interviewing three hundred seven- and eight-year-old students in England; they found no evidence that gender matches between teacher and
student have an effect on academic engagement.

Other recent studies tell a somewhat different story. Research using
data from the U.S. Air Force Academy—where students are randomly
assigned to science courses—found that women perform better when
they have female science teachers (Carrell, Page, and West 2010). South
Korea has an unusual school system in that secondary school districts
frequently have a mix of coeducational, all-boy, and all-girl schools, and
graduating middle school students are randomly assigned to high
schools within district, based on a public lottery. Hyunjoon Park and Jere
Behrman (2010) found that both boys and girls are significantly more
likely to attend four-year colleges when they attend single-sex high
schools than when they attend coeducational high schools. For girls, the
advantage from single-sex schooling is 3.5 percent (0.5 standard deviation increase), while for boys the effect is a larger 5.8 percent (a 0.8 standard deviation increase). The fact that girls do better in all-girl schools is
consistent with the research in the United States, but Park and Behrman's finding that boys do better in all-boy schools appears to contra-
dict other recent studies that suggest that both boys and girls benefit
from a larger proportion of girls in the classroom. The inconsistency is
largely resolved by Park and Behrman's further discovery that most of
the effect of attending all-boy schools stems from the fact that they have
a larger percentage of teachers who are male and that Korean boys respond favorably to male teachers. They found that every ten-percent-

age-point increase in the share of male teachers increases boys' four-year college attendance by 1.6 percent. Park and Behrman's results also suggest that boys in all-boy schools do not suffer the disadvantage found in heavily male classrooms in the United States. Perhaps Korean male high school students are less disruptive and more academically oriented than American male high school students. Clearly more work is needed to understand better the similarities and differences in the results obtained by Park and Behrman for South Korea and the results found in the United States and other Western settings.

Classroom Peers and Performance

In chapter 6, we argued that preadolescent and adolescent school cultures can have a significant impact on students' orientation to learning, especially for boys. We also argued that parental resources can mediate boys' responses to the peer culture by fostering development of a masculine self-image and providing them with strategies for accommodating their peer culture with an instrumental attachment to school. Similarly, the nature of the student body of a school affects students' academic orientation and thus their academic performance. The Coleman report (1966, 325) concluded that "the social composition of the student body is more highly related to achievement, independent of the student's own social background, than is any school factor." When the adolescent culture rewards academic performance, students are motivated to invest in their studies, both in order to gain status with their peers and to please significant others such as parents and teachers. The result, Coleman argued, is greater academic achievement returns to academic ability and higher average academic achievement in the class (Coleman 1960, 1961).[3] But when the adolescent culture values non-academic outcomes more highly (for example, sports, popularity, or opposition to school authority), and especially when the adolescent culture denigrates academic achievement, it draws energy away from students' academic achievement. Simply put, a highly motivated, achievement-oriented student body creates a learning-oriented peer culture (see also Sewell et al. 1969; Jencks and Mayer 1990; Rumberger and Palardy 2005; Baumert, Stanat, and Watermann 2006).

Much of the literature on male underachievement focuses on disincentives to engage with school that stem from adolescent conceptions of masculinity and their impact on behavior. Gender differentiation and the creation of separate play habits for boys and girls begin in early childhood, even before children experience school (Maccoby and Jacklin 1974; Maccoby 1998; Thorne 1993; Davies 1993, 2003). These gender-differentiated childhood cultures become both the basis for gender-differentiated adolescent cultures and—many argue—important influences on whether youths take school seriously and how hard they work as students (Steinberg et al. 1996).

Classroom observations and other ethnographic studies have documented how gender identities are constructed in the classroom and how these gender cultures affect boys' and girls' interactions and approaches to learning (Salisbury and Jackson 1996; Skelton 1997; Pickering 1997; Francis 2000). Masculinity is generally constructed as competitive, active, aggressive, and dominating, while femininity is viewed as passive and cooperative (Francis 2000, 48). Although not caused by school, these differentiated gender identities, especially for boys, interact with social class to create orientations that are quite relevant to students' school success.

In a classic study, Paul Willis (1981) argued that working for academic success conflicts with masculinity for working-class white boys. Michèle Cohen (1998) and many others (Mac an Ghaill 1994; Power et al. 1998; Epstein 1998; Murphy and Elwood 1998; Quenzel and Hurrelmann 2010) have argued that gender identities perpetuate the belief that girls have to work hard in order to learn, whereas boys are naturally gifted. Cohen shows that this belief is reflected in boys' casual if not reluctant attitude toward school. These studies show that boys are generally noisier, more physically active, and more distracted compared to girls (Spender 1982; Younger and Warrington 1996; Salisbury and Jackson 1996; Pickering 1997; Skelton 1997; Howe 1997; Younger et al. 1999; Francis 2000). Disruptive behavior is often encouraged by male peers insofar as it precipitates status gains in the adolescent peer group, while working for academic achievement is labeled as feminine and thereby stigmatized. Among girls, however, school work is typically viewed as acceptable and sometimes even encouraged. Based on her own and others' ethnographic work, Debbie Epstein (1998, 106) argues that "the main demand on boys from within their peer culture . . . is to appear to do little or no work," whereas for girls "it seems as if working hard at school is not only accepted, but is, in fact, wholly desirable." This is exemplified in a story told in one of Epstein's focus groups by Teresa, a student from a working-class school:

TERESA: We used to have one boy that we used to call [laughs] and abuse [laughs]. I was horrible, I was part of a horrible gang of girls that used to go round bullying everyone [laughter]. . . . No, really, like poof and queer and things like that. . . . They were directed specifically at this one boy.

OTHER PARTICIPANT: What was, what was he like?

TERESA: He was like really quiet and he was, um, he always used to get his homework done, used to have his school uniform on and then, none of us had a school uniform. He did. And this sort of thing. So he was just different I think just different. (Epstein 1998, 99)

Similar stories can be found throughout the ethnographic literature (see, for example, Morris 2008; Coleman 1961; Eitzen 1975; Steinberg et al. 1996). John Bishop and his colleagues (2003) argue that adolescents value the attributes that make one "cool" or popular and that in the adolescent subculture high status goes to the "jocks." Noguera (2008, 42) argues that black adolescents feel the need to project "toughness." In one survey, 20 percent of high school students said that they sometimes did not try as hard as they could in school because of worries about what their friends might think (Bishop et al. 2003). Those who responded this way were more likely to be middle schoolers, male, and nonwhite and to have lower-educated parents or only a single parent at home. Edward Morris (2008) reports a similar tendency by some boys who do not see good grades per se as inconsistent with masculinity, but think that academic "strivers" are "pussies"—that is, feminized males. The tendencies for both working-class parents and boys in general to disparage school are sometimes exaggerated in the literature. Nonetheless, persuasive evidence indicates that young boys construct masculinity partly in terms of resistance to school and teachers, and this attitude of resistance may be partly responsible for male underachievement in school (Salisbury and Jackson 1996; Pickering 1997; Skelton 1997; Francis 2000). At the same time, it is important to recall Coleman's central insight that adolescent cultures vary in their core values. In schools where academic performance is a route to the leading crowd, boys compete more for high grades and this competition produces a stronger connection between cognitive ability (as measured by standardized test scores) and school performance (Coleman 1960). Coleman (1960, 1961) also found that boys are more likely to report that they prefer to be remembered as an "athletic star" than as a "brilliant student." However, in all schools a significant minority of boys choose "brilliant student" over "athletic star" or "most popular."[4] Both girls and boys experience differentiated cultures based partly on social class and partly on athletics or other determinants of "popularity," with academic achievement having a variable connection to adolescent status across subcultures. However, variation in male subcultures seems especially influential on the academic performance of boys.

In the decades following Coleman's research, many studies have provided evidence that peers affect educational achievement (for example, Sewell et al. 1969; Jencks and Mayer 1990). Since Charles Manski's (1995) work on the "reflection problem," however, scholars have grown more sensitive to the challenge of accurately estimating the strength of peer effects, which is difficult because the characteristics of students within any school or classroom (such as average socioeconomic status) are generally correlated with unmeasured characteristics of the school or classroom (like teacher quality) that affect student outcomes (Angrist and Pischke 2008). Recent studies have used sophisticated strategies to overcome these challenges. One strategy uses natural experiments—such as the forced evacuation of Hurricane Katrina victims to Houston—to estimate the impact of changes in class composition on student outcomes.[5] A second strategy exploits the potentially random assignment of students to classes within schools, especially in European countries where it is difficult for parents to "teacher shop" (Ammermueller and Pischke 2009). A third strategy examines arguably random fluctuations in the gender and race composition of adjacent cohorts for the same school and grade (Hoxby 2000; Gould et al. 2010), though these studies have not examined peer effects related to socioeconomic characteristics. The estimated effects range from near zero to about 0.15 standard deviations, which is about the same magnitude as some of the most reliable estimates of teacher effects on academic or social and behavioral outcomes (Rivkin 1995; Rockoff 2004; Jennings and DiPrete 2010).[6] Other studies using estimation strategies that control for potential confounders (along with sensitivity analyses in the case of Crosnoe 2009) have similarly found peer effects of 0.15 of a standard deviation on test scores (Rumberger and Palardy 2005), though Robert Crosnoe 2009 has found negative "frog-pond" type effects of high-SES school composition on coursetaking and GPA for low-income students. However, these studies have not examined whether the character of classroom peer groups affects the size of the gender gap in educational performance.

Joscha Legewie and Thomas DiPrete (2012b) recently addressed precisely this question using strategies drawn from the recent causal effects literature. They employed standard regression techniques with large-scale data sets from Berlin, Germany, for secondary school (the PISA-I-Plus and PISA-E 2003 data) and a quasi-experimental design based on within-school variation across classrooms in the same elementary school grade (the ELEMENT data). In contrast to the United States, the lack of performance-based tracking in elementary schools and the smaller extent of parents' influence on classroom assignment allowed them to use a quasi-experimental identification strategy based on between-class variation within schools. Legewie and DiPrete (2012b) found that school context matters for the performance of boys. Specifically, they found that schools with higher average performance are also schools with small net effects of gender. Figure 7.1 illustrates this finding by plotting the empirical Bayes prediction of the random intercept (that is, average school performance) against the prediction for the random slope (the female advantage) from the model without covariates for about 1,100 schools in the PISA-E data. Whether all school types are taken together or considered separately, the female performance advantage is smaller in schools where the average performance is higher.

Their estimates from a multilevel model for the PISA-I-Plus (using random school effects) and from a fixed-effects model with the ELE-MENT and the PISA-I-Plus data (using fixed school effects) are compared in table 7.1 for the key coefficients of gender and the main effect of SES composition (at the school level for the multilevel model and at the classroom level for the fixed-effects models), plus interactions between SES composition and gender.[7]

The results in table 7.1 show that SES composition has a highly significant positive effect on reading test scores in all models, net of individual SES background. This conforms with previous findings on the effects of SES composition (Jencks and Mayer 1990; Rumberger and Palardy 2005; Baumert et al. 2006). In all models in table 7.1, the point estimate for the interaction between SES composition and female is negative and significant, which means that going to a higher-SES school helps boys more than girls. In light of the institutional and statistical evidence that students are allocated randomly to classes within elementary schools in Berlin, these estimates of the difference in the causal effect of SES composition for boys and girls imply that because boys are more sensitive to school resources, the gender gap is smaller in high-quality schools. Legewie and DiPrete (2012b) also demonstrated that part of the beneficial effect of high SES composition on boys' achievement works indirectly through the effect of SES composition on the achievement of low-performing students in general, of whom boys are the disproportionate share. However, they found that the effect of SES composition on male-specific achievement is statistically significant even after accounting for the association between gender and low achievement. Furthermore, Legewie and DiPrete found that males receive a relatively strong gain from classroom socioeconomic composition when working habits or the strength of the student's learning orientation are the dependent variables. These findings suggest mechanisms by which the local peer environment affects academic achievement for all students while at the same time providing especially strong gains for boys.

Legewie and DiPrete (2011) also examined academic performance for about 200,000 students in 584 public schools in Chicago. Berlin elementary schools enroll a very heterogeneous population, with roughly one-third of the students having an immigrant background. Chicago public schools, in contrast, have a disproportionately poor, nonwhite student population who are at high risk of academic failure. The Chicago data are administrative data supplemented with surveys of students and administrators. Although, unlike the Berlin data, the Chicago data cannot distinguish individual classrooms within grades, these data do have the advantage of following multiple cohorts of students as they progress

Figure 7.1   Empirical Bayes Predictions for Average School Performance and Gender Gap in Education

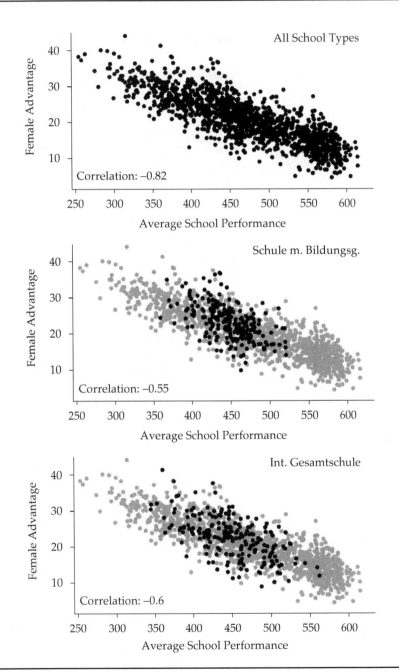

Source: Authors' compilation based on data from PISA-E (Prenzel et al. 2006).

Figure 7.1   (*continued*)

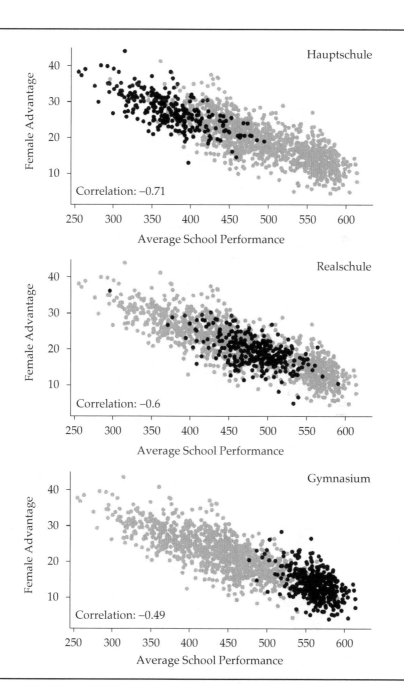

Table 7.1   Effect of Socioeconomic School/Class Composition for Boys and Girls, in Standard Deviations

	Female		SES Composition		SES Composition x Female	
	Coefficient	(Standard Error)	Coefficient	(Standard Error)	Coefficient	(Standard Error)
Multilevel model estimates (PISA-I-Plus 2003)	0.143	(0.11)	0.303***	(0.05)	−0.099*	(0.04)
Fixed effects estimates (ELEMENT)	0.120***	(0.03)	0.178***	(0.06)	−0.057*	(0.03)
Fixed effects estimates (PISA-I-Plus 2003)	0.196***	(0.03)	0.237***	(0.03)	−0.052*	(0.02)

Source: Authors' compilation based on Legewie and DiPrete (2012b).
Note: Standard errors in parentheses.
* $p < 0.05$, ** $p < 0.01$, *** $p < 0.001$

through the elementary grades. Because the Chicago data have a different structure, Legewie and DiPrete modified their estimation strategy and thereby exploited the quasi-random variation in the socioeconomic composition of successive cohorts within individual schools. Specifically, they estimated both linear and quadratic trends in SES composition in the first grade at the individual school level and used the residual variation in first-grade SES composition as an instrumental variable for fourth-grade SES composition, along with school and cohort fixed effects. They found that, net of third-grade performance on math and reading Iowa tests, boys gain a particularly strong benefit from being in a cohort with higher SES composition. These findings are consistent with the findings from Berlin in suggesting that locally strong academic climates boost both girls' and boys' performance, but that their net effect is to reduce the gender gap in achievement.

Because the gender gap in achievement is a prime determinant of the gender gap in educational attainment, school climate offers a potentially important policy lever in redressing the lower educational attainment of boys. Legewie and DiPrete's (2012b) findings direct attention to the question of whether school climate effects are long-lasting. Some teacher effects research suggests that the effects of any particular teacher tend to be relatively short-term (Jacob, Lefgren, and Sims 2010; Kane and Staiger 2008), while other research has found that good teaching has durable effects that last into adulthood (Chetty, Friedman, and Rockoff 2011). In addition, Raj Chetty and his colleagues (2010) have found with Project STAR data that a summary measure of class quality in the early grades has durable effects on noncognitive skills and improves the probability of attending college. Whether the relatively strong effects of high-SES peers for male students that were found by Legewie and DiPrete (2012b) and Legewie and DiPrete (2011) are durable remains an open question. We hypothesize that these effects cumulate across grades and that their durability is greater when the exposure to strong academic climates stretches across several years. Because high-SES students are inherently in short supply, schools also need to find ways to mimic the effects of socioeconomic composition through other mechanisms. These limitations notwithstanding, the literature increasingly suggests that the local environment is a source of gender gaps in educational achievement and college completion as well as a site of potential strategies for reducing these gender gaps.

Self-Esteem, Stereotypes, and Gender Differences in Performance

Up to this point we have focused on childhood and adolescent subcultures and their potential impact on a broad set of behaviors and psychological processes involving gender identity. Psychologists have posited an alternative, narrower form of peer influence in their effort to explain task choices and performance and, more concretely, to account for minorities' low performance relative to whites and women's low performance in math and science relative to men. Various psychological theories posit effects that arise less from concerns about acceptance by peer groups and more from internalizations of a gender identity and the anticipated psychological and cognitive consequences of this gender identity for performance.

According to the expectancy-value model (Fishbein 1963; Fishbein and Ajzen 1975), individuals' choices are influenced by their values regarding possible outcomes and their estimated probabilities of the outcomes. Jacquelynne Eccles and her colleagues used this theory to explain how gender differences in values, beliefs about their own competence, and expectations for success in alternative careers are related to gender differences in major choice and career plans (Eccles et al. 1983; Eccles 2005; Wigfield and Eccles 2000).The motivational process model of Carol Dweck (2000) emphasizes the relationship between individuals' beliefs about intelligence and the adaptive and maladaptive coping patterns that they display in the face of academic challenges. Some students believe that intelligence is a fixed and largely unchangeable personality attribute, while others believe that intelligence is malleable and increases with effort just as athletic abilities increase with physical training. According to Dweck, students who believe that intelligence is fixed also tend to believe that effort does not produce better results and are less likely to respond with effort-oriented strategies when they perform poorly on tests (Blackwell, Trzesniewski, and Dweck 2007).

Claude Steele and his associates have argued that blacks and women are aware of stereotypes that they are less capable at certain intellectual tasks (academics in general or mathematics in particular) and that they integrate this stereotype into beliefs about their own ability (Steele and Aronson 1995; Steele 1997). According to Steele, these stereotypes do not have a fixed effect on outcomes; rather, the effect can be enhanced or diminished by environmental cues that link the stereotype to specific performance.

According to expectation states theory, status-related beliefs develop when people of one status do better than those of another status because of some material or social advantage that causes the belief that the advantaged-status members have greater competence. This belief then shapes individuals' beliefs about their own competence, which, in turn, affect both their actual performance and their evaluations of their performance in comparison with advantaged-status members (Berger, Cohen, and Zelditch 1972; Ridgeway and Berger 1986). With respect to gender, the theory predicts that males will have advantages over females in mixed-sex settings when the task in question is seen as stereotypically masculine and that females will have advantages over males if the task is seen as stereotypically feminine. Cecilia Ridgeway, Shelley Correll, and Lynn Smith-Lovin have developed this theory as an explanation for the widespread—albeit diminishing—beliefs about men as more instrumentally competent than women (Ridgeway and Smith-Lovin 1999; Ridgeway and Correll 2004; Ridgeway and Bourg 2004). This theory has also been applied to math performance. If math skills are viewed as masculine, observers (like teachers or employers) will presume that males have higher ability than equally performing females, and students will share this conception. Observers will attribute females' performance to greater effort, which is seen as disadvantaging women in the context of advancement in scientific careers (Ridgeway and Bourg 2004; Correll 2001, 2004; Nosek, Banaji, and Greenwald 2002).

Taken together, these studies assert that if some factor causes one group to perform a task better than another group, then this difference can be magnified or maintained through psychological expectations about one's own and others' performance, even if the factor in question dies away. Consequently, this literature suggests the practical value of strategies to raise the collective sense of efficacy among disadvantaged groups in order to improve their performance. Some of the laboratory studies utilizing these strategies yield impressive results. For example, Catherine Good, Joshua Aronson, and Michael Inzlicht (2003) found that randomized interventions early in seventh grade that encourage subjects to view intelligence as malleable result in significantly better performance on math tests at the end of seventh grade for students in the experimental group compared to the control group. Meanwhile, the experimental interventions of Geoffrey Cohen and his colleagues (Cohen et al. 2006; Cohen et al. 2009) suggest that low-performing minority students could improve their performance through an intervention that asks randomly selected students to complete a series of structured writing assignments that reflect on an important personal value.

Despite the impressive results of these experiments in the laboratory, it is difficult to establish the size of these psychological reinforcement effects and thereby judge the potential impact of intervention strategies based on enhancing self-esteem and confidence in classroom settings. Inspirational teachers can raise student expectations and improve their confidence and performance. But expectations are themselves shaped by performance. Students' expectations for high performance are likely to decline if their own performance fails to meet expectations. Moreover, this literature has focused largely on the performance gap between whites and minority students and on the (relatively small) average female deficit on standardized math tests. Whether these interventions apply to the more general male deficit in academic performance is unknown. It is unclear whether the boys' underperformance stems from their tendency to believe that boys are intellectually inferior to girls.[8] If the academic gender gap arises instead from male developmental delays, from male deficits in social and behavioral skills, or from cultural forces that interfere with male motivations to expend effort in school, then strategies such as those outlined earlier in this book are likely to be more fruitful for reducing the gender gap in educational achievement.

Conclusion

This chapter has examined the impact of the school environment on the gender gap in educational performance. First, we evaluated three claims about schools as the source of the gender gap that have been asserted in prior research: that the gender gap in educational performance is a consequence of teacher bias in favor of girls; that schools have created a "feminine" environment that disadvantages boys; and that the gender gap in academic performance is attributable to coeducation. Although social constructivists argue that teachers evaluate girls more favorably than boys because of gender bias, we believe that teachers accurately observe gender differences in social and behavioral skills, which affect both learning and the academic products that factor into the evaluation process. The story that middle-class female teachers tend to favor students like themselves (middle-class girls) does not align with the pattern of differences in rated social and behavioral skills found in elementary school; instead, girls' superior social and behavioral skills produce a strong female advantage in course grades, especially when grades are determined through the use of "well-rounded" academic evaluative criteria. Others argue that coeducational schools are "feminized" and that most boys would be better served in single-sex schools. Although the debate about the benefits of single-sex education has gone on for decades, recent studies using experimental and quasi-experimental variation in student assignment conclude that both boys and girls appear to benefit from classrooms that have higher proportions of female students. Thus, existing evidence suggests that single-sex schooling would do little to close the gender gap in academic performance.

Consistent with the perspective developed in chapter 6, we then argued that schools with strong academic climates typically shrink the gender gap by raising the boys' academic performance without harming girls' academic performance. Much of the male disadvantage can be traced to the peer culture that provides status rewards for an oppositional attitude toward school. Recent evidence from the United States and Europe suggests that schools with stronger academic climates differentially raise the academic performance of both elementary and secondary school-age boys.

Finally, we considered the recent literature on stereotype threat as a potential cause of the gender gap in academic performance. Stereotype threat has been posited as a plausible mechanism for the academic underperformance of nonwhite children and of girls on standardized math and science tests. Stereotype threat might even emerge as a barrier to performance for boys if—following increased awareness of the gender gap in academic performance—a cultural stereotype of boys as less academically capable than girls takes root in society. To date, however, we know of no research that makes a plausible case for stereotype threat as a source for boys' lower academic performance relative to girls.

Chapter 8

Gender, College Major, and Postgraduate Education

OUR FOCUS to this point has been on the growing advantage that women have over men in attaining bachelor's degrees and on the determinants of this advantage in the environment and earlier life course. It is striking that the rise of the female advantage in four-year college completion has occurred without a steady convergence in the fields of study undertaken by females and males. Fields of study in college have a strong effect on postgraduate education, on the occupational trajectories of men and women, and on the gender gap in earnings (Brown and Corcoran 1997; Blau and Kahn 2000). Understanding the full character of gender stratification in education requires attention to both the content of postsecondary education and educational and occupational trajectories beyond completion of a bachelor's degree.

This chapter compares trends in rates of college completion with trends in the distribution of college majors and trends in rates of postgraduate degrees. Much of the gender difference in college majors concerns science, technology, engineering, and mathematics (STEM) fields, in terms of both the fraction of males and females who major in STEM fields and gender differences in the specific fields of study within STEM. Throughout this book, we have developed the argument that gender differences in educational performance in elementary and secondary school have their basis in the global environment and the local environment that encompass families, peers, and schools. Similarly, we maintain that gender differences in field of study in college are also linked to the environment, including both the global environment and the local environment defined by family, peers, and school.

Gender Segregation in Fields of Study

Not long ago, women college students were concentrated in a very narrow range of fields of study. In the early 1960s, more than 70 percent of female undergraduates majored in education, English, fine arts, nursing, history, or home economics (Jacobs 1996). The degree of gender segregation across majors can be measured by the index of dissimilarity, which captures the percentage of women who would have to change majors in order for there to be parity for men and women in the distributions; 100 percent indicates complete segregation, and 0 percent indicates identical distributions. In 1965 the dissimilarity index calculated across all fields of study indicated that 40 percent of women would have had to change major fields in order to achieve gender parity. Gender segregation of major fields declined most dramatically during the 1970s. Sarah Turner and William Bowen (1999) show that a substantial movement of women out of education, coupled with a large influx of women into business programs, accounted for much of this reduction in the total dissimilarity index.

As we noted in chapter 2, there has been very little change in the overall index of dissimilarity since the early 1980s (see figure 2.9). Mann and DiPrete (2012) found that the dissimilarity had dropped to 23 as of 1984 for college sophomores from the High School and Beyond study. Since then, the level of dissimilarity has remained about the same: for the college sophomores in 1994 from NELS, the index was 24, and for the college sophomores in 2006 from ELS, the index remained at 24.

Summary measures sometimes hide change that is occurring within specific fields of study. The most salient example concerns the life sciences. Using data from the National Science Foundation CASPAR database, Mann and DiPrete (2012) found a small continual increase in the fraction of science majors who are female; this change has been driven partly by the trend for women to make up a greater share of all college students and partly by the increase in the popularity of life sciences majors for women. As shown in figure 8.1, the number of undergraduate female science and engineering majors has increased consistently since 1966, such that by 2001 women had garnered slightly more than half of all bachelor's degrees in science and engineering. Inspection of specific fields within the broad category of science and engineering reveals great variation in women's representation. The majority of students in the biological and social sciences, with the exception of economics, are now women. They are approaching parity in chemistry, but they remain the minority in nearly all other sciences. Their underrepresentation in all fields within engineering is particularly striking.

Analysis of graduate degrees provides further evidence of both substantial change and persisting gender-specific patterns of study.[1] The number of advanced degrees earned by women has increased dramatically across all fields even as gender segregation in undergraduate fields of study has persisted (England and Li 2006; England et al. 2007). Figure 8.2 breaks down the trends according to whether the degree is a profes-

Figure 8.1   Bachelor's Degrees in Science and Engineering Awarded to Men and Women

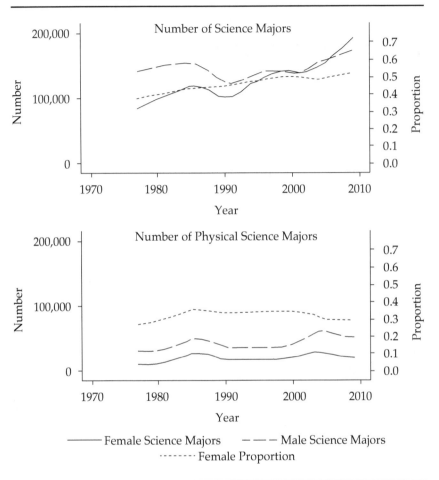

Source: Mann and DiPrete (2012), based on CASPAR data (National Science Foundation 2012).

sional degree in medicine, dentistry, or law or a master's or doctoral-level degree in business, social science or humanities, education or "other health" professions, life sciences, physical sciences or mathematics, or engineering. The number of degrees earned by women differs enormously across these fields (and therefore the counts are reported on a log scale). Women have increased the number of advanced degrees they earn in all fields since the early 1970s. Their share of advanced degrees has also grown (see figure A.12). Since the 1980s, women have earned more than 50 percent of the advanced degrees in the social sci-

Figure 8.1 (*continued*)

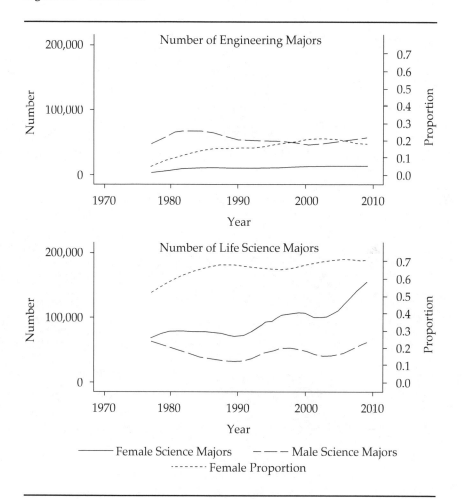

ences and humanities as well as in other health professions and education; the same has been true in social sciences and humanities since the
mid-1970s. In life sciences, women achieved parity and then surpassed
men in advanced degrees in the early years of the current decade. They
have nearly reached parity with men in the combined fields of medicine,
dentistry, and law, and they have been heading steadily toward parity in
advanced business degrees. Women's share of total degrees in physical
sciences and mathematics is lower than in these other fields, but their
steady gains in physical sciences and mathematics show no sign of pla-

Figure 8.2   Advanced Degrees Awarded to Women

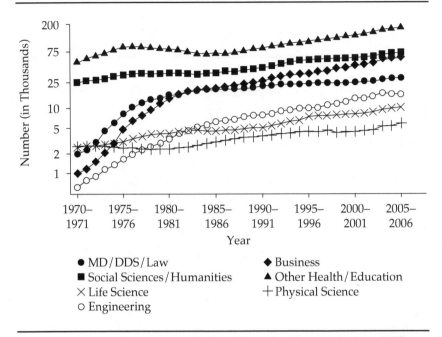

Source: Authors' compilation based on National Center for Education Statistics (2007).
Note: The Y axis is on a log scale.

teauing. Women had even made gains in engineering through the year 2000. Despite these gains, however, they obtain only about 25 percent of the total number of advanced engineering degrees, and there is evidence of a plateau from the year 2000 onward.

Figures 8.3 and 8.4 use the same data to examine the within-gender distribution of degrees by field. These figures demonstrate that sharp differences persist in the distribution of degrees within each gender. No single field of the seven dominates the male distribution, though business degrees have constituted the largest share since the late 1970s, while engineering and other health and education degrees constitute the second and third largest shares. The natural and life sciences constitute the smallest shares throughout the thirty-five-year period.

The trends for females in figure 8.4 look quite different than the trends for males. First, degrees in other health and in education constitute a much larger share of the degrees for women than for men. This category constituted over 60 percent of the degrees earned by women in the early 1970s, and its share fell toward 40 percent as opportunities for women increased in other fields. Over the past twenty years, however, this area has held a steady and even slightly increasing share of the advanced

Figure 8.3   Proportion of Male Advanced Degree Recipients in Indicated Specialty

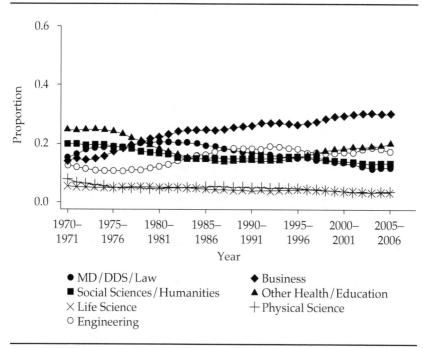

Year

● MD/DDS/Law   ◆ Business
■ Social Sciences/Humanities   ▲ Other Health/Education
✕ Life Science   + Physical Science
○ Engineering

Source: Authors' compilation based on Snyder and Dillow (2007).

degrees for women. Another prominent trend shown in figure 8.4 concerns business degrees, which constituted a rapidly growing share of degrees for women until the mid-1980s and a more gradually growing share thereafter. Degrees in medicine, dentistry, and law also constituted a growing share of all degrees earned by women until the mid-1980s, but since then their share has gradually fallen, even though the female share of all degrees awarded in these areas has grown continually throughout this period (see figure A.12). Degrees in physical science, mathematics, and engineering have constituted a relatively small share of all degrees earned by women from the early 1970s to the present day.

The trends shown in figures 8.3 and 8.4 are driven by two distinct forces: changes in the relative attractiveness of different fields for men and women and changes in the relative size of these fields. These forces are interconnected to some extent. Although the supply of degrees in some areas, such as medicine, is relatively rigid, at least in the short term (and thus not driven by the percentage of men or women who would like to obtain a medical degree if they could get into medical school), the supply of degrees in other areas is responsive to short-term changes in

Figure 8.4   Proportion of Female Advanced Degree Recipients in Indicated Specialty

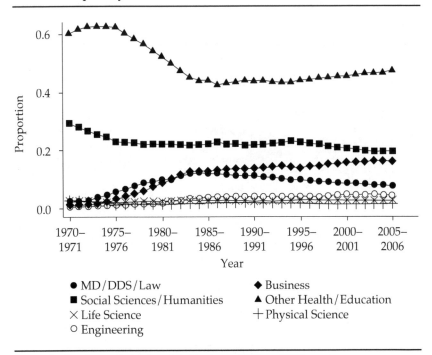

Source: Authors' compilation based on Snyder and Dillow (2007).

demand as well as to supply constraints. It is instructive, therefore, to examine the gender trends in degree distributions separately from trends in the changing share of degrees going to a particular field.

In figures 8.5 and 8.6, we fix the distribution of total (male plus female) degrees across fields at their 2005–2006 levels and exclude fields that have traditionally been most attractive to women (other health professions, education, social sciences, and humanities). Figure 8.6 demonstrates striking changes in the relative attractiveness or openness of the medical and legal professions, business, and sciences and engineering to women during the 1970s, followed by a high degree of stability from the early 1980s onward. In the 1970s, the fraction of women in these five field groups who entered business and the professions of medicine, dentistry, and law rose at the expense of women who were entering the life sciences and the physical sciences, even as women's *numerical* increase in all these areas was strong. Since the early 1980s, the distribution of women across these five areas has been highly stable; there has only

Figure 8.5   Proportion (Standardized) of Male Advanced Degree Recipients in the Indicated Specialty

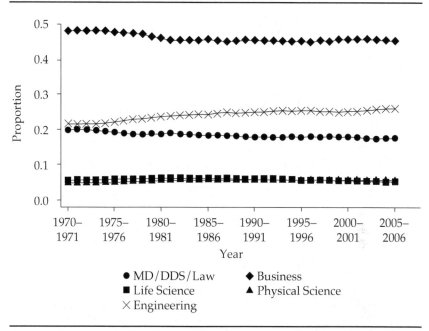

Source: Authors' compilation based on Snyder and Dillow (2007).
Notes: Education, social science, humanities, and other health excluded. Distribution of male and female degrees fixed at 2005–2006 levels. Proportions across all specialties sum to unity.

been a slight increase in the tendency of women to enter engineering instead of business or the professions of medicine, dentistry, or law. This highly stable pattern of entry stands in sharp contrast to the dramatic increases in the number of women—both absolutely and relative to men—who have entered all of these fields. This phenomenon is driven largely by the rising share of all bachelor's degrees that are awarded to women. However, women at the margin largely earn these degrees in the same proportion—at least on average—as do women who are far from this margin. Since the early 1980s, moreover, there have been very few changes in the relative attractiveness of these degrees to women, net of the overall attractiveness (or availability) of these degrees to men and women alike.

Women are more likely than men to enter health professions, education, the social sciences, and the humanities. When we consider only those women who do not enter these fields, figure 8.6 shows that women

Figure 8.6   Proportion (Standardized) of Female Advanced Degree
Recipients in the Indicated Specialty

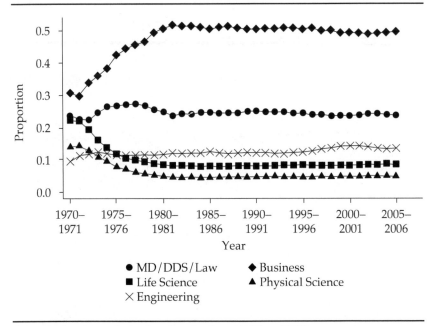

Source: Authors' compilation based on Snyder and Dillow (2007).
Notes: Education, social science, humanities, and other health excluded. Distribution of
male and female degrees fixed at 2005–2006 levels. Proportions across all specialties sum to
unity.

are more likely to enter business and the professions of dentistry, medicine, and law than engineering and the more mathematically oriented
physical sciences.[2] This pattern contrasts with the pattern for men, where
engineering dominates the professions of dentistry, medicine, and law
(see figure 8.5).

In summary, two sets of forces together account for the number of
women obtaining advanced science and engineering degrees. One set of
forces, which operates on both males and females, has rearranged the
gender composition of higher education and resulted in women gaining
a greater share of all degrees, both at the bachelor's level and at more
advanced levels. A second set of forces accounts for the distribution of
women among elite field groups and has produced, on average, relatively stable outcomes for the past twenty years. Growing opportunities
for women in medicine, law, business, and life sciences may be related to
the slower rates of women's progress in physical science and engineering, but no prior research has addressed this issue empirically.

The Causes of Gender Segregation in College Majors

Performance

At the undergraduate level, gender segregation in fields of study as measured by the index of dissimilarity has remained relatively stable for two decades, while at the PhD level gender segregation has not changed much in forty years (England and Li 2006; England et al. 2007). Why are women still underrepresented in physical science and engineering and overrepresented in the humanities and some of the social sciences? Many studies have examined the reasons for the low numbers of women in the hard sciences and engineering fields within universities (Fox and Stephan 2001; Long 2001). Research attempting to understand gender differences in choice of college major tend to focus on either differences in skill, such as academic performance, or differences in preferences and socialization. As noted earlier, most studies find small differences in mean mathematics test scores between males and females and a higher variance in the test scores of males than females (Hedges and Nowell 1995); moreover, the male lead in mathematics performance tends to widen in the upper end of the distribution. In other words, the gender disparity grows with the sensitivity of the test to extreme performance in mathematics, being about 2-to-1 among students scoring 800 on the math SAT (Ellison and Swanson 2010), 1.6-to-1 among those scoring in the 99th percentile of the math PISA test (Guiso et al. 2008), and 10-to-1 at the 99.9 percentile of the math ability distribution (Ellison and Swanson 2010).

While gender differences in the upper end of the math distribution are considerable, they do not have much to do with gender differences in STEM majors. In the NELS data, 10 percent of all males completing college majored in STEM fields, compared with 6 percent of all females. Gender differences in choice of major at the extreme upper end of the distribution would have relatively little impact on the overall gender difference in STEM majors. Turner and Bowen (1999) examined the degree to which gender differences in college major choices are associated with gender differences in precollege math performance as measured by math SAT scores.[3] They found that differences in SAT scores account for less than half of the total gender gap in choice of major. Consequently, Turner and Bowen concluded that differences in academic preparation provide only a small part of the explanation for the persistence of gender segregation in majors; other forces, "including differences in preferences, labor market expectations, gender-specific effects of college experience and unmeasured aspects of academic preparation account for the main part of today's gender gaps in choice of academic major" (Turner and Bowen 1999, 309). However, like most studies, their model left a large residual "unexplained" gender difference.

More recent studies come to largely the same conclusion. Using data from HSB, NELS, and ELS, Mann and DiPrete (2012) found that math test scores explain even less of the gender gap in physical science and engineering majors than was found in the College and Beyond data analyzed by Turner and Bowen (1999). Yu Xie and Kimberlee Shauman (2003) similarly assessed the most commonly asserted causes for women's underrepresentation in the hard sciences and engineering fields. Like Turner and Bowen (1999), Xie and Shauman concluded that the gender differences in science majors are not due to gender differences in math ability or math training in high school, since these gaps have closed. Nor are they due to girls' lower participation in high school math and science course work. Instead, they concluded, gender segregation within the sciences (for example, biology versus physics) and familial roles are the key barriers to women's successful career trajectories in science and engineering, though most of the gender difference in the decision to major in science is unexplained by available covariates. These findings are consistent with other studies that also find gender differences in math and science achievement, as indicated by standardized tests, to be too small to explain gender differences in math and science education or occupations (Hyde 2005; Hyde et al. 2008; Spelke 2005).

Attitudes, Values, and Expectations

Although there are only small gender gaps in math and science aptitude and preparation, beliefs about males' superiority in these domains persist in American culture. Cultural beliefs differentially bias how males and females evaluate their own competence at career-relevant tasks, such that females tend to underestimate their competence at mathematics relative to their equal-ability male counterparts, and this tendency in turn reduces their commitment to career trajectories in math and science (Correll 2001, 2004). As noted in chapter 7, the expectancy-value model (Eccles et al. 1983; Eccles 2005; Wigfield and Eccles 2000) asserts that individuals' expectations of success at a task and the value they attach to the task are directly related to their task choices. Gender differences in college major and career choices stem in part from gender differences in the intrinsic and utility values of different occupations. Intrinsic values constitute enjoyment derived from a task and the centrality of that task to confirming aspects of one's identity. Intrinsic value is a major predictor of participation in math courses in high school and college (Benbow and Minor 1986; Updegraff et al. 1996; Watt 2005). Evidence suggests that females are more interested in jobs involving people, social interactions, and helping others, and that males are more interested in jobs involving physical objects and abstract concepts (Bridges 1989; Hansen et al. 1993; Elizur 1994; Lippa 1998; Eccles 2007). Studies consistently find that young women attach greater importance to the intrinsic, altruistic, and social rewards associated with an occupation; young men place a higher value on extrinsic rewards such as money, prestige, and power (Beutel and Mooney Marini 1995; Bridges 1989; Johnson 2001; Davies and Guppy 1996; Konrad et al. 2000). Claude Montmarquette, Kathy Cannings, and Sophie Mahseredjian (2002) find that the elasticity on expected earnings of a college major is half as large for women as for men, suggesting that women make their choices based on intrinsic characteristics of the majors while men add an expectation of earnings. Thus, gender differences in attitudes and values might explain, in part, why adolescents' expectations of college majors and occupations remain quite gender-typed (Lueptow et al. 2001; Wilson and Boldizar 1990).

Young men and women also view their adult roles differently. Since boys and men are socialized to view work as their primary adult role, they tend not to experience conflict between their work and family roles (Arnold 1995; Eccles and Hoffman 1984). But because girls and women are socialized to put family roles first, conflict between work and familial roles is a prominent feature of women's lives (Duxbury and Higgins 1991; Williams 2000). Young women anticipate this career-family conflict long before they experience it firsthand (Shauman 2009). Even career-oriented women may take a contingency approach to planning their future by choosing career paths that they perceive to be compatible with future family roles (Almquist, Angrist, and Mickelsen 1980; Angrist and Almquist 1993). Women are also more likely than men to expect and experience breaks in employment (Felmlee 1993; Okamoto and England 1999) and to change their career plans in response to work-family conflicts (Gerson 1985; Seymour and Hewitt 1997).

However, recent research suggests that gender differences in values have little power to explain gender differences in choice of college major. As Mann and DiPrete (2012) note, values related to career-family conflict have not impeded the trend to full gender equality in law and medical schools, even if gender segregation persists in the choice of specialties within these two professions.[4] In a direct assessment of the role of values in choice of major, Mann and DiPrete used data from HSB, NELS, and ELS to assess the impact of three dimensions of values: aspirations toward having a family, the importance of money and success, and the importance of helping others. They found that students who value the importance of helping others and who have stronger family aspirations are less likely to major in the physical sciences or engineering, while those who value the importance of helping others are more likely to major in the biological sciences. However, these effects were small; they accounted for very little of the gender difference in majoring in STEM versus non-STEM fields and also very little of the gender difference in the distribution of majors within STEM fields.

The "Pipeline"

Much prior research on the underrepresentation of women in science uses a "pipeline" framework, which posits a structured sequence of educational and career stages constituting a science career. This literature examines whether and at what stages education and work environments contribute to the "leaking" of women from science. It concludes that women have higher rates of attrition than men at each stage in the pipeline (Berryman 1983). The popularity of this model has spawned many studies of women science majors and scientists (Long 2001; Seymour and Hewitt 1997; Sonnert 1995; Sonnert, Fox, and Adkins 2007; Schiebinger 1999), but its applicability to the educational life course appears limited.

Xie and Shauman (2003) provide a comprehensive analysis of gender differences in the educational and career trajectories in science and engineering from middle school through adulthood. They used HSB data to examine the educational trajectories leading to a bachelor's degree in a STEM field. In contrast to the "leaky pipeline" paradigm, they found that the two most frequently traveled pathways to a STEM degree are persistence in the trajectory from high school through college and entry from a non-STEM trajectory during college, with females most likely to take the second pathway. They found that nearly half of the gender gap in STEM degree attainment comes from the higher likelihood that males will declare STEM majors in the first two years of high school. Another 28 percent of the gender gap is due to males' higher likelihood of persisting in the STEM trajectory from high school to college. Finally, 28 percent is due to gender differences in expectations for a STEM major while in high school.

Legewie and DiPrete (2012a) reexamined Xie and Shauman's (2003) "pathways" analysis to locate the sources of the gender gap in science majors in terms of earlier expressed preferences and behaviors for a more recent sample of students with NELS data. They generalized Xie and Shauman's approach to account for the evolution of the gender gap in terms of "personal" and "behavioral" orientations to science while in high school. The personal orientation to science was defined in terms of high school seniors' stated plans for their college majors. The behavioral orientation to science was defined in terms of both the courses that students took and their performance in these courses. Legewie and DiPrete found that the pathways to a college degree in a STEM field depend on which of these measures is used as the orientation to STEM. When personal orientation is used, their analysis showed that 57 percent of the gender gap in STEM fields can be traced to personal orientation in high school, a much higher fraction than the 28 percent that was found by Xie and Shauman.[5] Much of the remaining gender difference comes from the greater tendency for males to shift into STEM fields from non-STEM fields. Differences in persistence (the so-called leaky pipeline) account for less than 2 percent of the overall gender gap in STEM majors. The problem is not that the pipeline leaks, but rather that a relatively small fraction of women express an interest in STEM fields (particularly physical science and engineering) while in high school.

In contrast to the results using personal orientation, results using behavioral orientations in high school show that only a modest 14 percent of the gender gap in STEM field majors can be attributed to different behavioral orientations to STEM fields while in high school. Forty-six percent of the gap is attributable to the greater persistence of men from a science-oriented pattern of high school courses to the receipt of a bachelor's degree in a STEM field. The different results when personal as opposed to behavioral orientation is used result from the smaller gender gap in high school course-taking behavior than in high school orientation toward majoring in a STEM field in college.

From a behavioral perspective, high school females have increasingly overtaken males: they passed their male classmates in the average number of science and math credits they took between the early 1980s and the early part of the past decade; they closed much of the gap in math test scores; and they now have higher GPAs in math and science (see figure A.9 and also Freeman 2004; Hyde et al. 2008). Legewie and DiPrete (2012a) found that the gender gap in math and science performance has not closed completely: males have higher math test scores and also take more AP math courses, and their lead is largest in the upper end of the mathematics test score distribution in the education panel data sets. However, as with other studies, both Legewie and DiPrete (2012a) and Mann and DiPrete (2012) found that test performance and course grades account for very little of the stronger male personal orientation toward STEM fields while in high school. Like Shelley Correll (2001), Legewie and DiPrete find that gender differences in self-evaluation of mathematics ability explain part of the gender difference in personal orientation, but their contribution is relatively small. College-oriented high school girls appear to take similar courses as boys, more as a strategy to get into selective colleges than to prepare themselves for a major in a STEM field. To put it another way, the underrepresentation of women in math and science majors and careers cannot be explained by gender differences in aptitude or preparation in math and science.

Orientations toward math and science arguably arise from the influence of gender stereotypes on emerging gender identity and the activities and attitudes associated with these stereotypes. Boys have higher self-efficacy in math by early elementary school (Eccles et al. 1993; Jacobs et al. 2002), and according to Jaap Denissen and his colleagues (2007), interest in science and math correlates positively with self-perceived ability. Other studies demonstrate that children as early as second grade associate being male with "liking math" (Cvencek, Meltzoff, and Green-wald 2011) and that children ages six to ten are aware of the gendered character of occupations (Martin, Wood, and Little 1990; Liben, Bigler, and Krogh 2001). At the same time, in elementary school girls express higher values for the task of doing math than do boys (Eccles et al. 1993; Jacobs et al. 2002).

Gender stereotypes regarding interest in math and science undoubt-edly come from the environment. For example, Janis Jacobs and Martha Bleeker (2004) found that children get gendered cues about math and science from their parents, who appear to spend more time on math ac-tivities with sons than with daughters. The extent to which these stereo-types control behavior at the individual level is less clear, as is whether mathematically talented girls maintain a consistent deficit in their self-concept of math ability relative to similarly talented boys through ele-mentary, middle, and high school. The relationship between self-ex-pressed interest in math and reading and subsequent choice of a college major is also unclear. Therefore, we do not know when during child-hood STEM orientations typically stabilize and produce long-term im-plications for academic degrees and occupational choices.

To answer this question, Legewie and DiPrete (2012a) carried out an investigation of the link between orientation toward mathematics in eighth grade and orientation toward a STEM major in twelfth grade. Eighth-graders in NELS were asked a number of questions about their attitudes toward math and science classes, including whether they usu-ally looked forward to these classes, whether they were often afraid to ask questions in these classes, and whether they thought that math and science would be useful in their future. They were also asked about their occupational expectations using about fifteen categories that included "science/engineering professional." Legewie and DiPrete used this in-formation, along with other background variables, in an attempt to ex-plain the gender gap in expressed intention to major in a STEM field in college. There is a strong association between students' expressed inten-tions in eighth grade to become a "science/engineering professional" and their choice of intended major in twelfth grade. However, eighth-grade science orientation explains only a small fraction of the gender difference in STEM degrees. Indeed, if the pathways through high school and college were simulated under the assumption that boys and girls have identical science orientations in eighth grade, the gender gap in STEM bachelor's degrees would be reduced by only about 10 percent. Attitudes and plans concerning a college major are largely formed in the high school years, and secondarily during college. Legewie and DiPrete showed that the gender gap in STEM degrees would be reduced by over two-thirds if females and males had the same science orientation at the end of high school. Their results suggest that the experiences between eighth grade and the end of high school are decisive in the formation of a science orientation. Their results also imply that females' orientations tend to become more "fixed" during high school than males' orientations. It is relatively common for males to transition into a STEM orientation from an earlier non-STEM orientation after high school. Females, in contrast, are much less likely to make this switch. Those who have asserted a STEM orientation in high school were just as likely as males to maintain this orientation through to a bachelor's degree. But females who had not expressed such a personal science orientation were much less likely than males to transition into such an orientation during college.

Finally, it is noteworthy that women have gradually increased their relative proportions in the biological sciences; this change, along with the overall rising trend of women's college enrollments, has greatly increased the absolute number of women majoring in these areas. Mann and DiPrete (2012) showed that the failure to close the gender gap in the physical science and engineering fields in recent years arises more from the different within-STEM choices of major that male and female STEM majors make than it does from women's reluctance to major in a STEM field per se.

The Impact of School Environments

In earlier chapters, we stressed the importance of the school environment in maintaining a gender gap in educational achievement. The school environment is also important in maintaining a gender gap in choice of college major. Legewie and DiPrete (2012a) estimated the impact of the local school environment on the formation of a STEM orientation by taking advantage of the clustered design of NELS at the high school level. NCES followed over 13,000 eighth-grade students through twelfth grade in over 1,200 high schools, with an average of about 10 students per high school. NCES then enriched the sample with about 250 high schools in order to allow a more detailed study of the role of high school characteristics in the educational process. This "high school effectiveness" study included about 9,100 students, with an average of about 37 students per high school. The high school effectiveness study data allow for a more precise school-specific estimate of the impact of high school on the formation of STEM orientations.[6]

Legewie and DiPrete (2012a) found strong evidence that high school environments play an important role in the STEM orientations of students during the adolescent years, when these orientations are most likely to form, even net of controls for middle school achievement and orientations. As they predicted, the effects of the local environment are stronger for girls than for boys. Generally speaking, a science-intensive school environment stimulates interest in science. Interestingly, however, it also reduces the power of gender stereotypes concerning STEM fields, because girls are more strongly influenced by science-intensive environments than boys are. Local environmental effects are quite strong: if the impact on STEM orientations of the top third of high schools were extended to the rest of the high schools, the size of the STEM gap in bachelor's degrees would be reduced by 25 percent. These effects are durable in the sense that leakage rates out of science are no greater for students who go to high schools with strong STEM effects than for students in the schools with weak STEM effects. Other specific factors that create a supportive environment for female interest in STEM remain to be uncovered.

Legewie and DiPrete's (2012a) results reported in chapter 7 show that boys especially benefit from schools with intense academic orientations. Their results about STEM orientations parallel the earlier results in finding that girls especially benefit from schools with more intense science curricula. In both cases, one gender is negatively affected by gender stereotypes. These stereotypes reduce academic achievement for elementary school boys and reduce the appeal of majoring in science and mathematics for high school girls. Their analyses showed that environments that reduce the power of stereotypes tend to benefit the disadvantaged group.

Gender Segregation in Fields of Study and College Completion

Since at least the 1970s, the grading curves have differed between science, social science, and humanities majors at most four-year colleges. Given that women are less likely to major in fields that give lower grades, it is reasonable to ask whether some fraction of their higher rates of college completion is related to gender segregation in college majors. The general consensus is that gender segregation of majors is not the cause of the gender gap in rates of college completion.

Buchmann and DiPrete (2006) examined this question in some detail using data from NELS. Table 8.1 shows the impact of large sets of covariates on the female effect on the probability of college completion. The large female advantage in college completion is reduced, but remains large, when college attributes (type, selectivity, and major) are included in model 2. When college GPA is added to model 3, however, essentially all of the completion gap is eliminated for whites. Table 8.1 suggests that blacks differ from whites in that a smaller proportion of the female advantage comes from gender differences in performance (19 and 48 percent, respectively). For blacks, more of the female advantage appears to be linked with gender differences in type of college and college major

Table 8.1   Logistic Regression Coefficients for College Completion

	Model 1	Model 2	Model 3	Model 4
Main effect of female				
Whites and blacks	0.479**	0.335**	0.025	−0.005
Whites only	0.419**	0.295*	−0.046	−0.075
Blacks only	1.105**	0.507	0.319	0.303
Included covariates				
Social background	Yes	Yes	Yes	Yes
College attributes		Yes	Yes	Yes
College GPA			Yes	Yes
College GPA × major				Yes

Source: Authors' compilation based on Buchmann and DiPrete (2006).
Notes: Social background covariates include mother some college, father some college, father present; college attribute covariates include college type, selectivity, and major. Data are from NELS, 1988 to 2000 (National Center for Education Statistics 2003).
* $p \leq 0.05$; ** $p \leq 0.01$ (two-tailed tests)

selected, and a relatively large fraction of the female advantage in college completion rates is unexplained by college attributes or GPA. The more complex story for black students could be a consequence of the smaller sample size for blacks in the NELS. More research is needed to establish how the female advantage arises during college for nonwhite students.

More recently, Sigal Alon and Dafna Gelbgiser (2011) examined the impact of college major on college graduation rates using a sample of selective colleges (the College and Beyond data) and a large nationally representative study (the Beginning Postsecondary Study). Like Buchmann and DiPrete (2006), they found a significant gender gap in six-year graduation rates, and also like Buchmann and DiPrete, they found that the female advantage declines but is not eliminated when college major is controlled for in the model. Our conclusion is that gender segregation by major explains a relatively small fraction of the gender advantage in rates of college completion.

The Consequences of Gender Segregation

The research discussed in this chapter locates the primary source of gender differences in STEM majors in the high school years and secondarily in the transition to college or the transition from middle school to high school. Legewie and DiPrete's (2012a) results show that the STEM pipeline is not leaky when the pipeline is defined in terms of students' stated personal orientations and when attention is focused on the period leading up to the bachelor's degree. Process aside, however, gender segregation in fields of study has consequences for adult lives. Studies differ widely in the amount of the gender gap in wages they attribute to gender segregation of majors. Brown and Corcoran (1997), for example, found that college major accounts for between 20 and 30 percent of the wage gap between male and female college graduates, with much of this effect directly related to gender differences in the characteristics of the jobs of college graduates. Weinberger (1998) found that 20 percent of the black gender wage gap and about 40 percent of the white gender wage gap can be explained by college major, while Joy (2002) found that college major explains 27 percent of the wage gap. Meanwhile, Donna Bobbitt-Zeher (2007) found that 14 percent of the wage gap in the early career is attributable to college major. The models employed, the data sets, the time period, the age range, and the covered population differ among these studies,[7] but they all support the conclusion that horizontal stratification in education is an important phenomenon that offsets to some extent the advantage that women have obtained in their quantitative advancement in postsecondary education (Gerber and Schaefer 2004). Gender differences in the returns to majors must also be considered. For example, Linda Datcher Loury (1997) found that the gender gap in wage returns to specific fields such as business narrowed in the 1980s at the same time that women were increasing their share of graduates with a business degree.

Conclusion

Despite the tremendous increase in women's college enrollment and degree completion, gender segregation in college majors has not changed much in recent decades. Women continue to lag far behind men in engineering and physical science degrees even as they have achieved parity or an advantage in elite fields such as medicine, law, and the biological and life sciences. This chapter reported on trends in both bachelor's and advanced degrees using survey and administrative data from the National Center for Education Statistics and other sources. It evaluated the dominant theories that have been proposed to account for the gender gap in fields of study and finds that neither gender differences in mathematical skills nor gender differences in values concerning career and family provide comprehensive explanations. One important source, we argue, is the impact of the local environment on the development of stereotypes concerning gender and STEM fields during middle and high school.

Recent research demonstrates that college-bound girls largely form their orientations toward physical science, engineering, or mathematical fields of study by the end of high school. Girls who have signaled an intention to major in one of these fields by this point are just as likely as boys to graduate from college with a STEM degree. But girls are much less likely than boys to enter these fields in college if they have not already declared an interest in STEM by high school. In contrast, the orientations that girls and boys express toward the sciences while in middle school are only moderately predictive of the orientations they will express at the end of high school. It follows that the high school years are a very important period for the formation of a science or nonscience orientation by girls in particular. School environments differ in the extent to which they support the notion of STEM fields as attractive choices for women. Some schools may do an especially good job of eroding common stereotypes that link majoring in a STEM field with a masculine identity. Recent evidence suggests that schools with strong science and math curricula are particularly good at delinking STEM fields from masculine stereotypes.

Chapter 9

Enhancing Educational Attainment

THE GENDER reversal in educational attainment occurred during a period of history when a rising value of education coincided with a cultural transformation in gender roles. Profound shifts in gender attitudes during the 1960s and 1970s and declining discrimination against women produced strong incentives for them to get more education, and women responded to these incentives by completing ever-higher rates of college. Their rates of college completion surpassed those of men in the 1980s, and the female-favorable advantage in college completion grew even larger in the first decade of the twenty-first century. Changes in the labor market have enhanced the economic value of professional and managerial jobs and reduced economic opportunities for well-paid, blue-collar jobs. These changes have heightened Americans' anxiety about the need for more education in order to improve economic growth and global competitiveness, to strengthen America's middle class, and to sustain opportunities for upward mobility in a nation traditionally believed to offer widespread possibilities for material and cultural success. Aside from its considerable historical importance, the gender reversal in higher education offers insights into the nature of educational problems in the United States and suggests policies to counteract these problems.

A full understanding of the growing female advantage in educational attainment requires examination of the performance distributions of girls and boys at all stages of the educational life course as well as attention to the heterogeneity in mean academic differences across age groups, family situations, and schools. Understanding the sources of this heterogeneity provides insights into how to raise educational attainment in the United States via strategies that raise male academic performance without impeding the performance of females. Despite the similar ability distribution of boys and girls, educational gains for boys have been relatively stagnant for several decades. The male college completion deficit is certainly not the only educational problem facing the United

States. But policies to reduce the male disadvantage in college completion should benefit other students as well as expand the population of college graduates. Policies that target boys' educational deficits should be fruitful for both aiding boys in particular and raising college completion more generally.

Part I of this book examined the forces in the broader environment that have shaped the reversal of the gender gap in college completion from a male advantage to a female advantage. As labor market opportunities for women expanded during the twentieth century, their incentives to complete a college degree grew rapidly. Changes in marriage patterns, the rise in family instability, and the educational incentives for both males and females that emerged as a consequence of these changes also played a role. At the same time, we argued, changes in educational incentives alone did not produce the reversal of the gender gap in college completion. The female advantage emerged out of the *combination* of a persisting latent advantage in academic performance and the development of a more egalitarian society that raised the incentive for girls to obtain higher education.

In parts II and III, we examined the educational life course and its interaction with the local as well as the global environment. Our empirical findings in combination with other research culminate in seven stylized facts that provide an understanding of the male disadvantage in educational attainment and a sound foundation on which to develop policy interventions.

First, the distributions of male and female performance and attainment overlap substantially, and the ranges of academic performance within each gender are larger than those between males and females. That said, today in the United States and many other industrialized countries there exists a notable female-favorable gender gap in educational performance and attainment.

Second, the female advantage is cumulative over the educational life course. Elementary school girls generally perform better than boys in reading and get about the same evaluations from teachers in math, even though their test scores are somewhat lower on average. Girls continue to get higher grades in middle school, high school, and college. Their academic performance at each of these levels is better than one would predict solely from information about performance at earlier ages.

Third, boys on average do not put as much effort into their school work as do girls. This fact is reflected in self-reports and teacher reports about boys' level of interest, commitment, and attachment to school.

Fourth, part of the male disadvantage appears to be attributable to non-academic behaviors across a number of dimensions. The average male deficit in social and behavioral skills appears to produce males' lower educational performance and lower rates of learning.

Fifth, boys who live in households with highly educated parents and a biological father in the home gain important benefits in academically relevant social and behavioral skills and academic performance per se. In middle school, boys with highly educated fathers gain a gender-specific advantage in performance, but they do not gain a gender-specific advantage in reported attachment to school beyond that which comes from higher academic performance.[1]

Sixth, boys who regularly engage in extracurricular cultural activities such as music, art, drama, and foreign languages tend to have higher attachment to school than boys who do not engage in such activities. Not coincidentally, these activities are often denigrated as unmasculine by preadolescent and adolescent boys, especially those from working- or lower-class backgrounds.

Seventh, both boys and girls benefit from the presence of a strong academic climate at home and in school. However, low-performing students in general and boys in particular receive especially large benefits because a strong academic climate tends to erode stereotypes and weaken the disconnection between academic prowess and a healthy, multifaceted masculine identity. The ability of the school environment to erode gender stereotypes may also explain why high school girls are more likely to develop a positive orientation toward STEM fields in some high schools, especially those with strong science curricula, than in others.

These stylized facts suggest several important conclusions about the connection between gender and education. The first concerns where in the life course interventions are most appropriate; we conclude that, because much of the gender gap in college completion stems from a gender gap in educational achievement that is readily visible early on, policies intended to close the achievement gap should target elementary and middle school students. Although policies directed at high school and college students may be effective at raising college completion rates, such policies cannot replace interventions at earlier ages.

A second conclusion is that the gender gap in performance is partly sociocultural in origin and thus amenable to appropriate interventions. Elementary school and middle school boys may have high educational aspirations, but many boys—even those from high-socioeconomic backgrounds—may feel a conflict between their emerging masculine identity and a strongly expressed identification with school. Boys' lack of expressive attachment to school is accompanied by lower levels of effort relative to girls, as measured by teachers' ratings and student self-reports. At the same time, sons of highly educated parents often manage to form what we have termed an instrumental attachment to school, which enables them to perform well academically even when their expressive attachment to school is weak.

How do some boys manage to perform well in school, regardless of whether they express strong attachment to school or display emotional coolness toward school, while still others perform below their potential because of a lack of attachment to school? To answer this question, we must appreciate that the preadolescent and adolescent culture presents boys with multiple models of masculinity and boys use various strategies to deal with these sometimes competing conceptions of masculinity. The oppositional culture, which is often characterized as "hegemonic masculinity," depicts identification with school and willingness to work hard for good grades as unmasculine. Indeed, most boys, including those who perform well in school, sometimes pay superficial allegiance to oppositional hegemonic masculine values. Only a small minority of boys in middle and high school appear to repudiate the prescriptions of hegemonic masculinity by wholeheartedly pursuing high-culture interests.

At the same time, some boys, especially sons of managerial and professional fathers, appear to have internalized an alternative, more adult conception of masculinity that is better aligned with material success in contemporary industrialized societies. By internalizing this alternative conception of masculinity, boys can access a motivational framework to do well in school even as they accommodate adolescent cultural scripts for masculinity in other domains. For these boys, masculine identity is expressed not only through interest in sports or efforts at physical dominance but also through academic activities that lead to power and success via a high-status occupation and reasonably high income. During adolescence, they gain this understanding implicitly or explicitly from their fathers who have used their education to gain such positions. Masculinity is also connected to sexual power as represented by one's ability to attract romantic partners. In adolescent culture, such ability is enhanced by being popular and athletic, but sons of highly educated fathers may perceive that in the adult world potential romantic partners are attracted to successful men. For these boys, high performance in school is not inconsistent with their developing masculine identity.

These boys are also likely to appreciate a fact that is underappreciated by many of their peers: success in academics, like success in sports, requires a considerable investment of time and effort. The more you practice, the better you become. That boys in general do not appreciate this fact is readily apparent in the disconnect between the relatively low grades and the very high educational aspirations of the "middle third" of the boys in the academic hierarchy who expect to complete college but are unlikely to fulfill their expectations. They seem not to understand the low probability of completing four-year college (as distinct from enrolling in college) if they have attained only B's and C's in middle school. They do not seem to understand how hard it is to successfully raise one's performance standard later. Nor do they understand that their likelihood of attaining a college degree would be markedly enhanced by a serious commitment to school work even as early as elementary and middle school.

Middle school girls likewise do not fully understand the connection between performance and educational attainment. After all, they overpredict their educational attainment to about the same extent as do boys. But even if their lack of understanding is as large as boys' (which we doubt), it is arguably less consequential because of girls' greater expressive attachment to school. This attachment seems to arise more readily through the gratification they get from close relationships with their teachers and the greater satisfaction they get from pleasing their parents. In other words, girls may work harder in school because they receive greater intrinsic satisfaction from high academic performance than do boys.

To repeat, there are multiple models for masculinity in the preadolescent or adolescent culture. Some peer groups strongly value popularity rooted in opposition to authority; others value athletic prowess, others value displays of wealth, and still others value academic performance. Adolescents generally orient their behavior toward the reward system of their peers, and as a result, they generally invest more energy in academic performance when their peer group rewards such behavior. Boys appear to benefit even more than girls from academically oriented peers. The most plausible reason for this advantage is that academically oriented peers blunt the value of masculine identities that oppose school and interfere with school performance.

Americans in general are conditioned to view the education system as a "meritocratic" contest in which the best positions go to the graduates who "merit" them. Parents in the upper-middle class often seem especially competitive; in the guise of helicopter parents and "Tiger Moms," some of these parents push, monitor, and motivate their children toward success. American adolescents aiming for admission into Ivy League colleges and universities know full well that they are engaged in a contest from their early teens. Other adolescents, in contrast, appear to see school as a series of disconnected contests that is replete with second chances well into adulthood. In reality, outside of elite colleges and universities, American higher education is less a contest for a few coveted prizes than a certification process with minimum performance standards. Those who meet the standard can graduate with a bachelor's degree and a satisfactory transcript. Meeting this standard requires training and effort. Like any performance standard, the higher education standard takes less effort to achieve the better one is trained. Students entering college with a history of mediocre academic achievement do indeed have a second chance, but they are less likely to meet the performance standard and graduate than others who started school with the same cognitive ability but who have a long history of high academic engagement. The effort required to overcome their poor training is likely to be substantial, and as anyone knows who tries a sport they are not trained for, even substantial effort may produce mediocre results, which produces frustration and a higher probability of dropping out before graduation.

In addition to attaining a threshold of academic performance, completing college requires financial resources. Students need access to financial support from family, work, and grants or scholarships, but increasingly students need to be willing to take on debt in order to attain this performance standard for enough semesters to finish a degree. American college students must shoulder a double burden of high college expenses coupled with highly unequal access to the resources to pay these expenses. Although the variation in students' ability to shoulder the financial burden of college does not privilege one gender relative to the other, the financial burden could still have gender-specific consequences because, like the academic performance standard, it represents another hurdle that students must clear in order to earn a college degree. Males and females may differ in their motivation to clear this hurdle, just as they vary in the skill sets that make meeting the higher education performance standard easier or more difficult.

We distinguish motivation from skill not to make a point about the psychology of motivation, but to return to a theme raised in the introduction of this book. Because completing college requires both effort and financial resources, students need motivation to expend both of these resources, especially if they do not gain strong intrinsic satisfaction from academic work. Research on the returns to a college degree suggest that males have the same average expected rate of return to a college degree as do females, but knowledge of average returns to a college degree may not mean much for students who do not understand their own personal long-term returns to completing college versus the benefits of immediate employment without a degree. While the work of Attewell and Lavin (2007), Maurin and McNally (2008), and Brand and Xie (2010) suggests that marginal students can gain considerable benefit from college, there is great uncertainty as to how large these benefits are, to say nothing about the variation in effect size by student.[2] Because of continuing occupational sex segregation, young men and women have different labor market opportunities. Men clearly overestimate their chances relative to women for material success, even when they lack a four-year college degree (DiPrete 2007). But how much men underestimate their personal return to college (that is, the return they would get given their grades in college, their major, and their knowledge of how to use college to achieve their labor market and other goals) relative to women is an open question.

Academic performance and knowledge about pathways from schooling to careers are characteristics of individuals, but they are also products of educational institutions. We know little about the extent to which an individual's "returns to education" can be enhanced through greater knowledge about the workplace or different curricular choices while in school. We also know little about the extent to which educational institutions can enhance knowledge, affect curricular choices by improving guidance services, and offer alternative curricular paths to a degree. It is possible that the male performance deficit is entirely to blame for the gender gap in college completion. However, it is also possible that males are less likely than females to see viable routes to a college degree that lead to better opportunities than those available without a degree. Males may be more likely than females to lack good information about the job market, to underestimate the value of college, and to overestimate their labor market chances without a college degree.

Barbara Schneider and David Stevenson (2000, 79) have written about the importance of adolescents having "aligned ambitions," by which they mean "knowledge of what type of job they want and how much education is needed for it." Clear occupational goals and knowledge of the educational pathways that lead to them can be important motivators for educational investments. On the other hand, the perceived need for aligned ambitions can be an inhibiting factor for students who feel that they must have concrete occupational goals before they make a significant investment in college. Sometimes academically talented high school students from working-class, minority, or immigrant families are reluctant to enroll in college unless they have very clear occupational goals (Roderick et al. 2008). In contrast, many upper-middle-class students have what Eric Grodsky and Catherine Riegle-Crumb (2010) call a "college-going *habitus*," meaning that they expected to attain a college degree long before they formulated specific occupational plans. Students with a college-going habitus aspire not to a specific occupation, but rather to a particular class position that demands a college education; for such students, the details for attaining this position can be left for later. The difference between working- and middle-class orientations may lie in large part in the visibility of alternative routes through college and the awareness of the occupational opportunities they offer in comparison with pathways offered by lower levels of educational attainment.

This "visibility" problem may have especially detrimental consequences for young men, who may overestimate the opportunity for good blue-collar and skilled trade jobs and the opportunity to transition from such jobs to successful small businesses, just as boys overestimate the odds of becoming a professional athlete or a rock star and the odds of becoming "rich" during their working lives. If students were provided with more detailed information in middle and high school, they could gain greater understanding of the alternative routes to a college degree. Such information would benefit all students, but might be especially valuable for males. When schools clarify the occupational returns to educational investments, they provide further incentives to academically capable students from the middle third   who would benefit from college but may not fully understand the size of these benefits—to increase their efforts.

Another policy-relevant finding from our work is that socioeconomically enriched environments at home and in school strengthen students' academic orientations. Even though we see multiplier effects from exposing students to culturally enriched peer environments, there are practical limits to any such policy, since socioeconomic resources such as highly educated parents and high-SES peers are in limited supply. We must therefore find other means to foster stronger academic orientations among students in order to increase both their academic efforts and the quality of instruction they receive. Ideally, schools should enhance students' understanding of the labor market value of schooling while simultaneously helping them understand how future performance and success are enhanced by greater effort today. One important means to this end is to clarify the instrumental value of schooling for students' longer-term socioeconomic goals. Too many adolescents have lofty educational aspirations that they are unlikely to attain if they maintain low levels of effort in school. These are the adolescents who are getting B's and C's in middle school. Their relatively strong performance on standardized tests suggests that many of these students, especially boys, could improve their grades even by only modestly increasing their efforts. As a group, these students do not fully appreciate the link between practice (academic effort), proficiency (good performance in classes), and educational attainment. The fact that many universities have low entrance requirements is one source of confusion, which is compounded by a lack of appreciation of how skill enhancement comes primarily from practice rather than from "cognitive ability." This confusion exists for both males and females, but it appears to have greater negative consequences for boys because they lag behind girls in the day-to-day development of the academic and organizational skills that make it easier to get through college.

Students' confusion regarding the strong relationship between practice and school performance is exemplified in research based on student interviews by Andrea Venezia and her colleagues (2003), who find that students underestimate the difficulty of completing college once they are admitted. Schools themselves perpetuate students' confusion by using multiple assessments with different formats, content, and standards in elementary and secondary schools. Venezia and her colleagues argue that this multitude of different assessments creates variance in expectations about what students need to know in order to succeed in college. They urge school reforms that would provide students with accurate, high-quality information from teachers, guidance counselors, and colleges about courses that will help prepare them for college-level standards, and they urge greater access to such college prep courses for high school students. To provide clearer signals and incentives for students, they urge a greater alignment between K-12 exit-level standards and assessments, on the one hand, and postsecondary education standards and assessments, on the other.[3]

Researchers from the Consortium on Chicago School Research (Roderick et al. 2008) and William Bowen and his colleagues (2009) advance similar policy prescriptions. Their analysis of "undermatching" (students with high GPAs or test scores attending less selective institutions than they are capable of being admitted to) suggests that, in addition to having fewer financial resources, low-income and minority students have less information about higher education and do not understand how to navigate the college application process. Roderick and her colleagues (2008) find that undermatching and lower rates of timely college enrollment are more common in high schools with weak academic climates. For these researchers, the primary solution to these problems is to improve the academic climate of schools. They argue that successful schools have three important characteristics. First, they provide one-on-one interaction between students and their counselors and teachers. Second, successful schools engage in extensive college preparatory programming through college fairs, SAT/ACT preparatory classes, visits to colleges, and other related activities. Third, they have student cultures that encourage "peer-to-peer networking," meaning that students pass information about the college application process to each other.

The reforms advocated by Roderick and her colleagues (2008) might also reduce the gender gap in college enrollment. Recall from chapter 7 that the socioeconomic composition of the classroom particularly benefits boys' academic achievement. Although Roderick and her colleagues focus on the academic climate of high schools, in our view, improving the academic climate of middle schools would by itself raise the academic climate of high schools, since foundations in the academic orientations and work habits needed for completing college are laid in middle school. Both Roderick et al. (2008) and Bowen et al. (2009) emphasize knowledge deficits about the college admissions process, an issue that comes to the fore during high school. We argue that there is a need to address a second knowledge gap about the level of self-organization, effort, and performance required in middle and high school to be ready for the rigors of college. This second knowledge gap arguably has a greater impact on boys because they experience less immediate gratification from academic performance than do girls.

Books such as *Learning to Labor* (Willis 1981) and *Ain't No Makin' It* (MacLeod 2008) have argued that working-class kids act rationally when they tune out of school because they cannot compete successfully with middle-class children for the degrees that lead to professional and managerial jobs. But the fact that working-class girls manage to obtain bachelor's degrees at higher rates than boys contradicts this logic. Children in the middle third of the socioeconomic distribution do not come from families with extreme human capital deficits. Moderate increases in effort among these students could have considerable payoff in terms of educational attainment. Strategies that increase both student effort and teaching and guidance counseling should be especially effective with these "middle-third" students, even as they also benefit students from disadvantaged families. This is not to say that the road to a college degree is wide open for Americans. After all, ours is a nation where people who live in near poverty or below constitute about one-third of the population by some measures (Short 2011), while college costs continue to rise (Desrochers and Wellman 2011). However, because college completion depends substantially on academic performance as well as on financial resources, both policies that raise academic performance and policies that lower the financial costs of college should be pursued.

The male deficit in college completion points to four policy strategies to raise boys' achievement and attainment while also benefiting girls. First, improve students' academic performance by raising the quality of their education. Second, increase student willingness to invest more time and energy in learning by increasing the short-term rewards they get from peers, teachers, and parents for these investments. Third, provide students with a better understanding of the long-term payoffs of their learning investments in terms of better academic performance in college and greater chances of completing a college degree. Fourth, and finally, help students understand the value of specific skills and credentials in the labor market so that they can confidently plot a course of higher education that ensures that their investments will lead to career opportunities. Students already have high educational aspirations, but they underinvest in developing their educational skills because they do not receive immediate rewards for high academic performance and they do not understand the longer-term payoffs to developing these educational skills in middle and high school.

A key ingredient in this formula is improving the academic climate in schools. As we have already noted, the most obvious source of a strong academic climate is a classroom with students of high socioeconomic background. But because high-SES students are in limited supply and increasingly segregated from other students (Reardon and Bischoff 2011), schools need alternative strategies to increase the appeal of academics and the goal of high academic achievement in the adolescent culture. Middle school students' high educational aspirations suggest that schools do not need to increase the appeal of high educational attainment, but rather to increase educational quality while at the same time motivating students to invest more in order to achieve their goals.

Ever since the highly influential government report *A Nation at Risk* was published in 1983, one oft-touted strategy to build strong academic climates in schools has been to increase the rigor of the curriculum. *The Nation at Risk* emphasized "the [five] new basics" of English, mathematics, science, social studies, and computer science. Evidence from Pallas and Alexander (1983) and Alexander and Pallas (1984) showed that students who complete a more rigorous curriculum generally do better on standardized tests in those subject areas. Specifically, the female deficit in mathematics performance on the SAT is partly due to deficits in the high school mathematics curricula of girls. At the same time, Alexander and Pallas (1984) argued that the academic benefits of taking more rigorous high school courses are largely limited to those who do well in these courses. Although Attewell and Domina (2008) do not address the performance issue, they found that, net of sociodemographic measures, high school seniors in the top quintile in academic intensity perform better on standardized tests like the SAT than do students in the bottom quintile. All these analyses suffer from potential selection biases; for example, they beg the question of whether these students perform better because they take more rigorous courses, or whether they perform better because they have been better students from the outset. Nonetheless, these analyses suggest the possibility that a more rigorous curriculum achieves both greater rates of learning and greater student effort to learn. *A Nation at Risk* largely advocated curricular reform in high schools. Our work suggests that curricular reform is also needed in elementary and middle school.

Aside from better teaching and a more rigorous curriculum, schools could help overcome the information gap that is reflected in the extremely high educational aspirations of middle school and high school students. One problem in calibrating students' understanding of the effort required to complete college may be the problem of relative performance. In the American educational system, where large numbers of students do not graduate from high school within four years, students performing in the middle of the distribution may believe that they are doing well enough in school to achieve their goals. They know that, even if they are not at the top of the academic distribution, they are doing better than many other students. They will certainly graduate from high school and can enroll in community college or a less-selective four-year college. What they do not understand is the level of performance, the curriculum choices, and the other preparations required to increase their chances of completing a college degree.

A useful analogy can be made between educational performance behaviors and behaviors related to health. A large and growing literature examines why socioeconomic status and education are "fundamental causes" of one's own health (Link and Phelan 1995) and also the health of one's children (Elo 2009). One mechanism producing this connection appears to be knowledge about the health consequences of specific behaviors and "learned effectiveness" at applying this knowledge in the service of good health (Mirowsky and Ross 2003). Studies of the rapid reduction in smoking by more-educated women in response to information about the connection between smoking and lung cancer (Aizer and Stroud 2010) or cross-sectional studies of the relationship between education and treatment compliance among HIV-positive patients (Goldman and Smith 2002) are examples. At the same time, the discipline and motivation needed to apply this knowledge in the service of healthful behavior also play central roles.[4] In the case of schooling, it is no secret that greater effort produces higher grades. But very few students know the extent to which college completion in general depends on academic performance. They have only hazy knowledge about fields of study and their connection to the labor market. The analogy with health behaviors extends past the impact of one's own knowledge about cause and effect; "learned effectiveness" in academic behavior also requires discipline and social support. Knowledge can enhance motivation and discipline, but social support remains a necessary ingredient. In the case of male educational performance, the social support goes beyond discipline to allow for forms of masculinity that align positive educational behaviors with peer expectations and rewards. This support can come from parents (especially fathers) and peers, and it is probably the strongest when it comes from multiple sources.

For much of the twentieth century, white ethnic immigrants successfully encouraged their sons to accomplish more than their fathers, in order not only to fulfill their fathers' ambitions for them but also, in the process, to become successful men themselves. That pattern of generational progress began to falter for American males in the 1970s. Conversely, girls once linked the ideal of middle-class adult femininity with dating, courtship, and marriage followed by suburban living, child-rearing, and civic engagement through volunteer activities. Today's girls also connect a feminine identity with a career and see college and advanced degrees as the route to a better career. Boys almost seem weighed down by the lingering intergenerational memory of (white male) working-class affluence, which colors their conception of masculinity as well as their concrete strategies to transition into adulthood. There was no comparable intergenerational inertia for girls who adapted their conceptions of femininity to include both career and family.

Getting both boys and girls through four-year college is not the be-all and end-all educational policy. We agree with Rosenbaum (2001) that college is not the right goal for all students. For students struggling academically in middle and high school, a more appropriate policy is to ensure that they complete high school and then follow clear alternative pathways to good jobs. But raising college completion rates among the "middle third" of American students, most of whom are college-capable and already enroll in college in large numbers, is a laudable policy goal. These students do not enter the workforce with the skill levels that they could have achieved to enable them to obtain better and higher-paying jobs. It is the situation of these students that we seek to improve.

Appendix A: Figures and Tables

Figure A.1 Number of Master's Degrees Conferred by Gender, 1969–1970 to 2009–2010

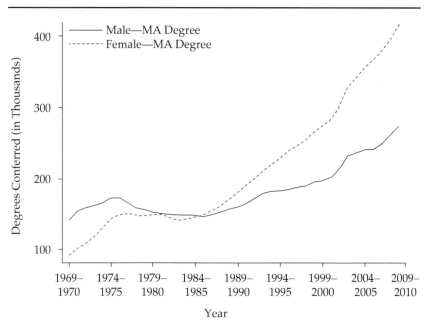

Source: Authors' compilation based on Snyder and Dillow (2012).

Figure A.2   Number of Doctoral and Professional Degrees Conferred by Gender, 1969–1970 to 2009–2010

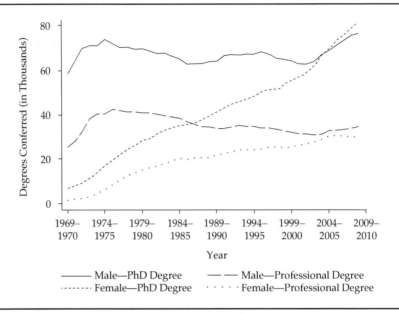

Source: Authors' compilation based on Snyder and Dillow (2012).

Figure A.3   The Effect of a Bachelor's Degree on Earnings for Thirty- to Thirty-Four-Year-Old Whites Working Full-Time/Full-Year, 1960 to 2000

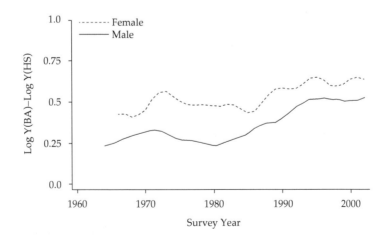

Source: DiPrete and Buchmann (2006).
Note: Log Y(BA) – Log Y(HS) = Log earnings given BA or more minus Log earnings given high school completion.

Figure A.4   Female/Male Odds Ratio of Bachelor's Degree Completion for Blacks Age Twenty-Five to Twenty-Eight, by Birth Year

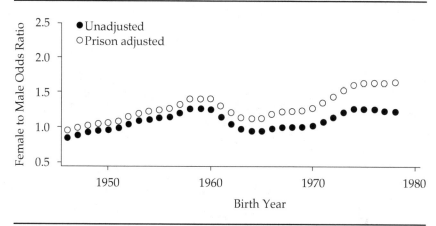

Source: McDaniel et al. (2011).
Note: Values are mean and median smoothed.

Figure A.5   Trends in Male-Female NAEP Reading Scores, Age Nine, 1971 to 2008

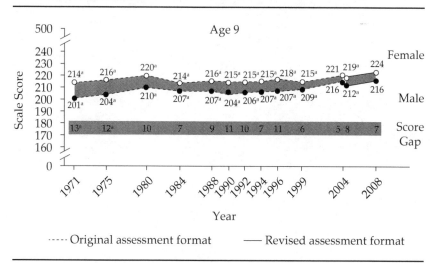

Source: Rampey et al. (2009).
[a]Significantly different (*p* < 0.05) from 2008.

Figure A.6   Trends in Male-Female NAEP Reading Scores, Ages Thirteen and Seventeen, 1971 to 2008

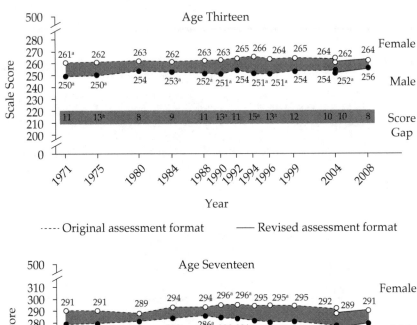

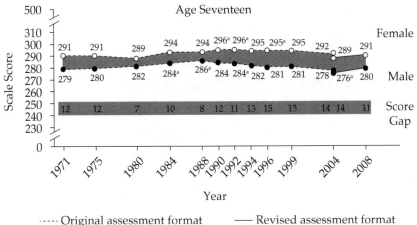

Source: Rampey et al. (2009).
Note: Score gaps are calculated based on differences between unrounded average scores.
[a]Significantly different (*p* < 0.05) from 2008.

Figure A.7   Trends in Male-Female NAEP Math Scores, Age Nine, 1973 to 2008

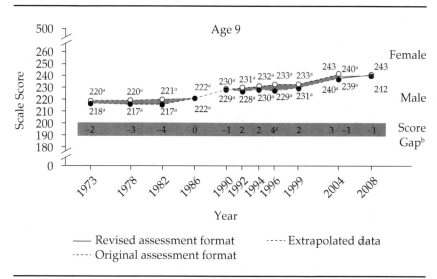

Source: Rampey et al. (2009).
Notes: Data for the years 1973 and 1978 are extrapolated. Top line indicates female scores for all years except for the years 1990–2004, when male scores are indicated by the top line.
[a]Significantly different ($p < 0.05$) from 2008.
[b]Rounds to zero.

Figure A.8   Trends in Male and Female NAEP Math Scores, Ages Thirteen and Seventeen

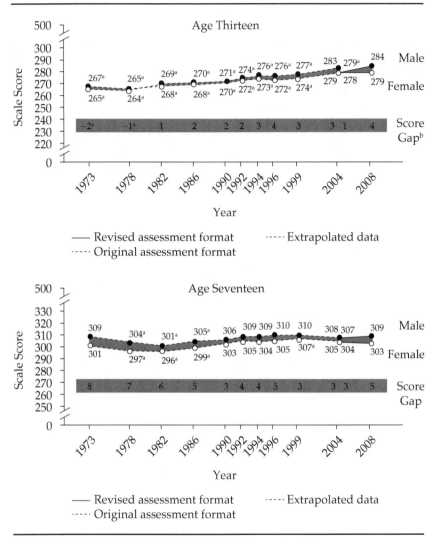

Source: Rampey et al. (2009).
Note: Score gaps are calculated based on differences between unrounded average scores.
[a]Significantly different ($p < 0.05$) from 2008.
[b]Rounds to zero.

Figure A.9   Course-Taking in High School for High School Seniors, 1972 to 2004

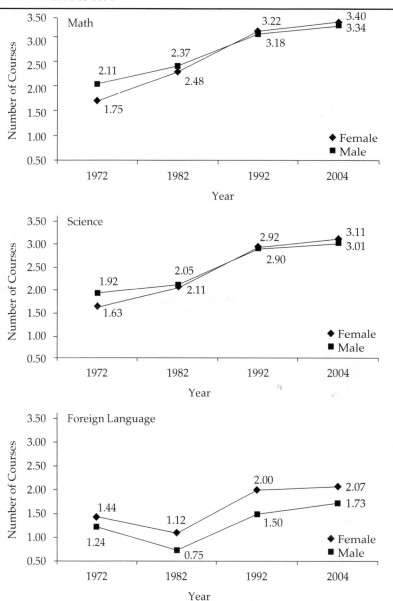

Source; Authors' compilation based on National Longitudinal Study of the High School Class of 1972, High School & Beyond, National Educational Longitudinal Study, and Educational Longitudinal Study (National Center for Education Statistics 1994, 1995, 2003, 2007). Data are weighted and pertain to high school seniors who subsequently graduated from high school. Data from NLS72 are from self-reports. Data from HSB, NELS, and ELS are from transcripts.

Figure A.10   Mean High School Grade Point Average by Race, 1972 to 2004

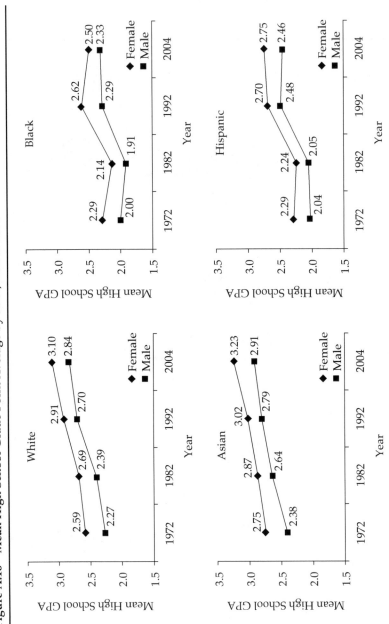

Source: Authors' compilation based on National Longitudinal Study of the High School Class of 1972, High School & Beyond, National Educational Longitudinal Study, and Educational Longitudinal Study (National Center for Education Statistics 1994, 1995, 2003, 2007). Data are weighted and pertain to high school seniors who subsequently graduated from high school. Data from NLS72 are from self-reports. Data from HSB, NELS, and ELS are from transcripts.
Note: All gender differences are significant at the 0.01 level.

Figure A.11   Percentage of All Master's and Doctoral Level Degree Recipients Who Are Female, 1970–1971 to 2005–2006

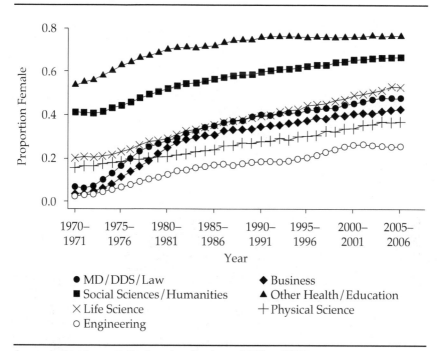

○ MD/DDS/Law   ◆ Business
■ Social Sciences/Humanities   ▲ Other Health/Education
✕ Life Science   + Physical Science
○ Engineering

Source: Authors' compilation based on Snyder and Dillow (2007).

Table A.1   Proportion Completing Four-Year College, by Age, Gender, Race, and Census Year, 1940 to 2007

			1940		1950		1960	
	Age		Male	Female	Male	Female	Male	Female
White	Twenty-two	%	0.0423	0.0433	0.0446	0.0685	0.0867	0.0723
		N	10,125	10,339	2,980	3,166	9,016	9,106
	Twenty-three	%	0.0611	0.0496	0.0650	0.0820	0.1272	0.0914
		N	10,036	10,178	3,014	3,184	8,797	8,868
	Twenty-four	%	0.0671	0.0510	0.0868	0.0690	0.1347	0.0927
		N	10,058	10,208	3,054	3,216	8,756	9,098
	Twenty-five	%	0.0739	0.0516	0.0957	0.0597	0.1448	0.0822
		N	10,091	10,218	3,135	3,384	8,975	9,336
	Twenty-six	%	0.0761	0.0508	0.1115	0.0602	0.1511	0.0830
		N	9,739	10,155	3,068	3,389	8,505	8,842
	Twenty-seven	%	0.0845	0.0528	0.1052	0.0617	0.1627	0.0836
		N	9,612	9,681	3,070	3,404	8,933	9,146
	Twenty-eight	%	0.0773	0.0535	0.1044	0.0668	0.1731	0.0819
		N	9,569	9,819	3,171	3,475	8,972	9,361
Black	Twenty-two	%	0.0118	0.0199	0.0085	0.0261	0.0101	0.0263
		N	1,136	1,344	355	421	1,186	1,259
	Twenty-three	%	0.0059	0.0073	0.0144	0.0344	0.0264	0.0468
		N	1,079	1,296	347	407	1,098	1,219
	Twenty-four	%	0.0137	0.0258	0.0229	0.0270	0.0307	0.0401
		N	1,092	1,292	349	408	1,106	1,322
	Twenty-five	%	0.0077	0.0131	0.0144	0.0245	0.0284	0.0458
		N	1,179	1,340	347	449	1,089	1,288
	Twenty-six	%	0.0134	0.0211	0.0279	0.0230	0.0379	0.0386
		N	1,022	1,304	358	434	1,057	1,217
	Twenty-seven	%	0.0162	0.0121	0.0108	0.0293	0.0392	0.0523
		N	1,085	1,171	371	409	1,149	1,337
	Twenty-eight	%	0.0105	0.0165	0.0207	0.0313	0.0426	0.0470
		N	1,080	1,322	384	416	1,009	1,296

Source: Authors' compilation based on IPUMS census data, 1940 to 2000 (Ruggles et al. 2010); American Community Survey, 2005 to 2007 (U.S. Census Bureau 2010).
Note: Sample sizes for 1950 are much smaller than other years owing to the sampling frame (uses sample-line, not universal frame, and has been weighted accordingly).

	1970		1980		1990		2000		2005–2007	
	Male	Female	Male	Female	Male	Female	Male	Female	Male	Female
	0.1451	0.1276	0.0990	0.1158	0.1160	0.1565	0.0993	0.1555	0.1188	0.2016
	13,965	14,823	16,346	11,649	12,067	11,850	10,869	10,751	31,399	31,715
	0.2041	0.1682	0.1741	0.1814	0.1874	0.2375	0.1914	0.2833	0.2132	0.3207
	13,954	14,759	16,205	15,899	12,573	12,600	10,621	10,321	30,896	32,187
	0.2106	0.1729	0.2058	0.1959	0.2192	0.2409	0.2416	0.3221	0.2571	0.3538
	10.827	11,375	16,101	16,184	12,964	12,854	10,434	10,378	31,346	32,098
	0.2132	0.1591	0.2237	0.2131	0.2322	0.2528	0.2714	0.3455	0.2641	0.3588
	11,126	11,520	15,965	15,672	13,932	14,397	10,727	10,781	32,025	32,858
	0.2208	0.1562	0.2519	0.2268	0.2458	0.2603	0.2967	0.3439	0.2838	0.3608
	11,679	11,829	15,359	15,590	14,673	14,910	10,420	10,599	31,069	33,013
	0.2267	0.1497	0.2632	0.2214	0.2436	0.2493	0.2912	0.3424	0.2856	0.3651
	12,184	12,249	15,309	15,314	15,140	15,312	11,171	11,406	31,374	33,026
	0.2253	0.1389	0.2832	0.2327	0.2555	0.2524	0.3099	0.3515	0.2936	0.3729
	10,719	10,970	14,721	14,951	14,835	15,164	12,033	12,206	30,856	32,612
	0.0316	0.0401	0.0373	0.0650	0.0444	0.0583	0.0440	0.0805	0.0532	0.0948
	1,613	1,922	2,492	2,752	1,877	2,105	2,310	2,440	5,566	5,966
	0.0523	0.0678	0.0678	0.1049	0.0610	0.0916	0.0787	0.1256	0.0913	0.1566
	1,435	1,813	2,404	2,707	1,872	2,158	2,133	2,327	5,440	5,748
	0.0450	0.0726	0.0772	0.0998	0.0809	0.1105	0.1114	0.1520	0.1153	0.1682
	1,379	1,583	2,357	2,726	1,876	2,198	2,082	2,365	5,171	5,729
	0.0483	0.0652	0.0964	0.1152	0.0856	0.1164	0.1164	0.1748	0.1235	0.1836
	1,304	1,641	2,293	2,726	2,024	2,319	2,054	2,309	5,321	6,049
	0.0642	0.0764	0.1024	0.1155	0.0888	0.1209	0.1272	0.1688	0.1407	0.1955
	1,308	1,577	2,216	2,494	2,007	2,382	1,944	2,343	4,967	6,155
	0.0630	0.0841	0.0988	0.1242	0.1034	0.1255	0.1192	0.1757	0.1453	0.1960
	1,380	1,558	2,115	2,488	1,974	2,356	2,039	2,457	5,036	6,166
	0.0830	0.0743	0.1223	0.1197	0.0934	0.1429	0.1319	0.1841	0.1447	0.2099
	1,217	1,426	2,011	2,305	1,953	2,407	2,201	2,536	4,870	5,735

Table A.2   Effects of Parental Characteristics and Family Structure on Eighth-Grade Reading and Math Scores (Standard Deviation Units)

	Reading	Math
Female	0.042***	–0.01
No biological father in house in kindergarten	–0.02	–0.046***
No father/stepfather in house in kindergarten	–0.008	0.016
SES in kindergarten	0.058***	0.056***
Age in kindergarten	0.013***	0.004
Parental help with reading and math in third grade	–0.011	–0.006
Average hours of TV on weekdays, third and fifth grades	0.0003	–0.001
Does homework 5 or more days/week in third and fifth grades	–0.007	–0.003
Female* father has BA or higher	–0.039**	–0.032*
English as second language	–0.02	–0.017
Hispanic	–0.023	–0.003
Black	–0.096***	–0.10***
Asian	0.009	0.034*
Constant	0.03	0.047
N	7,740	7,780

Source: Authors' compilation based on DiPrete and McDaniel (2011).
Note: ECLS-K sample size counts are rounded to the nearest 10.
* $p < .05$; ** $p < .01$; *** $p < .001$.

Notes

Chapter 1

1. See, for example, "Colleges Look for Ways to Reverse a Decline in Enroll-ment of Men," *Chronicle of Higher Education* (November 26, 1999); "The Male Minority," *Time,* December 2, 2000; "The New Gender Gap," *Business Week,* May 26, 2003; "Male Students' College Achievement Gap Brings Concern," *Washington Post,* August 31, 2003; "Diversity in Academe: The Gender Issue," *Chronicle of Higher Education* (November 2, 2012).
2. For convenience, we use the terms "completing college" and "completing a bachelor's degree" interchangeably. We sometimes use "BA" as shorthand for "bachelor's degree," though colleges and universities actually award many types of bachelor's degrees—most notably a bachelor of science (BS), but also a bachelor of engineering (BE), a bachelor of science in engineering (BSE), a bachelor of business administration (BBA), a bachelor of nursing (BN), and a bachelor of fine arts (BFA), as well as many other variants, de-pending on the student's major and university.
3. It is hard to predict how the gender wage gap will change in the future, even as women's educational attainment continues to rise. Blau and Kahn (2007b) maintain that the remaining wage gap is almost completely unaccounted for by the main predictors of wages—education and labor market experience—contained in the classic human capital earnings function.
4. Conor Dougherty, "Young Women's Pay Exceeds Male Peers," *Wall Street Journal,* September 1, 2010.
5. This calculation applies to men age twenty-five to sixty-four years old who were in the civilian labor force at the time of the ACS survey, and it assumes that the observed return to higher education is an accurate measure of the aggregate economic value of a hypothetical increased supply of higher edu-cation in the male population.
6. This shortfall of 9.4 percent amounts to $5,000 per male worker, on average. Recently, Robin Harding of the *Financial Times* determined that the share of U.S. national income that goes to workers as wages rather than to investors as profits and interest has fallen to its lowest level since records first began to be kept on this statistic shortly after World War II ("Pay Gap a $740bn Threat to U.S. Recovery," *Financial Times,* December 15, 2011, 1, 8). According to Harding, it would require a wage increase of $5,000 per worker to raise this share from its current value of 58 percent to the average postwar value of 63

percent, which amounts to $740 billion in additional wages. The plausible gain from equalizing the current education difference between twenty-five- to thirty-four-year-old men and women would account for more than half of the current pay gap.

7. Only 68 percent of males and 77 percent of females who attended only a four-year college successfully attained a bachelor's degree by age twenty-six. Some commentators assert that even college graduates suffer from educational deficits. One recent study (Arum and Roksa 2011) found that nearly 50 percent of a representative sample of college students showed no measurable increase in "critical thinking, complex reasoning, and writing skills" as measured by the College Learning Assessment between the fall of their freshman year and the spring of their sophomore year. The Spellings Commission on the Future of Higher Education (2006) found that fewer than one-third of college graduates were "proficient" in literacy tests involving prose, documents, and quantitative material. Taking a more extreme stance, Charles Murray (2009) argues that only 10 to 15 percent of any cohort has the academic ability to do well in college, which he operationalizes as the upper half of the distribution of students who presently manage to complete a bachelor's degree. Because Murray sees academic ability as largely genetic in origin, he views this number as relatively immutable and argues for postsecondary reforms in order to provide students outside of this elite group with a more useful vocational experience. Rosenbaum (2001) would probably reject Murray's 85 percent line, but he also argues that it does no good to push unprepared students toward higher education.

8. For comparisons with more OECD countries, see figure 2.3.

9. One contemporary example of this logic can be found in Japan, where men retain a large educational advantage over women. According to family economy theory, Japanese parents should be motivated to favor sons over daughters in their educational decisions because labor markets still favor men. Hiroshi Ono (2004) found that while siblings in general dilute family resources and lower the chances for educational attainment, Japanese daughters with male siblings are especially disadvantaged.

10. A detailed examination of the sources of these changes is beyond the scope of this book; see Goldin (1990) and Thistle (2006).

11. Girls also made progress in closing the gender gap in the upper end of the mathematics performance distribution (Wai et al. 2010). Curricular intensification may have played a small role in the equalization of male and female course-taking patterns, though boys continued to outperform girls in the top end of the distribution in math tests (Wai et al. 2010; Ceci, Williams, and Barnett 2009; Ellison and Swanson 2010). Although the gender gap at the upper end of the math and science distribution is potentially important for the gender gap in science, technology, engineering, and mathematics (STEM) fields, it pertains to very few students and has little to do with the gender gap in rates of college completion.

12. We do not rule out the possibility that some students drop out of college because they do not see a route through college that would allow them to realize its value. This perception could stem from inadequate counseling or in-

adequate linkage between some fields of study and the labor market, but academic preparation may be a contributing factor in these cases as well.

13. In various places in this book, we report on research from collaborative papers with these students (Jennings and DiPrete 2010; DiPrete and Jennings 2012; McDaniel et al. 2011; Legewie and DiPrete 2009; Legewie and DiPrete 2012a; Legewie and DiPrete 2012b; Mann and DiPrete 2012; DiPrete and McDaniel 2011), and also from Anne McDaniel's dissertation (McDaniel 2011).

14. The gender gap is even larger than these numbers imply, because the 2003 Gallup poll also found that men thought one needed a higher income (a median of $150,000, versus $100,000 for women) and greater assets (a median of $1 million, versus $500,000 for women) to be considered "rich."

15. Louis Uchitelle, "U.S. Manufacturing Gains Jobs as Wages Retreat," *New York Times*, December 29, 2011.

Chapter 2

1. Parts of this chapter were published previously in Claudia Buchmann. 2009. "Gender Inequalities in the Transition to College." *Teachers College Record* 111(10): 2320–51, and Anne McDaniel, Thomas A. DiPrete, Claudia Buchmann, and Uri Shwed. 2011. "The Black Gender Gap in Educational Attainment: Historical Trends and Racial Comparisons." *Demography* 48(3): 889–914.

2. An alternative calculation makes use of OECD tertiary "graduation rates" (Organization for Economic Cooperation and Development 2011, chart A3.2). In 1995 the United States was tied for first place with New Zealand among OECD countries in rates of tertiary completion. By 2009 it had slipped to eleventh place among countries reporting data for 1995, and fifteenth overall. The OECD calculates these rates either by summing the age-specific rates across the population or (if these data are not available) by summing the total graduates and dividing by the current year's population for the cohort at the "typical" graduation age. These methods are somewhat similar to the way fertility rates are calculated, and like fertility rates, they are sensitive to historical change in population size and in the timing of degree completion. Beyond these issues, the "graduation rate" reports for some countries (for example, the Slovak Republic and New Zealand) are implausibly higher than the "attainment rate" calculations reported in table A1.3a of the OECD (2011) report.

   Comparing educational attainment rates across countries is not straightforward because educational systems differ across countries. The OECD uses the International Standard Classification of Education (ISCED) to distinguish between the "tertiary type A" (ISCED 5A) and "tertiary type B" (ISCED 5B) standards. Tertiary type B programs are more vocationally oriented and typically take two or three years to complete, and thus they correspond roughly to the associate's degrees given out by U.S. community colleges. We are mainly interested in tertiary type A programs, which correspond to four-year college degrees in the American system. These comparisons might not tell the full story, because countries may differ in the extent to which training for male-dominated careers is done primarily in tertiary type B tracks. However, country comparisons are similar regardless of whether type A or a combination of type A and type B is used. The OECD computes the graduation rate by summing across age-specific graduation rates if possible, or otherwise by dividing the total number of graduates by the total number of people in the cohort at the country's "typical" graduation age.

3. Some of the apparent male decline for the twenty-five- to thirty-four-year-olds may have come from delayed completion of a tertiary degree.

4. The figures in this chapter showing college completion by year of birth for twenty-six- to twenty-eight-year-olds are drawn with a kernel-weighted local polynomial smoother.

5. The appearance of crossing in the early birth cohorts for blacks is an artifact of the statistical smoothing of the figures.

6. Small sample sizes for these three groups limit our ability to document trends prior to 1980.

7. The BA completion rates reported in this chapter do not always match the OECD reported rates (for a critique of OECD methodology, see Adelman 2009). The OECD tables do not break out non-Hispanic whites separately, but we can see by comparing figures 2.5 and 2.7 that non-Hispanic white graduation rates are five to six percentage points higher than the graduation rates for the entire cohort. If we added five percentage points to the male rate in figure 2.4 and six percentage points to the female rate, U.S. males would still rank below Korea, Japan, Norway, the United Kingdom, and the Netherlands, and U.S. females would still rank below Norway, Denmark, Finland, and Poland. This simple adjustment is, of course, too large if intended for comparing the majority population group across countries because some of the comparison countries also have significant minority populations.

8. We estimated age effects that control for cohort by linearly interpolating rates of college completion at each age from twenty-two to twenty-eight for all birth cohorts, and we report simulated age-specific rates of college completion for cohorts that were twenty-two years of age each census year. In other words, we report results for the 1918, 1928, 1938, 1948, 1958, and 1968 birth cohorts, which correspond to individuals who were twenty-two years old in 1940, 1950, 1960, 1970, 1980, and 1990, and then we interpolate their experience through age twenty-eight. For the 2000 census, we report results for the 1974 birth cohort, using interpolated rates for ages twenty-one to twenty-five, exact rates for age twenty-six from the 2000 census, and extrapolated rates for ages twenty-seven and twenty-eight. We simulate using the 1974 birth cohort instead of the 1978 one in order to avoid excess extrapolation. Anne McDaniel and her colleagues (2011) provide additional information about the analyses discussed in this section.

9. Census data do not distinguish between these two routes to completing high school for most of the period covered by these figures. Because adolescents following these two routes are not equivalent in terms of the probability that they will complete college, and because the composition of high school graduates over these two alternative routes has changed over time, we do not present trends in rates of high school completion.

Chapter 3

1. Parts of this chapter were published previously in Anne McDaniel, Thomas A. DiPrete, Claudia Buchmann, and Uri Shwed. 2011. "The Black Gender Gap in Educational Attainment: Historical Trends and Racial Comparisons." *Demography* 48(3): 889–914, and Thomas A. DiPrete and Claudia Buchmann. 2006. "Gender Specific Trends in the Value of Education and the Emerging Gender Gap in College Completion." *Demography* 43(1): 1–24, and Claudia Buchmann, Thomas A. DiPrete, and Anne McDaniel. 2008. "Gender Inequalities in Education." *Annual Review of Sociology* 34: 319–37.

2. As of the time of this writing, the issue of whether the recession (and more specifically, the Obama administration's policies) had a greater effect on men than on women, or the other way around, had become an issue in the presidential campaign. For a discussion and evaluation of the opposing ways the issue was being framed by the Romney and Obama campaigns, see Fact-Check.org, "Obama's 'War on Women'?" April 12, 2012, available at: http://www.factcheck.org/2012/04/obamas-war-on-women.

3. David Leonhardt, "Men, Women, and the Great Recession," *New York Times*, July 8, 2011. Recent reports further suggest that women have been more likely than men to return to school in response to the weak job market in the current recession; see Catherine Rampell, "Young Women Go Back to School Instead of Work," *New York Times*, December 28, 2011.

4. Notably Title VII of the Civil Rights Act of 1964 and Title IX of the Education Amendments of 1972.

5. See also Sam Roberts, "For Young Earners in Big City, a Gap in Women's Favor," *New York Times*, August 3, 2007.

6. This finding is consistent with research by Andrew Beveridge, who shows that entry-level women on Wall Street are earning more than entry-level men (cited in Roberts, "For Young Earners in Big City, a Gap in Women's Favor," *New York Times*, August 3, 2007).

7. Earned income is deflated by the consumer price index for all urban consumers (CPI-U), published by the Bureau of Labor Statistics.

8. The CPS defines a family as a group of two or more people living together and related by birth, marriage, or adoption. Gross family income was also deflated by the CPI-U.

9. The number of persons in the family is measured at the time of the survey.

10. A family is defined as "not income-deprived" if it has at least a standard of living value of $9,000 in 1983–1984 dollars. This is about $16,000 in 2002 pre-tax dollars, which implies a family income of at least $16,000 for one person, $23,000 for two persons, $28,000 for a family of three, and $32,000 for a family of four. For comparison, the official poverty level thresholds in 2002 were $9,300 for a family of one, $12,000 for a family of two, $14,500 for a family of three, and $18,200 for a family of four.

11. See figure A.3 for the results from DiPrete and Buchmann (2006).

12. A related puzzle stimulated by this research concerns the now-established fact that women for many decades have had higher returns to education than men (Dougherty 2005; Hubbard 2011).

13. See figure A.4 for the results from the analysis in DiPrete and Buchmann (2006).

14. Caroline Hoxby (2009) notes that the increased selectivity applies to the top 10 percent of American colleges and universities when ranked by selectivity.

15. Another form of competition that may be affecting completion rates and quality at less-selective universities is the competition to get into courses where the number of available "seats" in the class is lower than the number of students trying to register for the course. Students who are closed out of required or elective courses may well have lower probabilities of graduating (or of graduating within four or five years) as a consequence. Unfortunately, the necessary data are currently not available to determine the impact of supply shortages at the level of individual courses either on overall college completion rates or on the gender gap in completion rates.

16. Early in the twentieth century, the college enrollments of female students were primarily limited by supply constraints. Goldin and Katz (2010) show that an increased number of coeducational institutions in a state increased the ratio of college-educated women to college-educated men in that state for cohorts born around the turn of the twentieth century. Janet Currie and Enrico Moretti (2003) show that the opening of new public colleges in a county in the 1940 to 1996 period increased women's education by an average of 0.08 years, but they did not investigate whether the increase for women was larger than that for men.

Chapter 4

1. Parts of this chapter were published previously in Claudia Buchmann, Thomas A. DiPrete, and Anne McDaniel. 2008. "Gender Inequalities in Education." *Annual Review of Sociology* 34: 319–37, and Claudia Buchmann and Thomas A. DiPrete. 2006. "The Growing Female Advantage in College Completion: The Role of Parental Resources and Academic Achievement." *American Sociological Review* 71(4): 515–41.

2. This conclusion is supported further by evidence of large national-level differences in the fraction of both boys and girls who score as proficient on math and reading tests in the Program for International Assessment (PISA). In 2009, 30 percent of fifteen-year-olds achieved one of the top three levels of reading proficiency in the United States. In some countries, the percentage of students scoring in the top three levels of proficiency was much higher, with 46 percent of Korean students and 45 percent of Finnish students attaining these levels of proficiency. Large discrepancies also emerge when only boys are compared across countries. Only 23 percent of boys in the United States scored in one of the top three proficiency levels, compared to 38 percent of boys in Korea. International proficiency gaps in mathematics are equally dramatic: while only 27 percent of American students achieved one of the top three proficiency levels in mathematics, 52 percent of Korean students and 48 percent of Finnish students achieved at this level. Although in both Korea and Finland the patterns of female advantage in reading and male advantage in math are also found, the higher levels of proficiency among boys and girls in these countries underscore an important point: gender dif-

ferences in cognitive ability per se are not the primary explanation for the relative stagnation in the college completion rates of American men (OECD 2010b).

3. Buchmann and DiPrete (2006, supplementary web tables) found using data from NELS88 that high school performance as measured by rank in class predicts four-year college enrollment and college GPA better than standardized test scores. With the same data, William Bowen and his colleagues (2009) found that high school grades predict college completion better than standardized tests. Using data from the Chicago Public Schools combined with data from the National Student Clearinghouse, Melissa Roderick and her colleagues (2006) found that high school grades are a better predictor than test scores that a student will enroll in a four-year college and graduate from a four-year college, though test scores are also predictive among students with the same course grades.

4. See Hyde (2005) for an update of the Maccoby and Jacklin (1974) meta-analysis.

5. Hedges and Nowell (1995) found a change from a 0.19 to a 0.15 standard deviation advantage for boys in math between 1978 and 1992 based on the NAEP for eleventh-graders, a change from a 0.33 to a 0.23 standard deviation advantage for boys in science, and essential stability in a 0.25 to 0.3 standard deviation disadvantage for boys in reading.

6. The gender gap in reading is stable at 0.14 standard deviations regardless of whether we compare respondents who have nonmissing reading scores at the start of kindergarten and the end of fifth grade (using panel weights) or if we compare the full samples who have reading scores at the beginning of kindergarten with the full sample who have reading scores at the end of fifth grade (in each case using cross-sectional weights).

7. George Farkas and his colleagues (1990) reported that some studies had found evidence that girls receive higher grades than their aptitude scores would predict at various points in the school career (Brophy and Good 1974; Rehberg and Rosenthal 1978; Alexander and Eckland 1980), but that others had not found this to be true (Entwisle and Hayduk 1982; Natriello and Dornbusch 1983; Leiter and Brown 1985).

8. Goldin and her colleagues (2006) found that the class rank of the median girl among Wisconsin high school seniors in 1957 was twenty-one percentile points higher than the rank of the median boy, and in 1992 the median senior girl in the NELS survey was sixteen percentile points ahead of the median boy.

9. Because students tend to inflate their GPA relative to their transcript-reported GPA, we adjusted these self-reports downward by 0.4. We use 0.4 because it is the average difference between self-reported high school grades and transcript grades in HSB.

10. Our findings differ from those of Daniel Koretz and Mark Berends (2001), who found only a slight increase in average grades between HSB and NELS, mainly among high-income students, but their study differs in sample and GPA measure from what we use here. Koretz and Berends excluded anyone who transferred during their high school years or was missing data on the school administrator survey, the student survey, or cognitive testing. We in-

cluded the entire sample of the original tenth-graders who were twelfth-graders in 1982 and who had valid transcript data. Also, we used the overall high school GPA (not the academic GPA) provided by NCES in the HSB data. It appears that Koretz and Berends calculated their own GPA measure from the course grades in the high school transcripts.

11. Grade gaps favoring females exist for each racial group and look very similar to the overall trends (see figure A.10).

12. Goldin and her colleagues (2006) further showed that very little of the male advantage in college completion in the 1957 cohort could be accounted for by courses, test scores, or academic performance; in other words, the male advantage was statistically unrelated to the academic variables that would be expected to account for college completion rates.

13. Figure A.9 shows the mean number of courses taken in math, science, and foreign languages by male and female students from 1972 to 2004. Just as for GPA, the data for course-taking for the 1972 graduating cohort are necessarily drawn from self-reports because, unlike the other three surveys, there are no transcript data on the total number of courses taken in the NLS. For this reason, we cannot determine whether the apparent higher average number of math and science courses taken by males relative to females in 1972 reflects a true male advantage in course-taking or a tendency for males to over-report the courses they have taken in high school. At any rate, the number of math, science, and foreign language courses taken in high school has increased over time for all students.

14. Figure 4.7 is based on self-reported grades. While self-reported grades do not exactly match transcripts, they are reasonably accurate. In the Add Health study, for example, self-reported grades correlated around 0.7 with transcript grades (Kelly 2008, 49).

15. William Bowen and his colleagues (2009) recently found the same gender pattern in their analysis of student performance at "flagship" state universities.

16. Stephen Machin and Sandra McNally (2005) find a similar pattern in the United Kingdom. The gender gap in performance in secondary school widens and cannot be fully explained by the gender gap at age eleven. It is important to remember that we are speaking about averages and that academic performance for both males and females varies widely. High-performing boys do as well as high-performing girls in school, and high-performing boys do much better than most girls in the middle of the performance distribution. On average, however, the performance gap continues to grow over the educational life course.

17. The model underlying table 4.2 is very simple: it includes only college GPA. However, as we show in chapter 8, more complex models yield qualitatively similar findings, particularly for whites. Most of the higher completion rates for women in college come from their higher average academic performance.

Chapter 5

1. The "Approaches to Learning" scale assesses attentiveness, task persistence, eagerness to learn, learning independence, flexibility, and organization. The

"Self-Control" scale reflects teachers' ratings of children's ability to control their behavior by respecting the property rights of others, controlling their temper, accepting peer ideas for group activities, and responding appropriately to pressure from peers. The "Interpersonal Skills" scale rates the child's skill in forming and maintaining friendships, getting along with people who are different, comforting or helping other children, expressing feelings, ideas, and opinions in positive ways, and showing sensitivity to the feelings of others (National Center for Educational Statistics 1999).

2. Poverty is measured based on the preliminary census poverty thresholds for 1998 (Westat and Educational Testing Service 1998).

3. Trzesniewski and her colleagues (2006) find that the correlation between antisocial behavior and reading is significantly stronger for boys than for girls in the E-Risk Longitudinal Twin Study. Environmental rather than genetic factors explain most of the correlation between these variables. They further find that antisocial behavior may have a causal impact on reading for both genders, but that the reciprocal effect (poor reading leading to antisocial behavior) appears to apply only to boys.

4. Other studies suggest that only a subset of social and behavioral skills affects academic outcomes. For example, Dolan and his colleagues (1993) report no crossover effects of behavioral training on reading gains even though aggressive and shy behavior diminished.

5. For technical details, see DiPrete and Jennings (2012). They also report similar results using other estimation strategies.

6. The covariates in the models for table 5.4 are spring reading and test scores, gender, race, age, whether ever retained a grade, SES, whether biological father lives in the household, whether any father lives in the household, and third-grade social and behavioral skills. See DiPrete and Jennings (2012) for further details.

7. Gender differences concerning homework are the opposite of gender differences concerning television watching in the NLSY97: girls do 1.4 hours a week more homework than boys do even as they watch an average of two hours less television a week than boys do.

8. At the same time, Melissa Roderick and her colleagues (2008) find that students whose behavior with respect to college applications is inconsistent with their stated plans tend to be students with low GPA and SAT/ACT scores. Among students who have a realistic chance to complete college, the disconnect between aspirations and behavior is not so extreme.

Chapter 6

1. Richard Nisbett (2009) cites a large number of studies, including three French "natural experiments" in which (1) the SES of the child-rearing and biological families of adopted children was known; (2) one of a set of siblings of lower-SES families was adopted by an upper-middle-class family; and (3) abused low-IQ children at age four or five were adopted by families of varying SES and were retested at age fourteen. In all three studies, the estimated gap between the effects of high-SES and low-SES families was in the range of twelve to sixteen IQ points. Nisbett also calls attention to population change

over time in variables (such as height) that have very high heritability to demonstrate that even high heritability does not imply that environmental effects are weak.

2. In another study, we analyzed GSS data through 2004 (Buchmann and Di-Prete 2006). We update that analysis here with more recent data.

3. We operationalized "mother" to mean any female guardian and "father" to mean any male guardian.

4. Buchmann and DiPrete (2006) provide tests for the statistical significance of these effects.

5. Martha Bailey and Susan Dynarski (2011) argue that recent educational data show that the biggest gender gap in attainment is in the top income quartile. Their results, however, imply a nonlinear pattern across income quartiles, which is puzzling. When re-expressed as odds ratios, our reanalysis of the data presented in their figures shows that the biggest gender gap is actually in the quartile next to the bottom. When the data are collapsed into halves, our reanalysis shows that the gender gap is larger in the bottom half of the income distribution than in the top half of the distribution.

6. In summarizing a body of work on the effects of genes versus the environment, Nisbett (2009, 37) writes: "Moreover, we can place a number, or at least a range, on the degree to which environmental factors characteristic of lower-SES families reduce IQ below its potential: it is between 12 and 18 points. Whatever the estimates of heritability turn out to be, nothing is going to change this fact."

7. Jere Behrman and Mark Rosenzweig (2002) argue that in the United States highly educated women are more likely to work and this time spent away from child-rearing detracts from the positive effect of their education. But John Ermisch and Chiara Pronzato (2009) find this explanation implausible for Norway.

8. Widely used in research, PIAT measures word recognition and pronunciation ability in the reading test and basic math skills and concepts in the math test. We standardize both scores, with means of 100 and standard deviations of 15, and report only coefficients from the fixed-effects regression where meaningful variation in the independent variable between the siblings is plausible. Other control variables in the model are whether the current partner lived in the home, whether the current partner was a spouse, and the age of the child.

9. Father's education is not well measured in these data; the mother was asked about the education of her current spouse or partner, who was not necessarily the father of the children.

10. They are also roughly twice as likely as boys to get B's or better in eighth grade.

11. Carlson (2006) used measures of how often the father and child talked, whether the father spent enough time with the child, whether he listened to the child, whether the two shared ideas, whether the father typically knew where the child was, and so forth.

12. A common response scale is used for each item ("not true," "sometimes true," "often true"). Scores were summed across items and then standardized with a mean of 100 and a standard deviation of 15.

13. The other control variables in the regression were whether current partner lives in home, whether current partner is spouse, and age of the child.

14. After controlling for parental education and for parental religiosity, girls on average watched two fewer hours of television a week than boys in the NLSY97 data.

15. When children are asked the more concrete question, "Whom do you look up to and admire?" a clear majority choose people they know personally (Anderson and Cavallaro 2002). This pattern does not preclude these same children having emotional ties with celebrity or fantasy figures. Kristin Anderson and Donna Cavallaro also report that boys are less likely than girls (58 percent versus 67 percent) to name someone they know personally in response to the question about people they look up to and admire.

16. Many other recent action heroes (for example, Rocky Balboa, Axel Foley, and John Connor) are not or may not be well educated, though they typically retain intelligent, clever, crafty, and street-smart traits.

17. Recall that "my boy Bill" "does what he likes" and "wouldn't be President if he didn't wanna be . . . and you won't see nobody dare to try to boss him or toss him around!"

18. C. J. Pascoe (2006) and Jay MacLeod (2008) offer similar evidence that some adolescent males (or males in some social situations) treat "nerds"—or more generally, mental work—as unmasculine.

19. R. W. Connell (2005) argues that the highest-status form of masculinity is ideologically "hegemonic" and typically inegalitarian with respect to identities based on other gender orientations.

20. Using NELS data, Kao (1995) found that Asian American parents were significantly more likely to enroll their children in art, music, and computer classes than were white parents. She further found that enrollment in these specialized classes was associated with higher test scores net of a variety of background factors, including parental education and income. Roscigno and Ainsworth-Darnell (1999), who also analyzed NELS data, found that black students lagged behind white students in their taking of art, music, and dance classes, even net of family characteristics. They also found that these measures were associated with higher grade point averages net of controls for gender, family background, and school characteristics.

21. Other scholars (for example, Morgan 1998, 2005) have questioned the extent to which adolescent expectations are goals that in some sense are causing behavior as opposed to imperfect predictions about future outcomes. However, regardless of whether expectations are causes or predictions, the disconnect between mean educational expectations and mean educational attainment strongly suggests an informational failure in American education. Alleviation of this information failure would have multiple benefits that together might be described as a better alignment of effort and educational goals.

Chapter 7

1. A related argument has recently been made by Thomas Dee (2005), who examined whether the gender of middle school teachers affects the perception

and performance of same- and opposite-sex students. He found that middle school teachers on average provide more positive evaluations of students of the same gender and more negative evaluations of students of the opposite gender. Female teachers are more likely to see their male students as more disruptive, more frequently inattentive, and more likely to not complete homework, just as male teachers generally have more negative opinions of their female students. His findings of bias are symmetric with respect to gender and thus would affect boys more than girls to the extent that female teachers predominate. Taking elementary school and middle school together, men constitute only 18 percent of teachers, but this fraction increases to 45 percent in high school, according to current CPS data.

2. Laura Sokal and her colleagues (2007), for example, found that teacher gender does not matter for performance in elementary school and that boys' self-perceived ability is actually heightened when they have a female teacher.
3. Students may also learn more effectively in classrooms where their classmates are themselves more focused on learning.
4. Coleman (1960, 1961) found that students who had been named as members of the "leading crowd" were more likely than boys in general to choose "athletic star," in part because they were more likely to be athletic stars themselves.
5. In response to the influx, non-evacuee Houston students suffered a loss in academic performance and an increase in absenteeism (Imberman, Kugler, and Sacerdote 2009).
6. In one study, peer effect estimates ranged up to about a half a standard deviation gain (Hoxby 2000).
7. All coefficients are in standard deviation units. See Legewie and DiPrete (2012b) for the complete list of control variables for these analyses.
8. Moreover, stereotype threat–type arguments have predominantly involved standardized tests. The gender gap in performance, on the other hand, primarily concerns course grades, which arise from the cumulation of evaluation across the tests, homework assignments, and projects of an entire semester.

Chapter 8

1. These data are drawn from the 2007 *Digest of Education Statistics,* published online by the National Center for Education Statistics and based on the Higher Education General Information Survey (HEGIS) and the Integrated Postsecondary Education Data System (IPEDS). We converted the data from the field-specific trend tables of this report into a statistical database and re-analyzed them.
2. NCES data do not allow a trend breakdown, but other data show that the female deficit in physics is greater than the female deficit in chemistry.
3. Turner and Bowen (1999) used dummy variables for each fifty-point range of the math SAT in the College and Beyond sample, which consists primarily of highly selective colleges and universities.
4. Ann Boulis and Jerry Jacobs (2010) argue that perceptions of how supportive

the climate is for women play an important role in the continuing reluctance of women to pursue certain medical specialties, even after concerns about work-family incompatibility are taken into account.

5. The main reason for the difference in the fraction of the gender gap due to science orientation may be a consequence of coding decisions. Xie and Shauman (2003) filtered out all people who did not assert that they expected to obtain a BA.

6. A potential problem with the high school effectiveness study is that its data cannot reliably distinguish between high school effects and the effects of nonrandom, gender-specific selection into schools. Legewie and DiPrete (2012a) addressed this issue by using the broader NELS sample, which included a number of measures of student math and science orientations and performance while in eighth grade. These variables would be central predictors of any nonrandom assignment based on science aptitude or interest, and controlling for these "pretreatment" effects thus allows for arguably more accurate estimates of the causal effect of the high school environment on the formation of STEM orientations (Steiner et al. 2010; Steiner, Cook, and Shadish 2011).

7. Brown and Corcoran (1997) used the 1984 SIPP and the NLS72; Weinberger (1998) used 1985 National Survey or Recent College Graduates; Joy (2002) used 1993/93 Baccalaureate and Beyond; Bobbitt-Zeher (2007) used NELS.

Chapter 9

1. High-performing girls report greater levels of school attachment than do high-performing boys. Similarly, daughters of highly educated fathers report higher levels of attachment than do their brothers. Thus, the gender gap in reported attachment is not strongly affected by having a highly educated father or by level of academic performance.

2. Rosenbaum (2001) argues that students with mediocre high school grades on average get low returns from college. Brand and Xie (2010) argue that marginal students get high returns. David Card (2001) and Pedro Carneiro and his colleagues (2011) argue that unobservable variables play a strong role in selecting students into college graduation who on observable factors would seem to have a small probability of graduating, which implies that their observed returns do not readily generalize to other students who similarly would seem unlikely to graduate from college.

3. Venezia and her colleagues (2003) give the example of California high school graduation requirements (three years of English and two years of mathematics) versus the requirements to enter California public universities (four years of English and three years of mathematics).

4. Motivation and discipline are enhanced by social support from the environment, and higher-SES individuals get more effective support from their environment than do lower-SES individuals. For example, Anna Aizer and Laura Stroud (2010) found that educated women who live in more educationally segregated cities reduce their smoking more rapidly than do women in more educationally integrated cities. Similarly, more-educated HIV-positive men

are especially likely to follow good health maintenance regimes when they are married, which suggests that it is the combination of social support, one's own knowledge, and one's own discipline that produces the strongest behavioral response (Goldman and Smith 2002). Notably, HIV-positive women in this study did not gain an advantage from being married, a finding that suggests—like much other evidence—that the effects of social support are gendered.

References

Adelman, Clifford. 2006. *The Toolbox Revisited: Paths to Degree Completion from High School Through College.* Washington: U.S. Department of Education.
———. 2009. "The Spaces Between Numbers: Getting International Data on Higher Education Straight." Washington, D.C.: Institute for Higher Education Policy (November).
Aizer, Anna, and Laura Stroud. 2010. "Education, Knowledge, and the Evolution of Disparities in Health." Technical report. Cambridge, Mass.: National Bureau of Economic Research.
Alexander, Karl L., and Bruce K. Eckland. 1974. "Sex Differences in the Educational Attainment Process." *American Sociological Review* 39(5): 668–82.
———. 1980. "The Explorations in Equality of Opportunity Survey of 1955 High School Sophomores." *Research in Sociology of Education and Socialization* 1: 31–58.
Alexander, Karl L., Doris R. Entwisle, and Susan L. Dauber. 2003. *On the Success of Failure: A Reassessment of the Effects of Retention in the Early Grades.* New York: Cambridge University Press.
Alexander, Karl L., Doris R. Entwisle, and Maxine S. Thompson. 1987. "School Performance, Status Relations, and the Structure of Sentiment: Bringing the Teacher Back In." *American Sociological Review* 52(5): 665–82.
Alexander, Karl L., and Edward L. McDill. 1976. "Selection and Allocation Within Schools: Some Causes and Consequences of Curriculum Placement." *American Sociological Review* 41(6): 963–80.
Alexander, Karl L., and Aaron M. Pallas. 1984. "Curriculum Reform and School Performance: An Evaluation of the 'New Basics.'" *American Journal of Education* 92(4): 391–420.
Allensworth, Elaine M., and John Q. Easton. 2007. "What Matters for Staying on Track and Graduating in Chicago Public High Schools." Chicago: University of Chicago, Consortium on Chicago School Research.
Almquist, Elizabeth M., Shirley S. Angrist, and Richard Mickelsen. 1980. "Women's Career Aspirations and Achievements: College and Seven Years After." *Work and Occupations* 7(3): 367–84.
Alon, Sigal, and Dafna Gelbgiser. 2011. "The Female Advantage in College Academic Achievements and Horizontal Sex Segregation." *Social Science Research* 40(1): 107–19.

240   References

Alon, Sigal, and Marta Tienda. 2007. "Diversity, Opportunity, and the Shifting
Meritocracy in Higher Education." *American Sociological Review* 72(4): 487–511.

Alwin, Duane F., Michael Braun, and Jacqueline Scott. 1992. "The Separation of
Work and the Family: Attitudes Towards Women's Labour-Force Participation
in Germany, Great Britain, and the United States." *European Sociological Review*
8(1): 13–37.

Amato, Paul R., and Frieda Fowler. 2002. "Parenting Practices, Child Adjustment, and Family Diversity." *Journal of Marriage and Family* 64(3): 703–16.

Ammermueller, Andreas, and Jörn-Steffen Pischke. 2009. "Peer Effects in European Primary Schools: Evidence from the Progress in International Reading Literacy Study." *Journal of Labor Economics* 27(3): 315–48.

Anderegg, David. 2007. *Nerds: Who They Are and Why We Need More of Them.* New York: Penguin/Tarcher.

Anderson, Kristin J., and Donna Cavallaro. 2002. "Parents or Pop Culture? Children's Heroes and Role Models." *Childhood Education* 78(3): 161–68.

Angrist, Joshua D., and Jörn-Steffen Pischke. 2008. *Mostly Harmless Econometrics: An Empiricist's Companion.* Princeton, N.J.: Princeton University Press.

Angrist, Shirley S., and Elizabeth M. Almquist. 1993. "The Carnegie Mellon Class of 1968: Families, Careers, and Contingencies." In *Women's Lives Through Time: Educated American Women of the Twentieth Century,* edited by Kathleen Day Hulbert and Diane Tickton Schuster. San Francisco: Jossey-Bass.

Appelbaum, Eileen, Annette D. Bernhardt, and Richard J. Murnane. 2003. *Low-Wage America: How Employers Are Reshaping Opportunity in the Workplace.* New York: Russell Sage Foundation.

Armstrong, J. E. 1910. "The Advantages of Limited Sex Segregation in the High School." *The School Review* 18(5): 339–50.

Arnold, Karen D. 1995. *Lives of Promise: What Becomes of High School Valedictorians.* San Francisco: Jossey-Bass.

Arum, Richard, and Josipa Roksa. 2011. *Academically Adrift: Limited Learning on College Campuses.* Chicago: University of Chicago Press.

Attewell, Paul A., and Thurston Domina. 2008. "Raising the Bar: Curricular Intensity and Academic Performance." *Educational Evaluation and Policy Analysis* 30(1): 51.

Attewell, Paul A., and David E. Lavin. 2007. *Passing the Torch: Does Higher Education for the Disadvantaged Pay Off Across the Generations?* New York: Russell Sage Foundation.

Autor, David H. 2010. "The Polarization of Job Opportunities in the U.S. Labor Market: Implications for Employment and Earnings." Technical report. Washington, D.C.: Center for American Progress and the Hamilton Project.

Averett, Susan L., and Mark L. Burton. 1996. "College Attendance and the College Wage Premium: Differences by Gender." *Economics of Education Review* 15(1): 37–49.

Axinn, William G., and Arland Thornton. 2000. "The Transformation in the Meaning of Marriage." In *The Ties That Bind: Perspectives on Marriage and Cohabitation,* edited by Michelle Hindin, Arland Thornton, Elizabeth Thomson, Christine Bachrach, and Linda J. Waite. New York: Aldine Transaction.

Bachman, Jerald G. 2002. *The Decline of Substance Use in Young Adulthood: Changes in Social Activities, Roles, and Beliefs.* Mahwah, N.J.: Lawrence Erlbaum.

Bae, Yupin, Susan Choy, Claire Geddes, Jennifer Sable, and Thomas Snyder. 2000. "Trends in Educational Equity of Girls and Women." Technical report. Washington: U.S. Department of Education, National Center for Education Statistics.

Bahr, Stephen J., Suzanne L. Maughan, Anastasios C. Marcos, and Bingdao Li. 1998. "Family, Religiosity, and the Risk of Adolescent Drug Use." *Journal of Marriage and the Family* 60(4): 979–92.

Bailey, Martha J., and Susan M. Dynarski. 2009. "Inequality in Postsecondary Attainment: An Historical Perspective." In *Whither Opportunity? Rising Inequality, Schools, and Children's Life Chances,* edited by Greg J. Duncan and Richard Murnane. New York and Chicago: Russell Sage Foundation and Spencer Foundation.

———. 2011. "Gains and Gaps: Changing Inequality in U.S. College Entry and Completion." Technical report. Cambridge, Mass.: National Bureau of Economic Research.

Bailey, Susan, Lynn Burbidge, Patricia B. Campbell, Barbara Jackson, Fern Marx, and Peggy McIntosh. 1992. "The AAUW Report: How Schools Shortchange Girls: Executive Summary." Washington, D.C.: American Association of University Women Educational Foundation.

Baker, David P., and Deborah Perkins Jones. 1993. "Creating Gender Equality: Cross-National Gender Stratification and Mathematical Performance." *Sociology of Education* 66(2): 91–103.

Baumert, Jürgen, Petra Stanat, and Rainer Watermann. 2006. "Schulstruktur und die Entstehung differenzieller Lern- und Entwicklungsmilieus" ("School Structure and the Emergence of a Differential Learning and Development Environment"). In *Herkunftsbedingte Disparitäten im Bildungswesen: Differenzielle Bildungsprozesse und Probleme der Verteilungsgerechtigkeit: Vertiefende Analysen im Rahmen von PISA 2000 (The Origins of Disparities in Education: Differential Formation Processes and Problems of Distributive Justice: In-Depth Analysis of PISA 2000),* edited by Jürgen Baumert, Petra Stanat, and Rainer Watermann. Wiesbaden, Germany: VS Verlag für Sozialwissenschaften / GWV Fachverlage GmbH.

Baumrind, Diana. 1968. "Authoritarian Versus Authoritative Parental Control." *Adolescence* 3(11): 255–72.

Baydar, Nazli, and Jeanne Brooks-Gunn. 1991. "Effects of Maternal Employment and Child-Care Arrangements on Preschoolers' Cognitive and Behavioral Outcomes: Evidence from the Children of the National Longitudinal Survey of Youth." *Developmental Psychology* 27(6): 932.

Becker, Gary S. 1981. *A Treatise on the Family.* Cambridge, Mass.: Harvard University Press.

Behrman, Jere R., and Mark R. Rosenzweig. 2002. "Does Increasing Women's Schooling Raise the Schooling of the Next Generation?" *American Economic Review* 92(1): 323–34.

Beller, Michal, and Naomi Gafni. 1996. "The 1991 International Assessment of Educational Progress in Mathematics and Sciences: The Gender Differences Perspective." *Journal of Educational Psychology* 88(2): 365–77.

Bem, Sandra Lipsitz. 1981. "Gender Schema Theory: A Cognitive Account of Sex Typing." *Psychological Review* 88(4): 354.

Benbow, Camilla Persson, and Lola L. Minor. 1986. "Mathematically Talented Males and Females and Achievement in the High School Sciences." *American Educational Research Journal* 23(3): 425.

Berenbaum, Sheri A., Carol Lynn Martin, Laura D. Hanish, Phillip T. Briggs, and Richard A. Fabes. 2007. "Sex Differences in Children's Play." In *Sex Differences in the Brain: From Genes to Behavior,* edited by Jill B. Becker, Karen J. Berkley, Nori Geary, Elizabeth Hampson, James P. Herman, and Elizabeth A. Young. New York: Oxford University Press.

Berger, Joseph, Bernard P. Cohen, and Morris Zelditch Jr. 1972. "Status Characteristics and Social Interaction." *American Sociological Review* 37(3): 241–55.

Bergmann, Barbara R. 2005. *The Economic Emergence of Women.* London: Palgrave Macmillan.

Berryman, Sue E. 1983. *Who Will Do Science? Minority and Female Attainment of Science and Mathematics Degrees: Trends and Causes.* New York: Rockefeller Foundation.

Best, Raphaella. 1983. *We've All Got Scars: What Boys and Girls Learn in Elementary School.* Bloomington: Indiana University Press.

Beutel, Ann M., and Margaret Mooney Marini. 1995. "Gender and Values." *American Sociological Review* 60(3): 436–48.

Bianchi, Suzanne. 1999. "Feminization and Juvenilization of Poverty: Trends, Relative Risks, Causes, and Consequences." *Annual Review of Sociology* 25: 307–33.

Bianchi, Suzanne M., and John Robinson. 1997. "What Did You Do Today? Children's Use of Time, Family Composition, and the Acquisition of Social Capital." *Journal of Marriage and the Family* 59(2): 332–44.

Bianchi, Susan M., John P. Robinson, and Melissa A. Milkie. 2006. *Changing Rhythms of American Family Life.* New York: Russell Sage Foundation.

Bingley, Paul, Vibeke Myrup Jensen, and Annette Quinto Romani. 2009. "Intergenerational Transmission of Human Capital: Reform-Based Evidence from Denmark." Technical report. Copenhagen: Danish National Center for Social Research.

Bishop, John H., Matthew Bishop, Lara Gelbwasser, Shanna Green, Andrew Zuckerman, Amy Ellen Schwartz, and David F. Labaree. 2003. "Nerds and Freaks: A Theory of Student Culture and Norms." *Brookings Papers on Education Policy* 6: 141–213.

Björklund, Anders, Lena Lindahl, and Matthew J. Lindquist. 2008. "What More Than Parental Income? An Exploration of What Swedish Siblings Get from Their Parents." IZA Discussion Paper 3735. Bonn: Institute for the Study of Labor (IZA) (September).

Björklund, Anders, Mikael Lindahl, and Erik Plug. 2006. "The Origins of Intergenerational Associations: Lessons from Swedish Adoption Data." *Quarterly Journal of Economics* 121(3): 999–1028.

Black, Dan A., and Jeffrey A. Smith. 2004. "How Robust Is the Evidence on the Effects of College Quality? Evidence from Matching." *Journal of Econometrics* 121(1–2): 99–124.

Blackwell, Lisa S., Kali H. Trzesniewski, and Carol Sorich Dweck. 2007. "Implicit Theories of Intelligence Predict Achievement Across an Adolescent Transition: A Longitudinal Study and an Intervention." *Child Development* 78(1): 246–63.

Blau, Francine D., and Lawrence M. Kahn. 2000. "Gender Differences in Pay." *Journal of Economic Perspectives* 14(4): 75–99.

———. 2007a. "The Gender Pay Gap." *The Economists' Voice* 4(4): 5.

———. 2007b. "The Gender Pay Gap: Have Women Gone as Far as They Can?" *Academy of Management Perspectives* 21(1): 7–23.

Bobbitt-Zeher, Donna. 2007. "The Gender Income Gap and the Role of Education." *Sociology of Education* 80(1): 1.

Bogenschneider, Karen, and Laurence Steinberg. 1994. "Maternal Employment and Adolescents' Academic Achievement: A Developmental Analysis." *Sociology of Education* 67(1): 60–77.

Boulis, Ann K., and Jerry A. Jacobs. 2010. *The Changing Face of Medicine: Women Doctors and the Evolution of Health Care in America.* Ithaca, N.Y.: Cornell University Press.

Bound, John, Brad Hershbein, and Bridget Terry Long. 2009. "Playing the Admissions Game: Student Reactions to Increasing College Competition." *Journal of Economic Perspectives* 23(4): 119–46.

Bourdieu, Pierre. 1973. "Cultural Reproduction and Social Reproduction." In *Knowledge, Education, and Cultural Change*, edited by Robert Brown. London: Routledge.

———. 1984. *Distinction: A Social Critique of the Judgement of Taste.* Cambridge, Mass.: Harvard University Press.

Boushey, Heather. 2009. "The New Breadwinners." In *The Shriver Report: A Woman's Nation Changes Everything* by Maria Shriver and the Center for American Progress, edited by Heather Boushey and Ann O'Leary. Washington, D.C.: Center for American Progress.

Bowen, William G., Derek C. Bok, James L. Shulman, and Glenn C. Loury. 1998. *The Shape of the River: Long-Term Consequences of Considering Race in College and University Admissions.* Princeton, N.J.: Princeton University Press.

Bowen, William G., Matthew M. Chingos, and Michael S. McPherson. 2009. *Crossing the Finish Line: Completing College at America's Public Universities.* Princeton, N.J.: Princeton University Press.

Bowles, Samuel, and Herbert Gintis. 1976. *Schooling in Capitalist America: Educational Reform and the Contradictions of Economic Life.* New York: Basic Books.

Bozick, Robert, and Stefanie DeLuca. 2005. "Better Late Than Never: Delayed Enrollment in the High School to College Transition." *Social Forces* 84(1): 531.

Bradley, Karen, and Francisco O. Ramirez. 1996. "World Polity and Gender Parity: Women's Share of Higher Education, 1965–1985." *Research in Sociology of Education and Socialization* 11: 63–91.

Brand, Jennie E., and Yu Xie. 2010. "Who Benefits Most from College? Evidence for Negative Selection in Heterogeneous Economic Returns to Higher Education." *American Sociological Review* 75(4): 273–302.

Brewster, Karin L., and Irene Padavic. 2000. "Change in Gender-Ideology, 1977–1996: The Contributions of Intracohort Change and Population Turnover." *Journal of Marriage and Family* 62(2): 477–87.

Bridges, Judith S. 1989. "Sex Differences in Occupational Values." *Sex Roles* 20(3): 205–11.

Brint, Steven. 2008. "Remarks on Paul Attewell and David E. Lavin, *Passing the*

Torch: Does Higher Education for the Disadvantaged Pay Off Across the Generations?" Unpublished paper, University of California, Irvine.

Bronte-Tinkew, Jacinta, Kristin A. Moore, and Jennifer Carrano. 2006. "The Father-Child Relationship, Parenting Styles, and Adolescent Risk Behaviors in Intact Families." *Journal of Family Issues* 27(6): 850.

Brookhart, Susan M. 1993. "Teachers' Grading Practices: Meaning and Values." *Journal of Educational Measurement* 30(2): 123–42.

Brophy, Jere E., and Thomas L. Good. 1974. *Teacher-Student Relationships: Causes and Consequences.* New York: Holt, Rinehart and Winston.

Brown, B. Bradford 1990. "Peer Groups and Peer Cultures." In *At the Threshold: The Developing Adolescent,* edited by S. Shirley Feldman and Glen R. Elliott. Cambridge, Mass.: Harvard University Press.

Brown, B. Bradford, Nina Mounts, Susie D. Lamborn, and Laurence Steinberg. 1993. "Parenting Practices and Peer Group Affiliation in Adolescence." *Child Development* 64(2): 467–82.

Brown, Charles, and Mary Corcoran. 1997. "Sex-Based Differences in School Content and the Male-Female Wage Gap." *Journal of Labor Economics* 15(3): 431–65.

Buchmann, Claudia. 2009. "Gender Inequalities in the Transition to College." *Teachers College Record* 111(10): 2320–51.

Buchmann, Claudia, and Ben Dalton. 2002. "Interpersonal Influences and Educational Aspirations in Twelve Countries: The Importance of Institutional Context." *Sociology of Education* 75(2): 99–122.

Buchmann, Claudia, and Thomas A. DiPrete. 2006. "The Growing Female Advantage in College Completion: The Role of Family Background and Academic Achievement." *American Sociological Review* 71(4): 515–41.

Buchmann, Claudia, Thomas A. DiPrete, and Anne McDaniel. 2008. "Gender Inequalities in Education." *Annual Review of Sociology* 34: 319–37.

Buchmann, Claudia, and Hyunjoon Park. 2009. "Stratification and the Formation of Expectations in Highly Differentiated Educational Systems." *Research in Social Stratification and Mobility* 27(4): 245–67.

Burkhauser, Richard V. 2012. "A 'Second Opinion' on the Economic Health of the American Middle Class." *National Tax Journal* 65(1): 7–32.

Bussey, Kay, and Albert Bandura. 1999. "Social Cognitive Theory of Gender Development and Differentiation." *Psychological Review* 106(4): 676–713.

Byrnes, James P., David C. Miller, and William D. Schafer. 1999. "Gender Differences in Risk Taking: A Meta-Analysis." *Psychological Bulletin* 125(3): 367.

Cancian, Maria, and Deborah Reed. 2001. "Changes in Family Structure: Implications for Poverty and Related Policy." In *Understanding Poverty,* edited by Sheldon H. Danziger and Robert H. Haveman. Cambridge, Mass. and New York: Harvard University Press and Russell Sage Foundation.

Card, David. 2001. "Estimating the Return to Schooling: Progress on Some Persistent Econometric Problems." *Econometrica* 69(5): 1127–60.

Card, David, and Thomas Lemieux. 2001. "Going to College to Avoid the Draft: The Unintended Legacy of the Vietnam War." *American Economic Review* 91(2): 97–102.

Carlson, Jennifer. 2011. "Subjects of Stalled Revolution: A Theoretical Consideration of Contemporary American Femininity." *Feminist Theory* 12(1): 75.

Carlson, Marcia Jeanne. 2006. "Family Structure, Father Involvement, and Adolescent Behavioral Outcomes." *Journal of Marriage and Family* 68(1): 137–54.

Carneiro, Pedro, James J. Heckman, and Edward J. Vytlacil. 2011. "Estimating Marginal Returns to Education." *American Economic Review* 101(6): 2754–81.

Carrell, Scott E., Marianne E. Page, and James E. West. 2010. "Sex and Science: How Professor Gender Perpetuates the Gender Gap." *Quarterly Journal of Economics* 125(3): 1101–44.

Carrington, Bruce, Becky Francis, Merryn Hutchings, Christine Skelton, Barbara Read, and Ian Hall. 2007. "Does the Gender of the Teacher Really Matter? Seven- to Eight-Year-Olds' Accounts of Their Interactions with Their Teachers." *Educational Studies* 33(4): 397–413.

Ceci, Stephen J., Wendy M. Williams, and Susan M. Barnett. 2009. "Women's Underrepresentation in Science: Sociocultural and Biological Considerations." *Psychological Bulletin* 135(2): 218.

Charles, Kerwin Kofi, and Ming-Ching Luoh. 2003. "Gender Differences in Completed Schooling." *Review of Economics and Statistics* 85(3): 559–77.

Charles, Maria, and Karen Bradley. 2002. "Equal but Separate? A Cross-National Study of Sex Segregation in Higher Education." *American Sociological Review* 67(4): 573–99.

Charles, Maria, and David B. Grusky. 1995. "Models for Describing the Underlying Structure of Sex Segregation." *American Journal of Sociology* 100(4): 931–71.

Cherlin, Andrew, and Pamela B. Walters. 1981. "Trends in United States Men's and Women's Sex-Role Attitudes: 1972 to 1978." *American Sociological Review* 46(4): 453–60.

Chetty, Raj, John N. Friedman, Nathaniel Hilger, Emmanuel Saez, Diane Whitmore Schanzenbach, and Danny Yagan. 2010. "How Does Your Kindergarten Classroom Affect Your Earnings? Evidence from Project STAR." Technical report. Cambridge, Mass.: National Bureau of Economic Research.

Chetty, Raj, John N. Friedman, and Jonah Rockoff. 2011. "The Long-Term Impacts of Teachers: Teacher Value-Added and Student Outcomes in Adulthood." Working Paper 17699. Cambridge, Mass.: National Bureau of Economic Research (December).

Chinoy, Ely. 1955. *Automobile Workers and the American Dream.* Garden City, N.Y.: Doubleday.

Cho, Donghun. 2007. "The Role of High School Performance in Explaining Women's Rising College Enrollment." *Economics of Education Review* 26(4): 450–62.

Clarke, Edward Hammond. 1875. *Sex in Education: or, A Fair Chance for the Girls.* Boston: J. R. Osgood.

Clotfelter, Charles T., Helen F. Ladd, and Jacob L. Vigdor. 2006. "Teacher-Student Matching and the Assessment of Teacher Effectiveness." *Journal of Human Resources* 41(4): 778.

Cochran, John K., and Leonard Beeghley. 1991. "The Influence of Religion on Attitudes Toward Nonmarital Sexuality: A Preliminary Assessment of Reference Group Theory." *Journal for the Scientific Study of Religion* 30(1): 45–62.

Cohen, Geoffrey L., Julio Garcia, Nancy Apfel, and Allison Master. 2006. "Reducing the Racial Achievement Gap: A Social-Psychological Intervention." *Science* 313(5791): 1307–10.

Cohen, Geoffrey L., Julio Garcia, Valerie Purdie-Vaughns, Nancy Apfel, and Patricia Brzustoski. 2009. "Recursive Processes in Self-Affirmation: Intervening to Close the Minority Achievement Gap." *Science* 324(5925): 400–403.

Cohen, Michèle. 1998. "A Habit of Healthy Idleness: Boys' Underachievement in Historical Perspective." In *Failing Boys? Issues in Gender and Achievement*, edited by Debbie Epstein, Jannette Elwood, Valerie Hey, and Janet Maw. Buckingham, U.K.: Open University Press.

Coie, John D., and Gina Krehbiel. 1984. "Effects of Academic Tutoring on the Social Status of Low-Achieving, Socially Rejected Children." *Child Development* 55(4): 1465–78.

Coleman, James S. 1960. "The Adolescent Subculture and Academic Achievement." *American Journal of Sociology* 65(4): 337–47.

———. 1961. *The Adolescent Society*. New York: Free Press.

———. 1966. *Equality of Educational Opportunity*. Washington: U.S. Department of Health, Education, and Welfare, Office of Education.

Conley, Dalton. 2000. "Sibship Sex Composition: Effects on Educational Attainment." *Social Science Research* 29(3): 441–57.

Connell, R. W. 2005. *Masculinities*. Berkeley: University of California Press.

Cook, Glenn. 2006. "Boys at Risk: The Gender Achievement Gap." *American School Board Journal* 193(4): 4–6.

Cooksey, Elizabeth C., and Michelle M. Fondell. 1996. "Spending Time with His Kids: Effects of Family Structure on Fathers' and Children's Lives." *Journal of Marriage and the Family* 58(3): 693–707.

Corbett, Christianne, Catherine Hill, and Andresse St. Rose. 2008. *Where the Girls Are: The Facts About Gender Equity in Education*. Washington, D.C.: American Association of University Women.

Correll, Shelley J. 2001. "Gender and the Career Choice Process: The Role of Biased Self-Assessments 1." *American Journal of Sociology* 106(6): 1691–1730.

———. 2004. "Constraints into Preferences: Gender, Status, and Emerging Career Aspirations." *American Sociological Review* 69(4): 93–113.

Crosnoe, Robert. 2009. "Low-Income Students and the Socioeconomic Composition of Public High Schools." *American Sociological Review* 74(5): 709–30.

Crouter, Ann C., Susan M. McHale, and W. Todd Bartko. 1993. "Gender as an Organizing Feature in Parent-Child Relationships." *Journal of Social Issues* 49(3): 161–74.

Currie, Janet, and Enrico Moretti. 2003. "Mother's Education and the Intergenerational Transmission of Human Capital: Evidence from College Openings." *Quarterly Journal of Economics* 118(4): 1495–1532.

Cvencek, Dario, Andrew N. Meltzoff, and Anthony G. Greenwald. 2011. "Math-Gender Stereotypes in Elementary School Children." *Child Development* 82(3): 766–79.

Dale, Reginald R. 1969. *Mixed or Single-Sex School?* London: Routledge & Kegan Paul Books.

Dalton, Ben, Steven J. Ingels, Jane Downing, and Robert Bozick. 2007. *Advanced Mathematics and Science Coursetaking in the Spring High School Senior Classes of 1982, 1992 and 2004*. Washington: U.S. Department of Education.

Davies, Bronwyn. 1993. *Shards of Glass: Children Reading and Writing Beyond Gendered Identities*, rev. ed. New York: Hampton Press.

————. 2003. *Frogs and Snails and Feminist Tales: Preschool Children and Gender*, rev. ed. New York: Hampton Press.

Davies, Scott, and Neil Guppy. 1996. "Fields of Study, College Selectivity, and Student Inequalities in Higher Education." *Social Forces* 75(4): 1439–62.

Dee, Thomas S. 2005. "A Teacher Like Me: Does Race, Ethnicity, or Gender Matter?" *American Economic Review* 95(2): 158–65.

————. 2006. "The Why Chromosome." *Education Next* 6(4): 68.

Dee, Thomas S., and Brian A. Jacob. 2006. "Do High School Exit Exams Influence Educational Attainment or Labor Market Performance?" Working Paper 12199. Cambridge, Mass.: National Bureau of Economic Research.

DeNavas-Walt, Carmen, Bernadette D. Proctor, and Jessica C. Smith. 2010. "Income, Poverty, and Health Insurance Coverage in the United States." *Current Population Reports* P60-238. Washington: U.S. Census Bureau.

Denissen, Jaap J. A., Nicole R. Zarrett, and Jacquelynne S. Eccles. 2007. "I Like to Do It, I'm Able, and I Know I Am: Longitudinal Couplings Between Domain-Specific Achievement, Self-Concept, and Interest." *Child Development* 78(2): 430–47.

Department for Education and Skills. 2007. "Gender and Education: The Evidence on Pupils in England." Technical report. London: HM Government, Department for Education and Skills.

Desai, Sonalde, P. Lindsay Chase-Lansdale, and Robert T. Michael. 1989. "Mother or Market? Effects of Maternal Employment on the Intellectual Ability of Four-Year-Old Children." *Demography* 26(4): 545–61.

Desrochers, Donna M., and Jane V. Wellman. 2011. "Trends in College Spending: 1999–2009: Where Does the Money Come From? Where Does It Go? What Does It Buy?" Technical report. Washington, D.C.: Lumina Foundation for Education.

DiMaggio, Paul. 1982. "Cultural Capital and School Success: The Impact of Status Culture Participation on the Grades of U.S. High School Students." *American Sociological Review* 47(2): 189–201.

DiPrete, Thomas A. 2007. "Is This a Great Country? Upward Mobility and the Chance for Riches in Contemporary America." *Research in Social Stratification and Mobility* 25(1): 89–95.

DiPrete, Thomas A., and Claudia Buchmann. 2006. "Gender-Specific Trends in the Value of Education and the Emerging Gender Gap in College Completion." *Demography* 43(1): 1–24.

DiPrete, Thomas A., and Greg M. Eirich. 2006. "Cumulative Advantage as a Mechanism for Inequality: A Review of Theoretical and Empirical Developments." *Annual Review of Sociology* 32: 271–97.

DiPrete, Thomas A., and Jennifer L. Jennings. 2012. "Social and Behavioral Skills and the Gender Gap in Early Educational Achievement." *Social Science Research* 41(1): 1–15.

DiPrete, Thomas A., and Anne McDaniel. 2011. "Family, Gender, and Educational Outcomes in Elementary and Middle School." Paper presented to the 2011 meeting of the Population Association of America. Washington, D.C. (April 1).

DiPrete, Thomas A., Chandra Muller, and Nora Cate Shaeffer. 1982. *Discipline and Order in American High Schools*. Washington: U.S. Department of Education, National Center for Education Statistics.

Dolan, Lawrence J., Sheppard G. Kellam, C. Hendricks Brown, Lisa Werthamer-Larsson, George W. Rebok, Lawrence S. Mayer, Jolene Laudolf, Jaylan S. Turkkan, Carla Ford, and Leonard Wheeler. 1993. "The Short-Term Impact of Two Classroom-Based Preventive Interventions on Aggressive and Shy Behaviors and Poor Achievement." *Journal of Applied Developmental Psychology* 14(3): 317–45.

Dougherty, Christopher. 2005. "Why Are the Returns to Schooling Higher for Women Than for Men?" *Journal of Human Resources* 40(4): 969.

Dougherty, Conor. 2010. "Young Women's Pay Exceeds Male Peers." *Wall Street Journal*, September 1, 2010. Available at: http://online.wsj.com/article/SB100 01424052748704421104575463790770831192.html.

Downey, Douglas B., and Brian Powell. 1993. "Do Children in Single-Parent Households Fare Better Living with Same-Sex Parents?" *Journal of Marriage and the Family* 55(1): 55–71.

Dryler, Helen. 1998. "Parental Role Models, Gender, and Educational Choice." *British Journal of Sociology* 49(3): 375–98.

Duckworth, Angela L., Christopher Peterson, Michael D. Matthews, and Dennis R. Kelly. 2007. "Grit: Perseverance and Passion for Long-Term Goals." *Journal of Personality and Social Psychology* 92(6): 1087–1101.

Duckworth, Angela Lee, and Martin E. P. Seligman. 2006. "Self-Discipline Gives Girls the Edge: Gender in Self-Discipline, Grades, and Achievement Test Scores." *Journal of Educational Psychology* 98(1): 198–208.

Dumais, Susan A. 2002. "Cultural Capital, Gender, and School Success: The Role of Habitus." *Sociology of Education* 75(1): 44–68.

Duncan, Otis D., David L. Featherman, and Beverly Duncan. 1972. *Socioeconomic Background and Achievement*. New York: Seminar Press.

Duxbury, Linda E., and Christopher A. Higgins. 1991. "Gender Differences in Work-Family Conflict." *Journal of Applied Psychology* 76(1): 60–74.

Dweck, Carol S. 2000. *Self-Theories: Their Role in Motivation, Personality, and Development*. London: Taylor & Francis Group.

Dweck, Carol S., William Davidson, Sharon Nelson, and Bradley Enna. 1978. "Sex Differences in Learned Helplessness: II. The Contingencies of Evaluative Feedback in the Classroom, and III. An Experimental Analysis." *Developmental Psychology* 14(3): 268–76.

Eaton, Warren O., and Alice Piklai Yu. 1989. "Are Sex Differences in Child Motor Activity Level a Function of Sex Differences in Maturational Status?" *Child Development* 60(4): 1005–11.

Eccles, Jacquelynne S. 1987. "Gender Roles and Women's Achievement-Related Decisions." *Psychology of Women Quarterly* 11(2): 135–71.

———. 1989. "Bringing Young Women to Math and Science." In *Gender and Thought: Psychological Perspectives*, edited by Mary Crawford and Margaret Gentry. Berlin: Springer-Verlag.

———. 2005. "Studying Gender and Ethnic Differences in Participation in Math, Physical Science, and Information Technology Careers." In *Leaks in the Pipeline to Math, Science, and Technology Careers*, edited by Janis E. Jacobs and Sandra D. Simpkins. San Francisco: Jossey-Bass.

———. 2007. "Where Are All the Women? Gender Differences in Participation in Physical Science and Engineering." In *Why Aren't More Women in Science? Top*

Researchers Debate the Evidence, edited by Stephen J. Ceci and Wendy M. Williams. Washington, D.C.: American Psychological Association.

Eccles, Jacquelynne S., Terry F. Adler, Robert Futterman, Susan B. Goff, Caroline M. Kaczala, Judith L. Meece, and Carol Midgley. 1983. "Expectancies, Values, and Academic Behaviors." In *Achievement and Achievement Motivation,* edited by Janet T. Spence. San Francisco: W. H. Freeman.

Eccles, Jacquelynne S., and L. W. Hoffman. 1984. "Sex Roles, Socialization, and Occupational Behavior." In *Child Development Research and Social Policy,* vol. 1, edited by Harold William Stevenson and Alberta E. Siegel. Chicago: University of Chicago Press.

Eccles, Jacquelynne, Allan Wigfield, Rena D. Harold, and Phyllis Blumenfeld. 1993. "Age and Gender Differences in Children's Self- and Task Perceptions During Elementary School." *Child Development* 64(3): 830–47.

Ehrenberg, Ronald G., Daniel D. Goldhaber, and Dominic J. Brewer. 1995. "Do Teachers' Race, Gender, and Ethnicity Matter? Evidence from the National Educational Longitudinal Study of 1988." *Industrial and Labor Relations Review* 48(3): 547–61.

Eirich, Greg M. 2010. "Parental Religiosity and Children's Educational Attainment in the United States." PhD thesis, Columbia University, New York.

Eitzen, D. Stanley. 1975. "Athletics in the Status System of Male Adolescents: A Replication of Coleman." *Adolescence* 10(38): 267–76.

Elizur, Dov. 1994. "Gender and Work Values: A Comparative Analysis." *Journal of Social Psychology* 134(2): 201–12.

Ellison, Glenn, and Ashley Swanson. 2010. "The Gender Gap in Secondary School Mathematics at High Achievement Levels: Evidence from the American Mathematics Competitions." *Journal of Economic Perspectives* 24(2): 109–28.

Ellwood, David T., and Christopher Jencks. 2004. "The Uneven Spread of Single-Parent Families: What Do We Know? Where Do We Look for Answers?" In *Social Inequality,* edited by Katherine Neckerman. New York: Russell Sage Foundation.

Elo, I. T. 2009. "Social Class Differentials in Health and Mortality: Patterns and Explanations in Comparative Perspective." *Annual Review of Sociology* 35: 553–72.

England, Paula. 2010. "The Gender Revolution." *Gender and Society* 24(2): 149–66.

England, Paula, Paul Allison, Su Li, Noah Mark, Jennifer Thompson, Michelle J. Budig, and Han Sun. 2007. "Why Are Some Academic Fields Tipping Toward Female? The Sex Composition of U.S. Fields of Doctoral Degree Receipt, 1971–2002." *Sociology of Education* 80(1): 23–42.

England, Paula, and Su Li. 2006. "Desegregation Stalled: The Changing Gender Composition of College Majors, 1971–2002." *Gender and Society* 20(5): 657–77.

Entwisle, Doris R., Karl L. Alexander, and Linda Steffel Olson. 1994. "The Gender Gap in Math: Its Possible Origins in Neighborhood Effects." *American Sociological Review* 59(6): 822–38.

———. 1997. *Children, Schools, and Inequality.* Boulder, Colo.: Westview Press.

———. 2005. "First Grade and Educational Attainment by Age Twenty-Two: A New Story." *American Journal of Sociology* 110(5): 1458–1502.

———. 2007. "Early Schooling: The Handicap of Being Poor and Male." *Sociology of Education* 80(2): 114–38.

Entwisle, Doris R., and Leslie Alec Hayduk. 1982. *Early Schooling: Cognitive and Affective Outcomes.* Baltimore, Md.: Johns Hopkins University Press.

Epstein, Cynthia Fuchs. 1970. *Woman's Place: Options and Limits in Professional Careers.* Berkeley: University of California Press.

Epstein, Debbie. 1998. "Real Boys Don't Work: Underachievement, Masculinity, and the Harassment of Sissies." In *Failing Boys? Issues in Gender and Achievement,* edited by Debbie Epstein, Jannette Elwood, Valerie Hey, and Janet Maw. Buckingham, U.K.: Open University Press.

Epstein, Debbie, Jannette Elwood, Valerie Hey, and Janet Maw. 1998. "Schoolboy Frictions: Feminism and 'Failing' Boys." In *Failing Boys? Issues in Gender and Achievement,* edited by Debbie Epstein, Jannette Elwood, Valerie Hey, and Janet Maw. Buckingham, U.K.: Open University Press.

Ermisch, John, and Chiara Pronzato. 2009. "Causal Effects of Parents' Education on Children's Education (and Indications of Why They Exist)." Unpublished paper, University of Essex.

Fan, Xitao, and Michael Chen. 2001. "Parental Involvement and Students' Academic Achievement: A Meta-Analysis." *Educational Psychology Review* 13(1): 1–22.

Farkas, George. 2003. "Cognitive Skills and Noncognitive Traits and Behaviors in Stratification Processes." *Annual Review of Sociology* 29: 541–62.

Farkas, George, Robert Grobe, David Sheehan, and Yuan Shuan. 1990. "Cultural Resources and School Success: Gender, Ethnicity, and Poverty Groups Within an Urban School District." *American Sociological Review* 55(1): 127–42.

Felmlee, Diane H. 1993. "The Dynamic Interdependence of Women's Employment and Fertility." *Social Science Research* 22(4): 333–60.

Fischer, Claude S., and Michael Hout. 2006. *Century of Difference: How America Changed in the Last One Hundred Years.* New York: Russell Sage Foundation.

Fishbein, Martin. 1963. "An Investigation of Relationships Between Beliefs About an Object and the Attitude Toward That Object." *Human Relations* 16(3): 233–40.

Fishbein, Martin, and Icek Ajzen. 1975. *Belief, Attitude Intention, and Behavior: An Introduction to Theory and Research.* Reading, Mass.: Addison-Wesley.

Flynn, James R. 1994. "IQ Gains over Time." In *Encyclopedia of Human Intelligence,* edited by Robert J. Steinberg. New York: Macmillan.

———. 2007. *What Is Intelligence? Beyond the Flynn Effect.* Cambridge: Cambridge University Press.

Fordham, Signithia, and John U. Ogbu. 1986. "Black Students' School Success: Coping with the Burden of 'Acting White.'" *Urban Review* 18(3): 176–206.

Fox, Mary Frank, and Paula E. Stephan. 2001. "Careers of Young Scientists: Preferences, Prospects, and Realities by Gender and Field." *Social Studies of Science* 31(1): 109–22.

Francis, Becky. 2000. *Boys, Girls, and Achievement: Addressing the Classroom Issues.* London: Routledge Falmer.

Freeman, Catherine E. 2004. *Trends in Educational Equity of Girls and Women: 2004.* Washington: U.S. Department of Education, National Center for Education Statistics, Institute of Education Sciences.

Freeman, Richard B. 1976. *The Overeducated American.* Orlando, Fla.: Academic Press.

Freese, Jeremy, and Brian Powell. 1999. "Sociobiology, Status, and Parental Investment in Sons and Daughters: Testing the Trivers-Willard Hypothesis." *American Journal of Sociology* 104(6): 1704–43.

Fry, Richard. 2005. "Recent Changes in the Entry of Hispanic and White Youth into College." Washington, D.C.: Pew Hispanic Center.

Galbraith, John K. 1956. *American Capitalism: The Concept of Countervailing Power*. Boston: Houghton Mifflin.

Gallagher, Ann M., and James C. Kaufman. 2005. *Gender Differences in Mathematics: An Integrative Psychological Approach*. Cambridge: Cambridge University Press.

Gamoran, Adam, and Robert D. Mare. 1989. "Secondary School Tracking and Educational Inequality: Compensation, Reinforcement, or Neutrality?" *American Journal of Sociology* 94(5): 1146–83.

Gerber, Theodore P., and Sin Yi Cheung. 2008. "Horizontal Stratification in Postsecondary Education: Forms, Explanations, and Implications." *Annual Review of Sociology* 34: 299–318.

Gerber, Theodore P., and David R. Schaefer. 2004. "Horizontal Stratification of Higher Education in Russia: Trends, Gender Differences, and Labor Market Outcomes." *Sociology of Education* 77(1): 32–59.

Gerson, Kathleen. 1985. *Hard Choices: How Women Decide About Work, Career, and Motherhood*. Berkeley: University of California Press.

Gertz, David M. 2010. "Men's and Women's Earnings for States and Metropolitan Statistical Areas: 2009." Washington, D.C.: U.S. Census Bureau.

Gilliam, Walter S. 2005. "Prekindergarteners Left Behind: Expulsion Rates in State Prekindergarten Systems." Policy Brief Series. New York: Foundation for Child Development.

Goldin, Claudia. 1977. "Female Labor Force Participation: The Origin of Black and White Differences, 1870 and 1880." *Journal of Economic History* 37(1): 87–108.

———. 1990. *Understanding the Gender Gap: An Economic History of American Women*. New York: Oxford University Press.

———. 1992. "The Meaning of College in the Lives of American Women: The Past One-Hundred Years." Cambridge, Mass.: National Bureau of Economic Research.

Goldin, Claudia, and Lawrence F. Katz. 2000. "The Power of the Pill: Oral Contraceptives and Women's Career and Marriage Decisions." Cambridge, Mass.: National Bureau of Economic Research.

———. 2008. *The Race Between Education and Technology*. Cambridge, Mass.: Harvard University Press.

———. 2010. "Putting the Co in Education: Timing, Reasons, and Consequences of College Coeducation from 1835 to the Present." Working Paper 16281. Cambridge, Mass.: National Bureau of Economic Research.

Goldin, Claudia, Lawrence F. Katz, and Ilyana Kuziemko. 2006. "The Homecoming of American College Women: The Reversal of the College Gender Gap." *Journal of Economic Perspectives* 20(1): 133–56.

Goldman, Dana P., and James P. Smith. 2002. "Can Patient Self-Management Help Explain the SES Health Gradient?" *Proceedings of the National Academy of Sciences* 99(16): 10929–34.

Goldrick-Rab, Sara Y. 2006. "Following Their Every Move: How Social Class Shapes Postsecondary Pathways." *Sociology of Education* 79(1): 61–79.

Golombok, Susan, John Rust, Karyofyllis Zervoulis, Tim Croudace, Jean Golding, and Melissa Hines. 2008. "Developmental Trajectories of Sex-Typed Behavior in Boys and Girls: A Longitudinal General Population Study of Children Aged 2.5–8 Years." *Child Development* 79(5): 1583–93.

Good, Catherine, Joshua Aronson, and Michael Inzlicht. 2003. "Improving Adolescents' Standardized Test Performance: An Intervention to Reduce the Effects of Stereotype Threat." *Journal of Applied Developmental Psychology* 24(6): 645–62.

Gottfredson, Michael R., and Travis Hirschi. 1990. *A General Theory of Crime.* Palo Alto, Calif.: Stanford University Press.

Gould, Eric D., Victor Lavy, M. Daniele Paserman, and M. Scopus. 2010. "Does Immigration Affect the Long-Term Educational Outcomes of Natives? Quasi-Experimental Evidence." *Economic Journal* 119(540): 1243–69.

Graham, Patricia Albjerg. 1978. "Expansion and Exclusion: A History of Women in American Higher Education." *Signs* 3(4): 759–73.

Graue, M. Elizabeth, and James DiPerna. 2000. "Redshirting and Early Retention: Who Gets the Gift of Time and What Are Its Outcomes?" *American Educational Research Journal* 37(2): 509–34.

Green, Kenneth C. 2011. "The 2011 *Inside Higher Ed* Survey of College and University Admissions Officers." Report available at: http://www.insidehigh ered.com/sites/default/server_files/files/9-20finaladmissionsreport.pdf (accessed September 17, 2012).

Grodsky, Eric, and Catherine Riegle-Crumb. 2010. "Those Who Choose and Those Who Don't: Social Background and College Orientation." *Annals of the American Academy of Political and Social Science* 627(1): 14–35.

Guiso, Luigi, Ferdinando Monte, Paola Sapienza, and Luigi Zingales. 2008. "Culture, Gender, and Math." *Science* 320(5880): 1164–65.

Gullo, Dominic F., and Christine B. Burton. 1992. "Age of Entry, Preschool Experience, and Sex as Antecedents of Academic Readiness in Kindergarten." *Early Childhood Research Quarterly* 7(2): 175–86.

Gurian, Michael, and Kathy Stevens. 2007. *The Minds of Boys: Saving Our Sons from Falling Behind in School and Life.* San Francisco: Jossey-Bass.

Hallinan, Maureen T. 1988. "Equality of Educational Opportunity." *Annual Review of Sociology* 14: 249–68.

Halpern, Diane F. 1997. "Sex Differences in Intelligence: Implications for Education." *The American Psychologist* 52(10): 1091–1101.

Hansen, Jo-Ida C., Rose C. Collins, Jane L. Swanson, and Nadya A. Fouad. 1993. "Gender Differences in the Structure of Interests." *Journal of Vocational Behavior* 42(2): 200–11.

Hansot, Elisabeth, and David Tyack. 1988. "Gender in American Public Schools: Thinking Institutionally." *Signs* 13(4): 741–60.

Hanushek, Eric A. 1981. "Throwing Money at Schools." *Journal of Policy Analysis and Management* 1(1): 19–41.

———. 1989. "The Impact of Differential Expenditures on School Performance." *Educational Researcher* 18(4): 45–62.

Harris, Kathleen Mullan, Frank F. Furstenberg Jr., and Jeremy K. Marmer. 1998.

"Paternal Involvement with Adolescents in Intact Families: The Influence of Fathers over the Life Course." *Demography* 35(2): 201–16.

Hauser, Robert M., Shu-Ling Tsai, and William H. Sewell. 1983. "A Model of Stratification with Response Error in Social and Psychological Variables." *Sociology of Education* 56(1): 20–46.

Haveman, Robert H., and Barbara L. Wolfe. 1995. *Succeeding Generations: On the Effects of Investments in Children*. New York: Russell Sage Foundation.

Hawkins, David A., and Jessica Lautz. 2007. "State of College Admission." Alexandria, Va.: National Association for College Admission Counseling.

Heard, Holly E. 2007. "Fathers, Mothers, and Family Structure: Family Trajectories, Parent Gender, and Adolescent Schooling." *Journal of Marriage and Family* 69(2): 435–50.

Heckman, James J., and Paul LaFontaine. 2007. "The American High School Graduation Rate: Trends and Levels." IZA Discussion Paper 3216. Bonn: Institute for the Study of Labor (IZA) (December).

Heckman, James J., Jora Stixrud, and Sergio Urzua. 2006. "The Effects of Cognitive and Noncognitive Abilities on Labor Market Outcomes and Social Behavior." *Journal of Labor Economics* 24(3): 411–82.

Hedges, Larry V., and Amy Nowell. 1995. "Sex Differences in Mental Test Scores, Variability, and Numbers of High-Scoring Individuals." *Science* 269(5220): 41–45.

Helbig, Marcel. 2010. "Sind Lehrerinnen für den geringeren Schulerfolg von Jungen verantwortlich?" ("Are Teachers Responsible for the Lower School Achievement of Boys?"), *Kölner Zeitschrift für Soziologie und Sozialpsychologie* (*Cologne Journal of Sociology and Social Psychology*) 62(1): 93–111.

Heriot, Gail, and Alison Somin. 2011. "Affirmative Action for Men? Strange Silences and Strange Bedfellows in the Public Debate over Discrimination Against Women in College Admissions." *Engage* 12(3): 14–22.

Hess, Beth B., and Myra Marx Ferree. 1987. *Analyzing Gender: A Handbook of Social Science Research*. Thousand Oaks, Calif.: Sage Publications.

Hetherington, E. Mavis, and John Kelly. 2003. *For Better or for Worse: Divorce Reconsidered*. New York: W. W. Norton & Co.

Hinshaw, Stephen P. 1992. "Externalizing Behavior Problems and Academic Underachievement in Childhood and Adolescence: Causal Relationships and Underlying Mechanisms." *Psychological Bulletin* 111(1): 127–55.

Hirschman, Charles. 1983. "America's Melting Pot Reconsidered." *Annual Review of Sociology* 9: 397–423.

———. 2001. "The Educational Enrollment of Immigrant Youth: A Test of the Segmented-Assimilation Hypothesis." *Demography* 38(3): 317–36.

Hoekstra, Mark. 2009. "The Effect of Attending the Flagship State University on Earnings: A Discontinuity-Based Approach." *Review of Economics and Statistics* 91(4): 717–24.

Hoff-Ginsberg, Erika, and Twila Tardif. 2002. "Socioeconomic Status and Parenting." In *Handbook of Parenting: Biology and Ecology of Parenting*, vol. 2, edited by Marc H. Bornstein. Mahwah, N.J.: Lawrence Erlbaum Associates.

Hofferth, Sandra L., and John F. Sandberg. 2001. "How American Children Spend Their Time." *Journal of Marriage and Family* 63(2): 295–308.

Hogan, Dennis P. 1981. *Transitions and Social Change: The Early Lives of American Men.* New York: Academic Press.

Holland, Spencer H. 1992. "Same Gender Classes in Baltimore: How to Avoid Problems Faced in Detroit/Milwaukee." *Equity and Excellence* 25(2–4): 93.

Holmlund, Helena, and Krister Sund. 2008. "Is the Gender Gap in School Performance Affected by the Sex of the Teacher?" *Labour Economics* 15(1): 37–53.

Horn, Laura, Mark D. Premo, Educational Resources Information Center (U.S.), and National Center for Education Statistics. 1995. *Profile of Undergraduates in U.S. Postsecondary Education Institutions, 1992–1993, with an Essay on Undergraduates at Risk.* Washington: U.S. Department of Education, Office of Educational Research and Improvement, Educational Resources Information Center.

Howe, Christine. 1997. *Gender and Classroom Interaction: A Research Review.* Edinburgh: Scottish Council for Research in Education.

Hoxby, Caroline. 2000. "Peer Effects in the Classroom: Learning from Gender and Race Variation." Working Paper 7867. Cambridge, Mass.: National Bureau of Economic Research.

———. 2009. "The Changing Selectivity of American Colleges." *Journal of Economic Perspectives* 23(4): 95–118.

Hubbard, William H. J. 2011. "The Phantom Gender Difference in the College Wage Premium." *Journal of Human Resources* 46(3): 568–86.

Hyde, Janet Shibley. 2005. "The Gender Similarities Hypothesis." *American Psychologist* 60(6): 581–92.

Hyde, Janet S., Sara M. Lindberg, Marcia C. Linn, Amy B. Ellis, and Caroline C. Williams. 2008. "Gender Similarities Characterize Math Performance." *Science* 321(5888): 494–95.

Imberman, S., A. Kugler, and B. Sacerdote. 2009. "Katrina's Children: A Natural Experiment in Peer Effects from Hurricane Evacuees." Working Paper 15291. Cambridge, Mass.: National Bureau of Economic Research.

Isen, Adam, and Betsey Stevenson. 2010. "Women's Education and Family Behavior: Trends in Marriage, Divorce, and Fertility." Cambridge, Mass.: National Bureau of Economic Research.

Jackson, James, and James Moore III. 2008. "Introduction: The African American Male Crisis in Education: A Popular Media Infatuation or Needed Public Policy Response?" *American Behavioral Scientist* 51(7): 847–53.

Jacob, Brian A., Lars Lefgren, and David P. Sims. 2010. "The Persistence of Teacher-Induced Learning." *Journal of Human Resources* 45(4): 915–43.

Jacobs, Janis E., and Martha M. Bleeker. 2004. "Girls' and Boys' Developing Interests in Math and Science: Do Parents Matter?" *New Directions for Child and Adolescent Development* 106(2): 5–21.

Jacobs, Janis E., Stephanie Lanza, D. Wayne Osgood, Jacquelynne S. Eccles, and Allan Wigfield. 2002. "Changes in Children's Self-Competence and Values: Gender and Domain Differences Across Grades One Through Twelve." *Child Development* 73: 509–27.

Jacobs, Jerry A. 1995. "Gender and Academic Specialties: Trends Among Recipients of College Degrees in the 1980s." *Sociology of Education* 68(2): 81–98.

———. 1996. "Gender Inequality and Higher Education." *Annual Review of Sociology* 22: 153–85.

———. 1999. "Gender and the Stratification of Colleges." *Journal of Higher Education* 70(2): 161–87.

Jencks, Christopher, and Susan E. Mayer. 1990. "The Social Consequences of Growing Up in a Poor Neighborhood." In Committee on National Urban Policy, National Research Council, *Inner-City Poverty in the United States*. Washington, D.C.: National Academies Press.

Jennings, Jennifer L., and Thomas A. DiPrete. 2010. "Teacher Effects on Social and Behavioral Skills in Early Elementary School." *Sociology of Education* 83(2): 135–59.

Johnson, M. K. 2001. "Social Origins, Adolescent Experiences, and Work Value Trajectories During the Transition to Adulthood." *Social Forces* 80(4): 1307–40.

Jordan, Ellen. 1995. "Fighting Boys and Fantasy Play: The Construction of Masculinity in the Early Years of School." *Gender and Education* 7(1): 69–86.

Joy, Lois. 2002. "Salaries of Recent Male and Female College Graduates: Educational and Labor Market Effects." *Industrial and Labor Relations Review* 56(4): 606–21.

Kalmijn, Maithijs. 1994. "Mother's Occupational Status and Children's Schooling." *American Sociological Review* 59(2): 257–75.

Kane, T. J., and D. O. Staiger. 2008. "Estimating Teacher Impacts on Student Achievement: An Experimental Evaluation." Working Paper 14607. Cambridge, Mass.: National Bureau of Economic Research.

Kao, Grace. 1995. "Asian Americans as Model Minorities? A Look at Their Academic Performance." *American Journal of Education* 103(2): 121–59.

Karabel, Jerome. 2005. *The Chosen: The Hidden History of Admission and Exclusion at Harvard, Yale, and Princeton*. New York: Houghton Mifflin.

Keith, Timothy Z., Christine Diamond-Hallam, and Jodene Goldenring Fine. 2004. "Longitudinal Effects of In-School and Out-of-School Homework on High School Grades." *School Psychology Quarterly* 19(3): 187.

Kelly, Sean. 2004. "Do Increased Levels of Parental Involvement Account for Social Class Differences in Track Placement?" *Social Science Research* 33(1): 626–59.

———. 2008. "What Types of Students' Effort Are Rewarded with High Marks?" *Sociology of Education* 81(1): 32–52.

Kerckhoff, Alan C. 1977. "The Realism of Educational Ambitions in England and the United States." *American Sociological Review* 42(4): 563–71.

Kimmel, Michael S. 2008. *Guyland: The Perilous World Where Boys Become Men*. New York: HarperCollins.

Kindlon, Dan J., and Michael Thompson. 2000. *Raising Cain: Protecting the Emotional Life of Boys*. New York: Ballantine Books.

King, Jacqueline E. 2000. *Gender Equity in Higher Education: Are Male Students at a Disadvantage?* Washington, D.C.: American Council on Education.

Kleykamp, Meredith A. 2006. "College, Jobs, or the Military? Enlistment During a Time of War." *Social Science Quarterly* 87(2): 272–90.

———. 2010. "Where Did the Soldiers Go? The Effects of Military Downsizing on College Enrollment and Employment." *Social Science Research* 39(3): 477–90.

Kobrin, Jennifer L., Viji Sathy, and Emily J. Shaw. 2007. "A Historical View of Subgroup Performance Differences on the SAT Reasoning Test." New York: College Entrance Examination Board.

Kochhar, Rakesh. 2011. "Two Years of Economic Recovery: Women Lose Jobs, Men Find Them." Washington, D.C.: Pew Research Center, Social and Demographic Trends (July 6).

Kohlberg, Lawrence. 1966. *A Cognitive-Developmental Analysis of Children's Sex-Role Concepts and Attitudes.* Palo Alto, Calif.: Stanford University Press.

Konrad, Alison, M., J. Edgar Ritchie, Jr., Pamela Lieb, and Elizabeth Corrigall. 2000. "Sex Differences and Similarities in Job Attribute Preferences: A Meta-Analysis." *Psychological Bulletin* 126(4): 593–641.

Koretz, Daniel, and Mark Berends. 2001. "Changes in High School Grading Standards in Mathematics, 1982–1992." Report prepared for the College Entrance Examination Board. Santa Monica, Calif.: RAND Corporation.

Krueger, Alan B., and Diane M. Whitmore. 2001. "Would Smaller Classes Help Close the Black-White Achievement Gap?" Working Paper 451. Princeton, N.J.: Princeton University, Industrial Relations Section,.

Ladd, Gary W., Sondra H. Birch, and Eric S. Buhs. 1999. "Children's Social and Scholastic Lives in Kindergarten: Related Spheres of Influence?" *Child Development* 70(6): 1373–1400.

Lahaderne, Henriette M. 1976. "Feminized Schools: Unpromising Myth to Explain Boys' Reading Problems." *The Reading Teacher* 29(8): 776–86.

Langan, Patrick A. 1991. "America's Soaring Prison Population." *Science* 251(5001): 1568.

Lareau, Annette. 2000. *Home Advantage: Social Class and Parental Intervention in Elementary Education.* Lanham, Md.: Rowman & Littlefield.

———. 2003. *Unequal Childhoods: Class, Race, and Family Life.* Berkeley: University of California Press.

Laub, John H., and Robert J. Sampson. 1993. "Turning Points in the Life Course: Why Change Matters to the Study of Crime." *Criminology* 31(3): 301–25.

Lavy, Victor, and Analía Schlosser. 2007. "Mechanisms and Impacts of Gender Peer Effects at School." Working Paper 13292. Cambridge, Mass.: National Bureau of Economic Research.

Leahy, Erin, and Guang Guo. 2001. "Gender Differences in Mathematical Trajectories." *Social Forces* 80(2): 713–32.

Lee, Valerie E. 1995. *Gender Equity and the Organization of Schools.* New York: Garland.

Lee, Valerie E., and Anthony S. Bryk. 1989. "A Multilevel Model of the Social Distribution of High School Achievement." *Sociology of Education* 62(3): 172–92.

Lee, Valerie E., and Helen M. Marks. 1990. "Sustained Effects of the Single-Sex Secondary School Experience on Attitudes, Behaviors, and Values in College." *Journal of Educational Psychology* 82(3): 578–92.

Legewie, Joscha, and Thomas A. DiPrete. 2009. "Family Determinants of the Changing Gender Gap in Educational Attainment: A Comparison of the U.S. and Germany." *Schmollers Jahrbuch (Journal of Applied Social Science Studies)* 129(2): 1–13.

———. 2011. "Gender Differences in the Effect of Peer SES: Evidence from a Second Quasi-Experimental Case Study." Working paper. New York: Columbia University.

———. 2012a. "High School Environments, STEM Orientations, and the Gender

Gap in Science and Engineering Degrees." Working paper. New York: Columbia University.

———. 2012b. "School Context and the Gender Gap in Educational Achievement." *American Sociological Review* 77(3): 463–85.

Leiter, Jeffrey, and James S. Brown. 1985. "Determinants of Elementary School Grading." *Sociology of Education* 58(3): 166–80.

Liben, Lynn S., Rebecca S. Bigler, and Holleen R. Krogh. 2001. "Pink- and Blue-Collar Jobs: Children's Judgments of Job Status and Job Aspirations in Relation to Sex of Worker." *Journal of Experimental Child Psychology* 79(4): 346–63.

Lin, Huey-Ling, Frank R. Lawrence, and Jeffrey Gorrell. 2003. "Kindergarten Teachers' Views of Children's Readiness for School." *Early Childhood Research Quarterly* 18(2): 225–37.

Link, Bruce G., and Jo Phelan. 1995. "Social Conditions as Fundamental Causes of Disease." *Journal of Health and Social Behavior* 35 (extra issue): 80–94.

Lippa, Richard. 1998. "Gender-Related Individual Differences and the Structure of Vocational Interests: The Importance of the People-Things Dimension." *Journal of Personality and Social Psychology* 74(4): 996–1009.

Livingston, Gretchen, and D'Vera Cohn. 2010. "Childlessness Up Among All Women; Down Among Women with Advanced Degrees." Washington, D.C.: Pew Research Center.

Long, J. Scott, ed. 2001. *From Scarcity to Visibility: Gender Differences in the Careers of Doctoral Scientists and Engineers.* Washington, D.C.: National Academies Press.

Lopez, Nancy. 2003. *Hopeful Girls, Troubled Boys: Race and Gender Disparity in Urban Education.* London: Routledge.

Loury, Linda Datcher. 1997. "The Gender Earnings Gap Among College-Educated Workers." *Industrial and Labor Relations Review* 50(4): 580.

Lueptow, Lloyd B., Lori Garovich-Szabo, and Margaret B. Lueptow. 2001. "Social Change and the Persistence of Sex Typing: 1974–1997." *Social Forces* 80(1): 1–35.

Mac an Ghaill, Mairtin Mac, ed. 1994. *The Making of Men: Masculinities, Sexualities, and Schooling.* Buckingham, U.K.: Open University Press.

Maccoby, Eleanor E. 1998. *The Two Sexes: Growing Up Apart, Coming Together.* Cambridge, Mass.: Harvard University Press.

———. 2003. *The Two Sexes: Growing Up Apart, Coming Together.* Cambridge, Mass.: Belknap Press of Harvard University Press.

Maccoby, Eleanor E., and Carol N. Jacklin. 1974. *The Psychology of Sex Differences.* Stanford, Calif.: Stanford University Press.

Maccoby, Eleanor E., and J. A. Martin. 1983. "Socialization in the Context of the Family: Parent-Child Interaction." In *Handbook of Child Psychology*, vol. 4, *Socialization, Personality, and Social Development*, 4th ed., edited by Paul H. Mussen and E. Mavis Hetherington. New York: Wiley.

Machin, Stephen, and Sandra McNally. 2005. "Gender and Student Achievement in English Schools." *Oxford Review of Economic Policy* 21(3): 357–72.

Machin, Stephen, and Tuomas Pekkarinen. 2008. "Assessment: Global Sex Differences in Test Score Variability." *Science* 322(5906): 1331.

MacLean, Alair. 2005. "Lessons from the Cold War: Military Service and College Education." *Sociology of Education* 78(3): 250–66.

MacLean, Alair, and Glen H. Elder Jr. 2007. "Military Service in the Life Course." *Sociology* 33(1): 175–96.

MacLeod, Jay. 2008. *Ain't No Makin' It: Aspirations and Attainment in a Low-Income Neighborhood.* Boulder, Colo.: Westview Press.

Malone, Lizabeth M., Jerry West, Kristin Denton Flanagan, and Jen Park. 2006. "The Early Reading and Mathematics Achievement of Children Who Repeated Kindergarten or Who Began School a Year Late." Washington: U.S. Department of Education, National Center for Education Statistics.

Mandara, Jelani. 2006. "The Impact of Family Functioning on African American Males." *Teachers College Record* 108(2): 206–23.

Mann, Allison, and Thomas A. DiPrete. 2012. "Trends in Gender Segregation in the Choice of Science and Engineering Majors." Working paper. New York: Columbia University.

Manski, Charles F. 1995. *Identification Problems in the Social Sciences.* Cambridge, Mass.: Harvard University Press.

Mare, Robert D. 1981. "Change and Stability in Educational Stratification." *American Sociological Review* 46(1): 72–87.

———. 1991. "Five Decades of Educational Assortative Mating." *American Sociological Review* 56(1): 15–32.

Marks, Gary N. 2007. "Accounting for the Gender Gaps in Student Performance in Reading and Mathematics: Evidence from Thirty-One Countries." *Oxford Review of Education* 34(1): 89–109.

Martin, Carol Lynn, and Richard A. Fabes. 2001. "The Stability and Consequences of Young Children's Same-Sex Peer Interactions." *Developmental Psychology* 37(3): 431.

Martin, Carol Lynn, and Charles F. Halverson. 1981. "A Schematic Processing Model of Sex Typing and Stereotyping in Children." *Child Development* 52(4): 1119–34.

Martin, Carol Lynn, Diane N. Ruble, and Joel Szkrybalo. 2002. "Cognitive Theories of Early Gender Development." *Psychological Bulletin* 128(6): 903.

Martin, Carol Lynn, Carolyn H. Wood, and Jane K. Little. 1990. "The Development of Gender Stereotype Components." *Child Development* 61(6): 1891–1904.

Martin, Steven P. 2005. "Growing Evidence for a 'Divorce Divide'? Education and Marital Dissolution Rates in the U.S. Since the 1970s." Unpublished paper. University of Maryland, Department of Sociology.

Martino, Wayne. 1999. "'Cool Boys,' 'Party Animals,' 'Squids,' and 'Poofters': Interrogating the Dynamics and Politics of Adolescent Masculinities in School." *British Journal of Sociology of Education* 20(2): 239–63.

Mason, Karen Oppenheim, and An-Magritt Jensen. 1995. *Gender and Family Change in Industrialized Countries.* New York: Oxford University Press.

Mathews, T. J., and Brady E. Hamilton. 2009. "Delayed Childbearing: More Women Are Having Their First Child Later in Life." Technical Report 21. Hyattsville, Md.: U.S. Department of Health and Human Services, Centers for Disease Control and Prevention, National Center for Health Statistics.

Maurin, Eric, and Sandra McNally. 2008. "Vive la Revolution! Long-Term Educational Returns of 1968 to the Angry Students." *Journal of Labor Economics* 26(1): 1–33.

McDaniel, Anne. 2009. "Cross-National Gender Gaps in Educational Expectations: The Influence of National-Level Gender Ideology and Educational Systems." *Comparative Education Review* 54(1): 27–50.

———. 2011. "Three Essays on Cross-National Gender Gaps in Education." PhD thesis, Ohio State University.

McDaniel, Anne, Thomas A. DiPrete, Claudia Buchmann, and Uri Shwed. 2011. "The Black Gender Gap in Educational Attainment: Historical Trends and Racial Comparisons." *Demography* 48(3): 889–914.

McHugh, Maureen C., and Irene Hanson Frieze. 1997. "The Measurement of Gender-Role Attitudes." *Psychology of Women Quarterly* 21(1): 1–16.

McLanahan, Sara, and Christine Percheski. 2008. "Family Structure and the Reproduction of Inequalities." *Annual Review of Sociology* 34: 257–76.

McLanahan, Sara, and Gary Sandefur. 1994. *Growing Up with a Single Parent: What Hurts, What Helps.* Cambridge, Mass.: Harvard University Press.

McLanahan, Sara, Aage Sørensen, and D. Watson. 1989. "Sex Differences in Poverty, 1950–1980." *Signs* 15(1): 102–22.

McLeod, Jane D., and Karen Kaiser. 2004. "Childhood Emotional and Behavioral Problems and Educational Attainment." *American Sociological Review* 69(5): 636.

McMillan, James H., Steve Myran, and Daryl Workman. 2002. "Elementary Teachers' Classroom Assessment and Grading Practices." *Journal of Educational Research* 95(4): 203–13.

Mickelson, Roslyn Arlin. 1989. "Why Does Jane Read and Write So Well? The Anomaly of Women's Achievement." *Sociology of Education* 62(1): 47–63.

Mirowsky, John, and Catherine E. Ross. 2003. *Education, Social Status, and Health.* Berlin: Aldine de Gruyter.

Mischel, Walter. 1966. "A Social-Learning View of Sex Differences in Behavior." In *The Development of Sex Differences,* edited by Roy G. D'Andrade. Palo Alto, Calif.: Stanford University Press.

Mishel, Lawrence, and Joydeep Roy. 2006. *Rethinking High School Graduation Rates and Trends.* Washington, D.C.: Economic Policy Institute.

Montmarquette, Claude, Kathy Cannings, and Sophie Mahseredjian. 2002. "How Do Young People Choose College Majors?" *Economics of Education Review* 21(6): 543–56.

Morgan, S. Philip, Diane N. Lye, and Gretchen A. Condran. 1988. "Sons, Daughters, and the Risk of Marital Disruption." *American Journal of Sociology* 94(1): 110–29.

Morgan, Stephen L. 1998. "Adolescent Educational Expectations: Rationalized, Fantasized, or Both?" *Rationality and Society* 10(2): 131–62.

———. 2005. *On the Edge of Commitment: Educational Attainment and Race in the United States.* Palo Alto, Calif.: Stanford University Press.

Morris, Edward W. 2008. "'Rednecks,' 'Rutters,' and 'Rithmetic': Social Class, Masculinity, and Schooling in a Rural Context." *Gender and Society* 22(6): 728–51.

Morse, Linda W., and Herbert M. Handley. 1985. "Listening to Adolescents: Gender Differences in Science Classroom Interaction." In *Gender Influences in Classroom Interaction,* edited by Louise C. Wilkinson and Cora Bagley Marrett. Orlando, Fla.: Academic Press.

Morse, Susan. 1998. *Separated by Sex: A Critical Look at Single-Sex Education for*

Girls. Washington, D.C.: American Association of University Women Educational Foundation.

MTA-Cooperative-Group. 1999. "A Fourteen-Month Randomised Clinical Trial of Treatment Strategies for Attention-Deficit/Hyperactivity Disorder." *Archives of General Psychiatry* 56(12): 1073–86.

Mundy, Liza. 2012. *The Richer Sex: How the New Majority of Female Breadwinners Is Transforming Sex, Love, and Family*. New York: Simon & Schuster.

Murphy, Joseph. 1991. *Restructuring Schools: Capturing and Assessing the Phenomena*. New York: Teachers College Press.

Murphy, Patricia, and Jannette Elwood. 1998. "Gendered Experiences, Choices, and Achievement: Exploring the Links." *International Journal of Inclusive Education* 2(2): 95–118.

Murray, Charles. 2009. "Intelligence and College." *National Affairs* (Fall): 95–106.

Muter, Valerie. 2003. *Early Reading Development and Dyslexia*. London: Whurr.

National Center for Education Statistics. 1994. "National Longitudinal Study of the High School Class of 1972" [NLS; Machine-readable database]. Available at: http://nces.ed.gov/surveys/nls72/ (accessed August 30, 2012).

———. 1995. "High School and Beyond Survey" [HSB; Machine-readable database]. Available at: http://nces.ed.gov/surveys/hsb/ (accessed August 30, 2012).

———. 1999. "Users' Manual for *ECLS-K Base Year Data Files and Electronic Codebook*." Washington: U.S. Department of Education.

———. 2003. "National Education Longitudinal Study of 1988" [NELS; Machine-readable database]. Available at: http://nces.ed.gov/surveys/nels88/ (accessed August 30, 2012).

———. 2007. "Education Longitudinal Study of 2002" [ELS; Machine-readable database]. Available at: http://nces.ed.gov/surveys/els2002/ (accessed August 30, 2012).

———. 2009. Early Child Longitudinal Study, Kindergarten Class of 1998–1999" [ECLS-K; Machine-readable database]. Available at: http://nces.ed.gov/ecls/kindergarten.asp (accessed August 30, 2012).

National Science Foundation. 2012. "Integrated Science and Engineering Data System" [WebCASPAR; Machine-readable database]. Available at: https://webcaspar.nsf.gov/ (accessed August 31, 2012).

Natriello, Gary, and Sanford M. Dornbusch. 1983. "Bringing Behavior Back In: The Effects of Student Characteristics and Behavior on the Classroom Behavior of Teachers." *American Educational Research Journal* 20(1): 29–43.

Neugebauer, Martin, Marcel Helbig, and Andreas Landmann. 2010. "Unmasking the Myth of the Same-Sex Teacher Advantage." *European Sociological Review* 27(5): 669–89.

Newcomer, Mabel. 1959. *A Century of Higher Education for American Women*. New York: Harper.

Nisbett, Richard E. 2009. *Intelligence and How to Get It: Why Schools and Culture Count*. New York: W. W. Norton & Co.

Noguera, Pedro A. 2003. "The Trouble with Black Boys: The Role and Influence of Environmental and Cultural Factors on the Academic Performance of African American Males." *Urban Education* 38(4): 431–59.

——. 2008. *The Trouble with Black Boys: And Other Reflections on Race, Equity, and the Future of Public Education.* San Francisco: Jossey-Bass.

Nosek, Brian A., Mahzarin R. Banaji, and Anthony G. Greenwald. 2002. "Math= Male, Me = Female, Therefore Math ≠ Me." *Journal of Personality and Social Psychology* 83(1): 44–59.

Office of the Under Secretary of Defense, Personnel, and Readiness. 2012. "Population Representation in the Military Services, Fiscal Year 2010." Available at: http://prhome.defense.gov/rfm/MPP/ACCESSION%20POLICY/PopRep 2010/index.html (accessed September 17, 2012).

Okamoto, Dina, and Paula England. 1999. "Is There a Supply Side to Occupational Sex Segregation?" *Sociological Perspectives* 42(4): 557–82.

Ono, Hiroshi. 2004. "Are Sons and Daughters Substitutable? Allocation of Family Resources in Contemporary Japan." *Journal of the Japanese and International Economies* 18(2): 143–60.

Organization for Economic Cooperation and Development (OECD). 2006. *Education at a Glance: 2006.* Paris: OECD.

——. 2010a. *Education at a Glance: 2010.* Paris: OECD.

——. 2010b. *PISA 2009 Results: What Students Know and Can Do: Student Performance in Math, Reading, and Science,* vol. 1. Paris: OECD.

——. 2011. *Education at a Glance: 2011.* Paris: OECD. Available at: http://www.oecd.org/education/highereducationandadultlearning/48631582.pdf (accessed August 31, 2012).

Paley, Vivian Gussin. 1984. *Boys and Girls: Superheroes in the Doll Corner.* Chicago: University of Chicago Press.

Pallas, Aaron M. 2003. "Educational Transitions, Trajectories, and Pathways." In *Handbook of the Life Course,* edited by Jeylan T. Mortimer and Michael J. Shanahan. New York: Kluwer Academic/Plenum Publishers.

Pallas, Aaron M., and Karl L. Alexander. 1983. "Sex Differences in Quantitative SAT Performance: New Evidence on the Differential Coursework Hypothesis." *American Educational Research Journal* 20(2): 165–182.

Papanek, Hanna. 1985. "Class and Gender in Education-Employment Linkages." *Comparative Education Review* 29(3): 317–46.

Park, Hyunjoon, and Jere R. Behrman. 2010. "Causal Effects of Single-Sex Schools on College Attendance: Random Assignment in Korean High Schools." Working paper. Philadelphia: University of Pennsylvania.

Pascoe, C. J. 2006. *"Dude, You're a Fag": Masculinity in High School.* Berkeley: University of California Press.

Penner, Andrew M. 2008. "Gender Differences in Extreme Mathematical Achievement: An International Perspective on Biological and Social Factors." *American Journal of Sociology* 114(51): 138–70.

Penner, Andrew M., and Marcel Paret. 2008. "Gender Differences in Mathematics Achievement: Exploring the Early Grades and the Extremes." *Social Science Research* 37(1): 239–53.

Perkins, Robert, Brian Kleiner, Stephen Roey, and Janis Brown. 2004. *The High School Transcript Study: A Decade of Change in Curricula and Achievement, 1990–2000.* Washington: U.S. Department of Education.

Peterson, James L., and Nicholas Zill. 1986. "Marital Disruption, Parent-Child

Relationships, and Behavior Problems in Children." *Journal of Marriage and the Family* 48(2): 295–307.

Pettit, Becky, and Bruce Western. 2004. "Mass Imprisonment and the Life Course: Race and Class Inequality in U.S. Incarceration." *American Sociological Review* 69(2): 151–69.

Pickering, Jon. 1997. *Raising Boys' Achievement*. Stafford, U.K.: Network Educational Press.

Pinker, Susan. 2008. *The Sexual Paradox: Men, Women. and the Real Gender Gap*. New York: Scribner.

Pollack, William S. 1999. *Real Boys: Rescuing Our Sons from the Myths of Boyhood*. New York: Owl Books.

Powell, Brian, and Douglas B. Downey. 1997. "Living in Single-Parent Households: An Investigation of the Same-Sex Hypothesis." *American Sociological Review* 62(4): 521–39.

Powell, Mary Ann, and Toby L. Parcel. 1997. "Effects of Family Structure on the Earnings Attainment Process: Differences by Gender." *Journal of Marriage and the Family* 59(2): 419–33.

Power, Sally, Geoff Whitty, Tony D. Edwards, and Valerie Wigfall. 1998. "Schoolboys and Schoolwork: Gender Identification and Academic Achievement." *International Journal of Inclusive Education* 2(2): 135–53.

Prenzel, M., J. Baumert, W. Blum, R. Lehmann, D. Leutner, M. Neubrand, R. Pekrun, J. Rost, and U. Schiefele (Eds.). 2006. "PISA International Plus 2003" (PISA-Längsschnittstudie zur Entwicklung mathematisch-naturwissenschaftlicher Kompetenzen im Verlauf eines Schuljahres). Available via data contract at: http://www.iqb.hu-berlin.de/arbbereiche/fdz (accessed August 30, 2012).

Qian, Zhenchao, and Samuel H. Preston. 1993. "Changes in American Marriage, 1972 to 1987: Availability and Forces of Attraction by Age and Education." *American Sociological Review* 58(4): 482–95.

Quenzel, Gudrun, and Klaus Hurrelmann. 2010. "Geschlecht und Schulerfolg. Warum wird die schulische Leistungsbilanz von jungen Männern immer schlechter?" ("Gender and School Success: Why Is the School Performance of Young Men Getting Worse?"). *Kölner Zeitschrift für Soziologie und Sozialpsychologie* (*Cologne Journal of Sociology and Social Psychology*) 62(1): 61–91.

Raffaelli, Marcella, Lisa J. Crockett, and Yuh-Ling Shen. 2005. "Developmental Stability and Change in Self-Regulation from Childhood to Adolescence." *Journal of Genetic Psychology* 166(1): 54–76.

Raftery, Adrian E., and Michael Hout. 1993. "Maximally Maintained Inequality: Expansion, Reform, and Opportunity in Irish Education, 1921–1975." *Sociology of Education* 66(1): 41–62.

Raley, Sara, and Suzanne Bianchi. 2006. "Sons, Daughters, and Family Processes: Does Gender of Children Matter?" *Annual Review of Sociology* 32: 401–21.

Rampey, Bobby D., Gloria S. Dion, and Patricia L. Donahue. 2009. "NAEP 2008: Trends in Academic Progress." NCES 2009-479. Washington: U.S. Department of Education, National Center for Education Statistics (April).

Ready, Douglas D., Laura F. LoGerfo, David T. Burkam, and Valerie E. Lee. 2005. "Explaining Girls' Advantage in Kindergarten Literacy Learning: Do Classroom Behaviors Make a Difference?" *The Elementary School Journal* 106(1): 21–38.

Reardon, Sean F., Allison Atteberry, Nicole Arshan, and Michal Kurlaender. 2009. "Effects of the California High School Exit Exam on Student Persistence, Achievement, and Graduation." Working Paper 2009-12. Palo Alto, Calif.: Stanford University, Institute for Research on Education Policy and Practice.

Reardon, Sean F., and Kendra Bischoff. 2011. "Growth in the Residential Segregation of Families by Income, 1970–2009." Technical report. New York: Russell Sage Foundation.

Rehberg, Richard A., and Evelyn R. Rosenthal. 1978. *Class and Merit in the American High School: An Assessment of the Revisionist and Meritocratic Arguments.* White Plains, N.Y.: Longman.

Ridgeway, Cecilia L., and Joseph Berger. 1986. "Expectations, Legitimation, and Dominance Behavior in Task Groups." *American Sociological Review* 51(5): 603–17.

Ridgeway, Cecilia L., and Chris Bourg. 2004. "Gender as Status: An Expectation States Theory Approach." In *The Psychology of Gender*, edited by Alice H. Eagly, Anne E. Beall, and Robert J. Sternberg. New York: Guilford Press.

Ridgeway, Cecilia L., and Shelley J. Correll. 2004. "Unpacking the Gender System: A Theoretical Perspective on Gender Beliefs and Social Relations." *Gender and Society* 18(4): 510–31.

Ridgeway, Cecilia L., and Lynn Smith-Lovin. 1999. "The Gender System and Interaction." *Annual Review of Sociology* 25: 191–216.

Rivkin, Steven G. 1995. "Black/White Differences in Schooling and Employment." *Journal of Human Resources* 30(4): 826–52.

Rivkin, Steven G., Eric A. Hanushek, and John F. Kain. 2005. "Teachers, Schools, and Academic Achievement." *Econometrica* 73(2): 417–58.

Rockoff, Jonah E. 2004. "The Impact of Individual Teachers on Student Achievement: Evidence from Panel Data." *American Economic Review* 94(2): 247–52.

Roderick, Melissa, Jenny Nagaoka, Elaine Allensworth, with Vanessa Coca, Macarena Correa, and Ginger Stoker. 2006. "From High School to the Future: A First Look at Chicago Public School Graduates: College Enrollment, College Preparation, and Graduation from Four-Year Colleges." Chicago: University of Chicago, Consortium on Chicago School Research (April).

Roderick, Melissa, Jenny Nagaoka, Vanessa Coca, Eliza Moeller, et al. 2008. "From High School to the Future: Potholes on the Road to College." Chicago: University of Chicago, Consortium on Chicago School Research.

Roscigno, Vincent J., and James W. Ainsworth-Darnell. 1999. "Race, Cultural Capital, and Educational Resources: Persistent Inequalities and Achievement Returns." *Sociology of Education* 72(3): 158–78.

Rosen, Bernard C., and Carol S. Aneshensel. 1978. "Sex Differences in the Educational-Occupational Expectation Process." *Social Forces* 51(1): 164–86.

Rosenbaum, James E. 2001. *Beyond College for All: Career Paths for the Forgotten Half.* New York: Russell Sage Foundation.

Rosenzweig, Mark R., and T. Paul Schultz. 1982. "Market Opportunities, Genetic Endowments, and Intrafamily Resource Distribution: Child Survival in Rural India." *American Economic Review* 72(4): 803–15.

Rostosky, Sharon Scales, Brian L. Wilcox, Margaret Laurie Comer Wright, and Brandy A. Randall. 2004. "The Impact of Religiosity on Adolescent Sexual Behavior: A Review of the Evidence." *Journal of Adolescent Research* 19(6): 677–97.

Ruble, Diane N., and Carol Lynn Martin. 2006. "Gender Development." In *Handbook of Child Psychology,* vol. 3, *Socialization, Personality, and Social Development,* 4th ed., edited by Paul H. Mussen and E. Mavis Hetherington. New York: Wiley.

Ruggles, Steven, J. Trent Alexander, Katie Genadek, Ronald Goeken, Matthew B. Schroeder, and Matthew Sobek. 2010. *Integrated Public Use Microdata Series: Version 5.0 (IPUMS)* [Machine-readable database]. Minneapolis: University of Minnesota.

Rumberger, Russell W., and Gregory J. Palardy. 2005. "Does Segregation Still Matter? The Impact of Student Composition on Academic Achievement in High School." *Teachers College Record* 107(9): 1999–2045.

Rury, John L. 2008. *Education and Social Change: Contours in the History of American Schooling.* New York: Taylor & Francis US.

Rutter, Michael, Avshalom Caspi, David Fergusson, L. John Horwood, Robert Goodman, Barbara Maughan, Terrie E. Moffitt, Howard Meltzer, and Julia Carroll. 2004. "Sex Differences in Developmental Reading Disability: New Findings from Four Epidemiological Studies." *Journal of the American Medical Association* 291(16): 2007–12.

Salisbury, Jonathan, and David Jackson. 1996. *Challenging Macho Values: Practical Ways of Working with Adolescent Boys.* London: Falmer Press.

Salomone, Rosemary C. 2003. *Same, Different, Equal: Rethinking Single-Sex Schooling.* New Haven, Conn.: Yale University Press.

———. 2006. "Single-Sex Programs: Resolving the Research Conundrum." *Teachers College Record* 108(4): 778–802.

Salomone, Rosemary C., Cornelius Riordan, and Janice Weinman. 1999. "Single-Sex Schooling: Law, Policy, and Research." *Brookings Papers on Education Policy* 2: 231–97.

Sax, Leonard. 2005. *Why Gender Matters: What Parents and Teachers Need to Know About the Emerging Science of Sex Differences.* New York: Doubleday.

Schiebinger, Londa. 1999. *Has Feminism Changed Science?* Cambridge, Mass.: Harvard University Press.

Schneider, Barbara L., and Venessa A. Keesler. 2007. "School Reform 2007: Transforming Education into a Scientific Enterprise." *Annual Review of Sociology* 33: 197–217.

Schneider, Barbara L., and David Stevenson. 2000. *The Ambitious Generation: America's Teenagers, Motivated but Directionless.* New Haven, Conn.: Yale University Press.

Schofield, Janet Ward. 1982. *Black and White in School: Trust, Tension, or Tolerance?* New York: Praeger.

Schrock, Douglas, and Michael Schwalbe. 2009. "Men, Masculinity, and Manhood Acts." *Annual Review of Sociology* 35: 277–95.

Schwartz, Christine R., and Robert D. Mare. 2005. "Trends in Educational Assortative Marriage from 1940 to 2003." *Demography* 42(4): 621–46.

Segal, David R., and Mady Wechsler Segal. 2004. "America's Military Population." *Population Bulletin* 59(4): 3–40.

Sewell, William H., Archibald O. Haller, and Alejandro Portes. 1969. "The Educational and Early Occupational Attainment Process." *American Sociological Review* 34(1): 82–92.

Sewell, William H., and Robert M. Hauser. 1975. *Education, Occupation, and Earnings: Achievement in the Early Career.* New York: Academic Press.

Sexton, Patrícia Cayo. 1969. *The Feminized Male: Classrooms, White Collars, and the Decline of Manliness.* New York: Random House.

Seymour, Elaine, and Nancy M. Hewitt. 1997. *Talking About Leaving: Why Undergraduates Leave the Sciences.* Boulder, Colo.: Westview Press.

Shanahan, Michael J. 2000. "Pathways to Adulthood in Changing Societies: Variability and Mechanisms in Life Course Perspective." *Annual Review of Sociology* 26: 667–92.

Shauman, Kimberlee A. 2009. "Are There Sex Differences in the Utilization of Educational Capital Among College-Educated Workers?" *Social Science Research* 38(3): 535–71.

Short, Kathleen. 2011. "Supplemental Poverty Measure: 2010." Technical Report P60-241. Washington: U.S. Census Bureau.

Simpson, Adelaide W., and Marilyn T. Erickson. 1983. "Teachers' Verbal and Nonverbal Communication Patterns as a Function of Teacher Race, Student Gender, and Student Race." *American Educational Research Journal* 20(2): 183–98.

Skelton, Christine. 1997. "Primary Boys and Hegemonic Masculinities." *British Journal of Sociology of Education* 18(3): 349–69.

Sluckin, Andy. 1981. *Growing Up in the Playground: The Social Development of Children.* London: Routledge & Kegan Paul.

Smith, Tom W., Peter V. Marsden, and Michael Hout. 2010. *General Social Survey, 1972–2010* [Cumulative File]. ICPSR31521-v1. Storrs, Conn.: Roper Center for Public Opinion Research, University of Connecticut/Ann Arbor, Mich.: Inter-university Consortium for Political and Social Research [distributors], 2011-08-05. doi:10.3886/ICPSR31521.v1. Available at: http://dx.doi.org/10.3886/ICPSR31521.v1 (accessed August 30, 2012).

Snyder, Thomas D., and Sally A. Dillow. 2007. *Digest of Education Statistics, 2006.* Washington: U.S. Department of Education, National Center for Education Statistics.

———. 2012. *Digest of Education Statistics, 2011.* Washington: U.S. Department of Education, National Center for Education Statistics. Available at: http://nces.ed.gov/pubsearch/pubsinfo.asp? pubid=2012001 (accessed August 30, 2012).

Snyder, Thomas D., Sally A. Dillow, and Charlene M. Hoffman. 2008. *Digest of Education Statistics, 2007.* Washington: U.S. Department of Education, National Center for Education Statistics. Available at: http://nces.ed.gov/pubsearch/pubsinfo.asp? pubid=2008022 (accessed August 30, 2012).

Sokal, Laura, Herb Katz, Les Chaszewski, and Cecilia Wojcik. 2007. "Good-bye, Mr. Chips: Male Teacher Shortages and Boys' Reading Achievement." *Sex Roles* 56(9): 651–59.

Solomon, Barbara Miller. 1985. *In the Company of Educated Women: A History of Women and Higher Education in America.* New Haven, Conn.: Yale University Press.

Sommers, Christina Hoff. 2001. *The War Against Boys: How Misguided Feminism Is Harming Our Young Men.* New York: Simon & Schuster.

Sonnert, Gerhard. 1995. *Who Succeeds in Science? The Gender Dimension.* New Brunswick, N.J.: Rutgers University Press.

Sonnert, Gerhard, Mary Frank Fox, and Kristen Adkins. 2007. "Undergraduate

Women in Science and Engineering: Effects of Faculty, Fields, and Institutions over Time." *Social Science Quarterly* 88(5): 1333–56.

Spelke, Elizabeth S. 2005. "Sex Differences in Intrinsic Aptitude for Mathematics and Science? A Critical Review." *American Psychologist* 60(9): 950–58.

Spellings Commission on the Future of Higher Education. 2006. *A Test of Leadership: Charting the Future of U.S. Higher Education.* Washington: U.S. Government Printing Office.

Spender, Dale. 1982. *Invisible Women: The Schooling Scandal,* 2nd ed. London: Writers and Readers.

Spera, Christopher. 2005. "A Review of the Relationship Among Parenting Practices, Parenting Styles, and Adolescent School Achievement." *Educational Psychology Review* 17(2): 125–46.

Stanley, Marcus. 2003. "College Education and the Midcentury GI Bills." *Quarterly Journal of Economics* 118(2): 671–708.

Stanworth, Michelle. 1984. *Gender and Schooling: A Study of Sexual Divisions in the Classroom.* London: Hutchinson.

Steele, Claude M. 1997. "A Threat in the Air: How Stereotypes Shape Intellectual Identity and Performance." *The American Psychologist* 52(6): 613–29.

Steele, Claude M., and Joshua Aronson. 1995. "Stereotype Threat and the Intellectual Test Performance of African Americans." *Journal of Personality and Social Psychology* 69(5): 797–811.

Steinberg, Laurence D., B. Bradford Brown, and Sanford M. Dornbusch. 1996. *Beyond the Classroom: Why School Reform Has Failed and What Parents Need to Do.* New York: Simon & Schuster.

Steiner, Peter M., Thomas D. Cook, and William R. Shadish. 2011. "On the Importance of Reliable Covariate Measurement in Selection Bias Adjustments Using Propensity Scores." *Journal of Educational and Behavioral Statistics* 36(3): 213–36.

Steiner, Peter M., Thomas D. Cook, William R. Shadish, and M. H. Clark. 2010. "The Importance of Covariate Selection in Controlling for Selection Bias in Observational Studies." *Psychological Methods* 15(3): 250–67.

Studer, Marlena, and Arland Thornton. 1987. "Adolescent Religiosity and Contraceptive Usage." *Journal of Marriage and the Family* 49(1): 117–28.

Tach, Laura Marie, and George Farkas. 2006. "Learning-Related Behaviors, Cognitive Skills, and Ability Grouping When Schooling Begins." *Social Science Research* 35(4): 1048–79.

Tanner, J. M. 1990. *Fetus into Man: Physical Growth from Conception to Maturity.* Cambridge, Mass.: Harvard University Press.

Teachman, Jay D. 2002. "Stability Across Cohorts in Divorce Risk Factors." *Demography* 39(2): 331–51.

Thistle, Susan. 2006. *From Marriage to the Market: The Transformation of Women's Lives and Work.* Berkeley: University of California Press.

Thomas, Gail E., Karl L. Alexander, and Bruce K. Eckland. 1979. "Access to Higher Education: The Importance of Race, Sex, Social Class, and Academic Credentials." *The School Review* 87(2): 133–56.

Thorne, Barrie 1993. *Gender Play: Girls and Boys in School.* New Brunswick, N.J.: Rutgers University Press.

Thornton, Arland, Duane F. Alwin, and Donald Camburn. 1983. "Causes and

Consequences of Sex-Role Attitudes and Attitude Change." *American Socio-logical Review* 48(2): 211–27.

Thornton, Arland, and Donald Camburn. 1987. "The Influence of the Family on Premarital Sexual Attitudes and Behavior." *Demography* 24(3): 323–40.

Thornton, Arland, and Deborah Freedman. 1979. "Changes in the Sex Role Attitudes of Women, 1962–1977: Evidence from a Panel Study." *American Sociological Review* 44(5): 831–42.

Toossi, Mitra. 2002. "A Century of Change: The U.S. Labor Force, 1950–2050." *Monthly Labor Review* 125(5): 15–28.

Trzesniewski, Kali H., Terrie E. Moffitt, Avshalom Caspi, Alan Taylor, and Barbara Maughan. 2006. "Revisiting the Association Between Reading Achievement and Antisocial Behavior: New Evidence of an Environmental Explanation from a Twin Study." *Child Development* 77(1): 72–88.

Turner, Sarah, and John Bound. 2003. "Closing the Gap or Widening the Divide: The Effects of the GI Bill and World War II on the Educational Outcomes of Black Americans." *Journal of Economic History* 63(1): 145–77.

Turner, Sarah E., and William G. Bowen. 1999. "Choice of Major: The Changing (Unchanging) Gender Gap." *Industrial and Labor Relations Review* 52(2): 289–313.

Twenge, Jean M. 1997. "Attitudes Toward Women, 1970–1995." *Psychology of Women Quarterly* 21(1): 35–51.

Tyre, Peg. 2009. *The Trouble with Boys*. New York: Random House.

United Nations Educational, Scienctific, and Cultural Organization (UNESCO). 2009. Institute for Statistics Data Center [Machine-readable database]. Montreal: UNESCO. Available at: http://stats.uis.unesco.org/unesco/tableviewer/document.aspx? ReportId=143 (accessed August 31, 2012).

———. 2012. *World Atlas of Gender Equality in Education*. Paris: UNESCO.

United States and National Commission on Excellence in Education. 1983. *A Nation at Risk: The Imperative for Educational Reform*. Washington, D.C.: National Commission on Excellence in Education.

Updegraff, Kim A., Jacquelynne S. Eccles, Bonnie L. Barber, and Kathryn M. O'Brien. 1996. "Course Enrollment as Self-Regulatory Behavior: Who Takes Optional High School Math Courses?" *Learning and Individual Differences* 8(3): 239–59.

U.S. Census Bureau. 2010. *American Community Survey, 2005–2010* [Machine-readable database]. Available at: http://www.census.gov/acs/www/data_documentation/public_use_microdata_sample (accessed August 31, 2012).

U.S. Department of Labor. U.S. Bureau of Labor Statistics. 2010a. *Women in the Labor Force: A Databook*. Technical Report 1026. Washington: U.S. Government Printing Office.

———. 2010b. "NLSY79 Children and Young Adults [database]. Available at: http://www.bls.gov/nls/nlsy79ch.htm (accessed August 30, 2012).

———. 2012. "National Longitudinal Surveys of Youth 1997 Cohort" [NLSY97; Machine-readable database]. Available at: http://www.bls.gov/nls/nlsy97.htm (accessed August 30, 2012).

Venezia, Andrea, Michael W. Kirst, and Anthony L. Antonio. 2003. "Betraying the College Dream: How Disconnected K-12 and Postsecondary Education Systems Undermine Student Aspirations." Final policy report from Stanford

University's Bridge Project. Stanford, Calif.: Stanford Institute for Higher Education Research.

Ventura, Stephanie J. 2009. "Changing Patterns of Nonmarital Childbearing in the United States." *NCHS* (National Center for Health Statistics) *Data Brief* 18(May): 1–8.

Vincent-Lancrin, Stephan. 2008. "The Reversal of Gender Inequalities in Higher Education–An On-Going Trend." *Higher Education to 2030,* Volume 1: Demography. Paris: OECD.

Wai, Jonathan, Megan Cacchio, Martha Putallaz, and Matthew C. Makel. 2010. "Sex Differences in the Right Tail of Cognitive Abilities: A Thirty-Year Examination." *Intelligence* 38(4): 412–23.

Walby, Sylvia. 1986. *Patriarchy at Work: Patriarchal and Capitalist Relations in Employment, 1800–1984.* Minneapolis: University of Minnesota Press.

Watson, Clifford, and Geneva Smitherman. 1991. "Educational Equity and Detroit's Male Academy." *Equity and Excellence* 25(2–4): 90–105.

Watt, Helen M. G. 2005. "Exploring Adolescent Motivations for Pursuing Maths-Related Careers." *Australian Journal of Educational and Developmental Psychology* 5: 107–16.

Weinberger, Catherine J. 1998. "Race and Gender Wage Gaps in the Market for Recent College Graduates." *Industrial Relations: A Journal of Economy and Society* 37(1): 67–84.

West, Jerry, Kristin Denton, and Lizabeth Reaney. 2000. "The Kindergarten Year." Washington: U.S. Department of Education.

Westat and Educational Testing Service. 1998. *ECLS-K Base Year Data Files and Electronic Codebook.* Washington: U.S. Department of Education.

Whitmore, Diane. 2005. "Resource and Peer Impacts on Girls' Academic Achievement: Evidence from a Randomized Experiment." *American Economic Review* 95(2): 199–203.

Wicherts, Jelte M., Conor V. Dolan, David J. Hessen, Paul Oosterveld, G. Caroline M. van Baal, Dorret I. Boomsma, and Mark M. Span. 2004. "Are Intelligence Tests Measurement Invariant over Time? Investigating the Nature of the Flynn Effect." *Intelligence* 32(5): 509–37.

Wigfield, Allan, and Jacquelynne S. Eccles. 2000. "Expectancy-Value Theory of Achievement Motivation." *Contemporary Educational Psychology* 25(1): 68–81.

Wilkinson, Louise C., and Cora Bagley Marrett, eds. 1985. *Gender Influences in Classroom Interaction.* Orlando, Fla.: Academic Press.

Williams, Joan. 2000. *Unbending Gender: Why Family and Work Conflict and What to Do About It.* Oxford: Oxford University Press.

Willingham, Warren W., and Nancy S. Cole. 1997. *Gender and Fair Assessment.* Mahwah, N.J.: Lawrence Erlbaum Associates.

Willis, Paul. 1981. *Learning to Labor: How Working-Class Kids Get Working-Class Jobs.* New York: Columbia University Press.

Wilson, Kenneth L., and Janet P. Boldizar. 1990. "Gender Segregation in Higher Education: Effects of Aspirations, Mathematics Achievement, and Income." *Sociology of Education* 63(1): 62–74.

Xie, Yu, and Kimberlee A. Shauman. 2003. *Women in Science: Career Processes and Outcomes.* Cambridge, Mass.: Harvard University Press.

Yeung, W. Jean, Greg J. Duncan, and Martha S. Hill. 2000. "Putting Fathers Back in the Picture: Parental Activities and Children's Adult Outcomes." *Marriage and Family Review* 29(2–3): 97–114.

Yeung, W. J., John F. Sandberg, Pamela E. Davis-Kean, and Sandra L. Hofferth. 2001. "Children's Time with Fathers in Intact Families." *Journal of Marriage and the Family* 63(1): 136–54.

Younger, Mike, and Molly Warrington. 1996. "Differential Achievement of Girls and Boys at GCSE: Some Observations from the Perspective of One School." *British Journal of Sociology of Education* 17(3): 299–313.

Younger, Michael, Molly Warrington, and Jacquetta Williams. 1999. "The Gender Gap and Classroom Interactions: Reality and Rhetoric?" *British Journal of Sociology of Education* 20(3): 325–41.

Zaleski, Ellen H., and Kathleen M. Schiaffino. 2000. "Religiosity and Sexual Risk-Taking Behavior During the Transition to College." *Journal of Adolescence* 23(2): 223–27.

Zill, N., and J. West. 2001. "Entering Kindergarten: A Portrait of American Children When They Begin School: Findings from the Condition of Education, 2000." Technical report. Washington: U.S. Department of Education, National Center for Education Statistics.

Index

Boldface numbers refer to figures and tables.

Made in the USA
San Bernardino, CA
02 February 2020